Police
A Field Guide

David Correia is a Professor of American Studies at the University of New Mexico. He is the author of *An Enemy Such as This: Larry Casuse and the Fight for Native Liberation in One Family on Two Continents over Three Centuries*.

Tyler Wall is Associate Professor in the Department of Sociology at the University of Tennessee in Knoxville.

Police
A Field Guide

David Correia and Tyler Wall

VERSO

London • New York

This paperback edition first published by Verso 2022

First published by Verso 2018

1 3 5 7 9 10 8 6 4 2

Verso
UK: 6 Meard Street, London W1F 0EG
US: 388 Atlantic Avenue, Brooklyn, NY 11217
versobooks.com

Verso is the imprint of New Left Books

ISBN-13: 978-1-83976-587-2
ISBN-13: 978-1-78663-013-1 (US EBK)
ISBN-13: 978-1-78663-012-4 (UK EBK)

British Library Cataloguing in Publication Data
A catalogue record for this book is available from the British Library

Library of Congress Cataloging-in-Publication Data
A catalog record for this book is available from the Library of Congress

Typeset in Arnhem by Biblichor Ltd, Edinburgh, Scotland
Printed and bound by CPI Group (UK) Ltd, Croydon, CR0 4YY

Contents

Foreword (Forward) to the Second Edition   ix
Preface to the Second Edition   xv
Introduction: Copspeak and the False Promise of Police Reform   1

1. **Weaponology: Technologies and Tactics of Police Violence**
   Gun   10
   Throw-Down Weapon   13
   Taser   13
   Tear Gas   17
   Handcuffs   20
   K-9   22
   Racial Profiling   24
   Stop and Frisk   27
   Rough Ride   31
   Body Cavity Search   33
   No-Knock Warrant   34
   Curfew   38
   Rape   41
   Lynching   43
   Starlight Tour   46
   Flashlight   48
   Rubber Bullets   50
   Nightstick   55
   Chokehold   58
   Lapel Camera   60
   Data Center   62
   Police Helicopter   70
   Traffic Stop   73
   Checkpoint   75
   Sound   77
   Pain Compliance   79

2. The Oath: Core Values of Police
Private Property   81
Order   83
Security   86
Pacification   89
Law   90
Crime   93
Violence   96
War   100
Force   102
Jurisdiction   104
The Badge   106
Thin Blue Line   110
Professionalization   113

3. Models of Policing: How the Police Are Organized and Defended
Police Gangs   116
Asset Protection Officer   118
Community Policing   122
Red Squads   123
Qualified Immunity   126
CRASH   128
COINTELPRO   130
Officer Friendly   132
SWAT   135
Militarization   139
Police Uniform   141
Slave Patrol   143
Rent-a-Cop   144
Police Oversight   146
Police Union   150
Dinkheller   151
Police Reform   155
Accountability   160

4. Using the Force: How Police Impose Order

Search   163

Armed Friendlies   165

Patrol   170

The Beat   172

Investigation   175

Discretion   176

Predictive Policing   178

CompStat   180

Ghetto   183

Gentrification   184

Broken Windows   186

Vagrancy   189

Interrogation   193

Good Cop, Bad Cop   195

Officer-Involved Domestic Violence   197

Pursuit   200

Crowds   201

Contempt of Cop   205

Police Brutality   207

Arrest   208

Kettling   210

Plain View   212

Asset Forfeiture   215

Testilying   218

Cop   219

5. Copspeak: How the Police See the World

Threat   222

Emergency   223

Bad Apple   224

Officer   227

Deterrence   228

Disproportionate   232

Ferguson Effect   235

Furtive Movements   236

Justified   238

No Humans Involved (NHI)   240

Deadname   242

Noncompliance   245

Officer-Involved Shooting   246

Challenge Coins   248

The Public   252

Reasonable Suspicion   255

Unarmed   257

Use-of-Force Continuum   258

Criminology   261

Epilogue:

On a World Beyond Police   264

Notes   269

Foreword (Forward)
to the Second Edition

You're holding a real field guide in your hands. What do field guides do? They help you name what you've been seeing. They help you see things you hadn't seen before. They provide brief descriptions of the objects you're seeing. They help you see the connections among things—the habitats or ecosystems these things depend on. And they encourage you to get outside and see more to understand more.

With the deluge of videos of police violence we're subjected to, you might imagine that we don't need a field guide. Surely we've seen enough to understand the problem, haven't we? David Correia and Tyler Wall argue we're not understanding much of what we're seeing. We're misunderstanding it because of the language we use to describe it. That language they call "Copspeak," and this field guide observes carefully how it is used, and what police behaviors are being misunderstood—or perhaps more accurately, covered up.

Credit: George Herriman

Protests following the police killings of Breonna Taylor and George Floyd were extraordinary. Masses of people took to the streets across the US (and elsewhere) for weeks, making the demonstrations what many called the biggest sustained set of protests in decades. This season of agitation brought "Defund the Police" into mainstream political discourse. Across the political spectrum, commentators expressed first surprise at how the demand/slogan had become so popular, then dismay. That various conservatives opposed Defund surprised no one. That so many liberals & people to their left dismissed the demand was more interesting, especially when so many police departments reacted to protests about police violence with escalating force.

That the demand was so unsettling tells us something about what is at stake in this fight, and as the *Field Guide* informs us, the terrain of the fight is in the intentionally fuzzy ground between what the police (and other law enforcement groups) do and how we and they describe what they do. Or properly and more broadly, the worlds in which policing happens.

One of the liberal responses was to explain that "Defund the Police" isn't actually a demand that the police be defunded, or that abolitionists aren't really trying to do away with police. It is a sign of the strength and visibility of the movement that a liberal newspaper like the *New York Times* would publish a response by organizer Mariame Kaba, one in which the headline writer(s) summarized the message pretty clearly:

YES, WE MEAN LITERALLY ABOLISH THE POLICE: BECAUSE REFORM WON'T HAPPEN

Others attacked the goal itself, as being unrealistic and/or not sufficiently popular—as though systemic change to a racist police system might be driven by public opinion polling.

The stakes were high enough that even former president Obama weighed in with comments that slid between policing practice and Copspeak:

If you believe, as I do, that we should be able to reform the criminal-justice system so that it's not biased and treats everybody fairly, I guess you can use a snappy slogan, like "defund the police."

But, you know, you lost a big audience the minute you say it, which makes it a lot less likely that you're actually going to get the changes you want done.

Obama seems to be talking only about the slogan, but in trying to hail protestors back to police reform and away from downsizing or abolishing the police, he's moved to policy and practices.

To Obama's left, Vivek Chibber attacked both slogan and demand. The slogan, he said, was bad because "you have to immediately explain that that's not really what you mean."[1] (See Mariame Kaba's headline above.) The demand, he argued, plays too easily into a politics of austerity that forces organizers to "immediately tell people not that you're trying to take away from public institutions right now and jumping on the austerity bandwagon." We'll leave aside for now that Defund is grounded in plans to spend money on life-supporting social services and public goods rather than death-dealing policing, not to "take away public institutions."

What dismissals of Defund have in common from the center to the left is that the idea of significantly fewer police (much less their abolition altogether) is *unthinkable* and therefore *unspeakable*. This *Field Guide* offers a means to think and say things that will destroy the blue wall of silence that shields the police and their privileged role in meting out violence to protect property and the race, class, gender and other hierarchies upon which racial capitalism depends. By changing how we think and speak about policing, it opens space for, as AbouMaliq Simone and Edgar Pieterse write, "new, formerly unthinkable possibilities to become visible and debatable—properly political."[2]

In addition to outright attacks on Defund, there were more "reasonable" and "realistic" counterproposals floated, the best known of which was #8CantWait: a package of eight police reforms promising significant reduction in police killings and other police-initiated violence. Abolitionists were quick to point out that a number of cities had already instituted many of the eight policies—Chicago, for example, had seven of the eight on the books already, and yet the Chicago PD is hardly a model of non-violent, non-racist policing. Abolitionists also released a set of counter policy proposals, #8toAbolition.

The almost immediate critique of #8CantWait and release of an alternative helped keep the Defund protestors from being pulled away from a potentially transformative political goal toward reforms that would have renewed and reinforced US policing. How did that work? We know that political change requires more than posting another document online, no matter how good it might be. Why was it that so many of the Portland moms (of whatever gender, parental status or location) rejected the advice of Obama, McKesson, *et.al.* and stuck with a Defund demand? It is not as though there has been a single, charismatic, national leader of Defund, shepherding their followers.

Rather, there have been dozens or hundreds of local organizers doing long-term political education as part of their core organizing strategy, people like Geri Silva and Pete White in Los Angeles or Vanessa Thompson in Frankfurt, and organizations like Plataforma Gueto in greater Lisbon. People using ideas like those in this *Field Guide* (and I don't doubt, many used the first edition of the *Field Guide* as well as a wealth of materials developed by abolitionist groups like Critical Resistance and Project NIA) to help local people, many of them new to protests and demands about their local police department, how better to see what the police do, what the police are, what changes are and aren't possible within current structures of race, property, gender, citizenship and borders, wealth. The fact that hundreds of thousands of people were in the streets for weeks insisting that fewer police would create a better, safer, more secure city was possible only once the hold of Copspeak on their collective minds was broken. Asha Ransby-Sporn of Defund CPD (Chicago) said, "political education is fundamental to building a base and growing a movement, because that's where you get people on the same page about what we're actually fighting for." One of the keys to that organizing has been to help people see that Defund (or abolish) is about much more than policing; the bigger targets are the hierarchies of racial capitalism and the death-producing austerities that are both its products and its infrastructure. "What we certainly have won is a great deal of people over to our side when it comes to not just defunding the police, but also connecting that to other issues that affect Black and Brown, and poor and working people in the city," said Ransby-Sporn.[3]

Copspeak is a language that exists so that we might misunderstand policing and the social, economic, and political structures that depend on it. Copspeak is not primarily about police lying or fabricating evidence, although of course we understand those to be basic components of everyday policing. Rather Copspeak is the dragnet of everyday speech we use to describe what policing is and does, one that reminds us constantly that despite the occasional bad apple the police exist to "serve and protect" the public.

The first edition of the *Field Guide* was published halfway through Trump's administration, and this, the second, will be released during Biden's. How, if at all, has the ecosystem of policing changed? How will this book be useful in the 2020s? There's no doubt that some significant number of those who have been in the streets protesting over the past four years imagine that with Trump gone, we're on our way to a return to normal that will diminish the number of people killed or beaten by the police, the number of people caged in local, state or federal systems and the number of people deported. But if by "normal" people imagine a return to, say, the Obama years, we're not going to see significant declines in high profile police violence (or deportations, detentions, incarceration). Instead of having virulent Trump to help us mobilize, we'll be seeing avuncular Biden.

Biden's policy platform suggests continuity with Obama's, and indeed with Trump's. He'll sympathize with protestors, comfort the families of those killed by cops, and offer police departments more money for training or diversification. His Justice Department will bring cases against a handful of police departments that they see

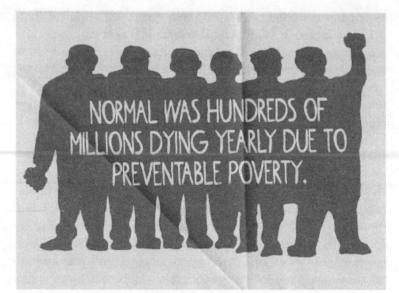

Autonomous Design Group

to be beyond the pale, basically applying the bad-apple theory not just to individual cops, but to whole departments. In short, we can expect them to roll out a lot of the classic reform playbook. And we, without the benefit of a lightning pole like Trump to draw people into the streets, have to push back hard on police reforms that simply re-entrench and re-legitimize policing. This book will be a very useful tool in that work.

There is one thing that sets this book apart from other field guides that have as a part of their purpose the conservation of their objects. *Police: A Field Guide* is a tool to disrupt, if not destroy, the ecosystem of Copspeak. It is written not for people who want simply to better understand the place the police have in our world, but for those who want to change this world and the police who are such key players in maintaining it. Use it well.

Craig Gilmore

Preface to the Second Edition

We began writing the first edition of *Police: A Field Guide* less than six months after the 2014 police murder of Mike Brown by a white, Ferguson, Missouri, cop. The uprisings that followed began in the summer and fall of 2015 and spread to cities through the US. We wrote the first edition of this book as a counterpoint to the police reformists who defended police, and whose work, like the work of police, has always served a counter-insurgency function. In our view, reformism functions as a common liberal technocratic response to all substantive challenges to police violence. It operates as a co-opting mode of political struggle, one that hijacks the energy of the anti-police violence movement in order to divert it from more radical proposals that call for the abolition of both police and the social conditions that make police appear necessary and even inevitable. Reformism defends the status quo through proposals that promise short-term fixes that always result in more cops, more weapons, larger police budgets, and more police violence. As we argued in the first edition, police reform never identifies the problem of police in the police mandate itself. Rather, police reform is always about you and your refusal to trust police; your refusal to have faith in police; your refusal to submit to the authority of police. Police reform is text-book hearts-and-minds stuff. Police promise to play nice, promise to build bridges in the community, but the real intent of police reform is to restore the legitimacy of police in crisis moments and, most importantly, to use the cover that reformism provides to in-crease and intensify the coercive capacity of police and the already expansive mandate of police. Police reform seeks a resolution to the crisis of police violence by treating it as a crisis of police legitimacy, never as a crisis that emerges from the racialized policing of the poor.

We started the second edition of this book in the middle of another uprising against police, this one after the police murders of Breonna Taylor and George Floyd. As millions of protestors filled the streets in the spring and summer of 2020, we received emails from family and comrades telling us how timely they found *Police: A Field Guide*. We thanked them, and then we explained that we didn't really deserve any credit. It's always timely to talk about police violence, after all. The police power and the prerogative to use violence produce a very specific, predictable result: where you find police, you find their victims. Cops kill, brutalize and harass people, overwhelmingly working-class people of color, every day. But there are differences between 2014 and 2020. The anti-police violence movement since the Ferguson uprising has worked to shake off its reformist elements. There are fewer calls to reform police, and more demands to put an end to the conditions that make police necessary. None of this was predictable. We were as surprised as anyone at the remarkable growth and popularity of police and prison abolition among groups, activists and organizers in the uprisings of 2020.

We wrote the second edition of this book as a response to the most recent reformist backlash against the police abolition movement. There's always backlash to any challenge to the authority of police because establishment order requires cops. We live in a world made in part by police, a death-dealing institution that exists for only one purpose: to build and defend a capitalist order defined by the unequal and racialized distribution of the conditions of life itself.

The second edition, like the first, is a book about copspeak, about the ways in which police patrol our streets and also the way they patrol, and constantly discipline, the language we have to talk about police and policing. Copspeak seeks to limit any discussion of police to one acceptable to cops and their allies. To speak in the language of copspeak is to submit to the fundamental principles, assumptions and illusions of policing. It is to accept the idea that police identify and manage threats, declare and resolve emergencies, and promise and provide security. Copspeak is the reformist's native tongue. Through it they invite us to see a world awash in fear and insecurity and flooded by threats and emergencies that only police can resolve. The uprisings of 2020, however, included a remarkable and collective refusal to see the world as police and police reformists do. Abolitionist organizers and groups throughout the US developed mutual aid efforts and community defense networks. These methods of community care exist in direct confrontation with police power, a power premised on the violence of the state to protect a racialized order of private property.

The uprisings of 2020 focused as much on reform and reformism as they did police, and for good reason. Reformists pretend to take police violence seriously. They acknowledge the crisis that police violence provokes and admit the everyday threat that police pose, particularly and overwhelmingly for working class communities of color. They offer themselves as ready and willing to confront the crisis of police violence, and they present their proposals as sober, practical solutions. After all, they constantly remind us, there is no alternative to reform because there is no alternative to police. The police, they claim, is nothing more than an essential, democratic institution gone temporarily awry.

It's not for nothing the uprisings of 2020 confronted not just police but also the reformist's claims about police. Unlike reformism, police abolition takes everyday police harassment seriously, not just the spectacular examples but also the grinding, harassing, dehumanizing, day-after-day violence of police. Abolitionist organizers and activists refused to compromise with reformists and instead opposed all their proposed reforms—all their promises of "improved" police training (whatever that means), all their calls for more lapel cameras (always deployed and controlled only by police), all their claims about community oversight (equally as vague, as all police reforms are meant to be), and all their talk about increased hiring standards (a constant refrain of reformists). Reformism seeks only a superficial recalibration of police violence into a "kinder, gentler" violence of lower death counts, fewer arrests, and less visible daily harassment. Proposals such as these only "fix" police if we understand "fix" to mean a version of police even more embedded in our communities.

But police will kill tomorrow, and they will kill the day after tomorrow, and so abolition requires bringing the future—one free of police—into the present. The demands to defund police, with their focus on budgets and legal tactics, confused or even frustrated some who called for the abolition of police. But the calls to defund police, at their best, understand the stakes clearly. These are what some call *non-reformist* reforms. These are not the familiar reformist proposals that always result in more cops and more weapons, but rather proposals that seek to rob the police of resources, personnel, and money. Any proposal that meaningfully limits police access to weapons and personnel might not challenge the logic of policing but limits the ability of police to kill and brutalize. Where police reform always ends up expanding the scale and scope of police and policing, non-reformist proposals promise to shrink police budgets and thus shrink the violence work of police. The demands to defund police, however, attracted not only abolitionists but also reformists, who saw in it an opportunity to smuggle the seductive power of reform into the language and proposals to defund. Cities throughout the US in the summer and fall of 2020 responded to demands to defund police by proposing reductions in police budgets and even, in the case of Minneapolis, to abolish police entirely. But these victories, at least from where we sit in September 2021, demonstrate just how adaptable the forces of order can be. Minneapolis backslid on this promise and has no real plan to abolish police. And cities like Albuquerque, which proposed a new Community Safety Department that its Democratic mayor said was developed in response to the uprisings, demonstrate how enduring the nature of the police power is, even during a profound crisis of legitimacy. The new department proposed in Albuquerque would slightly reduce the police budget, and in return we get a new department with the same mandate, same personnel, and same weapons as police.

The power of police, whether constituted in a police department or a community safety department, is a very particular type of power. It is a power some have described as a "patriarchal prerogative"; never meant to be "accountable" in any meaningful way, other than to capital. This is a power that James Baldwin called an "arrogant autonomy." This is not a book that seeks or offers alternatives to police violence. We do not propose replacing the coercive capacity of police with a new and different coercive institution. At the heart of the police powers—and of law itself—is a deadly mandate that must be abolished, in all its forms.

In addition to this introduction, and a new foreword by Craig Gilmore, an anti-prison organizer and co-founder of the California Prison Moratorium Project, the second edition includes nearly two dozen new entries. We included new terms and concepts familiar to anyone who paid attention to the uprisings of 2020. The sheer size of the uprising—by some estimates the largest social protest movement in US history—meant that the aggressive and violent tactics of police came suddenly into focus and were constantly on display, night after night, on television and social media. The images and video revealed that police don't just use weapons, police weaponize everything. Flashlights become clubs, cruisers become battering rams, handcuffs become portable prisons. And what's more, cops even reverse engineer their existing weapons. Police offer the taser as a less-lethal counterpart to the gun; they offer Tear gas as a friendlier truncheon. Police even develop less-lethal weapons for their less-lethal weapons, such as the use of K-9s in place of SWAT units. The development by police of what reformists call "less-lethal" weapons, and the violent, frenzied display of these weapons by police throughout 2020, reveal policing for what it is: a claim over life and death. Cops don't just patrol our streets, they patrol the line between life and death.

The order-maintenance imperative in policing manifests itself in the carefully calibrated coercion of routine, everyday policing. The principle or phrase that might best capture this is pain compliance. Pain, as we wrote in the first edition, is "the adjective that clarifies police power." The uprisings of 2020 showed that police carefully calibrate their use of violence. Consider the police weaponization of sound itself through the use of sound cannons and other auditory weapons. It's not a coincidence, as we write in this edition in a new entry titled "Sound," that we find the ubiquitous police siren on "a spectrum with acoustic vibrations designed to induce pain, panic, and terror." Everything about cops, from the uniforms they wear to the weapons they use to the cruisers they drive, serves a coercive function.

The uprisings also revealed how quickly police develop and deploy "new" police tactics. Consider kettling, for example, another new entry in this edition. Kettling is a common police tactic that police claim they're not familiar with and never use. In a kettling, as we define it, riot cops cordon and contain a crowd, squeezing it and squeezing it, and by doing so creating the very conditions that police claim their tactics diffuse. In the kettle we find an unresolvable contradiction to the cop claim that only police make order. It turns out that police fabricate order by creating the conditions for the disorder they use violence to resolve.

But police cannot be seen as the source of disorder and so police displace the disorder that policing creates onto the subjects of police violence. The uprisings of 2020 revealed the extensive help police get in doing this from vigilantes and right-wing, fascist militias. Fascists live in a world built by the violence of police, and therefore recognize their privileges as products of state violence. And so fascists organize with police and defend racialized property relations alongside police. We use the phrase "fascist militias" to describe this, but cops use a different term. "Armed friendlies" they call them, which we include as a new entry in this edition, defined as, "an all-encompassing index of the police powers. It describes the vast networks of actors, institutions and practices that bourgeois order requires." Armed friendlies, like the bad apples we wrote about in the first edition, are not the outliers or aberrations of police and policing, but rather its building blocks. Where you find police, you find armed friendlies.

The uprisings of 2020 included protests against the spectacular examples of police violence but also against the everyday harassment and intimidation that occupies the majority of police time and effort. We examine this in a series of new entries, including "Deadname," which details the many ways police dehumanize and demonize trans women, or in the entry on Challenge Coins, which offers another example of what we might call the aesthetics of police violence. Cops kill people and then mint collectible coins to celebrate and even commemorate their violence.

Cops appears impervious to the demands we place on them. There is nothing easy about confronting the violence of police; nothing politically expedient about refusing the promises of reformism. Police will respond to any challenge to their authority with a ruthless violence endorsed by law and sanctioned by reformists. Abolition seems a distant dream in the face of this violence. And so we weren't surprised to see references to the poet June Jordan throughout 2020. Jordan, born in Harlem in 1936 to Jamaican immigrant parents, wrote beautiful and uncompromising poetry that offered an unflinching, clear-eyed view of the stakes in this struggle. Hers were fierce and defiant words that somehow made the seemingly impossible—abolition—appear inevitable. Her poetry captured the fury that police violence produces and the promise that only personal refusal and collective solidarity might make possible. We begin the second edition of this book with her words as our guide. "I must become," she wrote in her 1973 poem of the same name, "a menace to my enemies":

I will no longer lightly walk behind
a one of you who fear me:
            Be afraid.
I plan to give you reasons for your jumpy fits
and facial tics
I will not walk politely on the pavements anymore
and this is dedicated in particular
to those who hear my footsteps
or the insubstantial rattling of my grocery
cart
then turn around
see me
and hurry on
away from this impressive terror I must be:
I plan to blossom bloody on an afternoon

surrounded by my comrades singing
terrible revenge in merciless
accelerating
rhythms

David Correia and Tyler Wall

Introduction:
Copspeak and the
False Promise of Police Reform

Police violence is not a new phenomenon. Nearly fifty years before Ferguson, Missouri erupted in anger at the police killing of Mike Brown in 2014, James Baldwin wrote that Black communities in the United States are "policed like occupied territory."

Fifty years before police demanded Black obedience to mostly white cops during anti-police violence protests in Baltimore, Milwaukee, Baton Rouge and dozens of other cities, Baldwin wrote in 1966 that "the law is meant to be my servant and not my master, still less my torturer and my murderer. To respect the law, in the context in which the American Negro finds himself, is simply to surrender his self-respect."

Nearly fifty years before Charlotte, North Carolina police refused to release the video of Keith Scott's killing because, as the cops claimed, they needed to finish their investigation of their own killing, Baldwin wrote, "I have witnessed and endured the brutality of the police many more times than once—but, of course, I cannot prove it. I cannot prove it because the Police Department investigates itself, quite as though it were answerable only to itself."

Fifty years before waves of police in riot gear used tear gas and truncheons to protect white-owned businesses in Minneapolis and New York from Black Lives Matter activists, Baldwin wrote that police are "present to keep the Negro in his place and to protect white business interests, and they have no other function. They are, moreover—even in a country which makes the very grave error of equating ignorance with simplicity—quite stunningly ignorant;

and, since they know that they are hated, they are always afraid. One cannot possibly arrive at a more surefire formula for cruelty."

2014 ushered in an era of police violence and anti–police violence activism and protest, but Baldwin reminds us that it is only the most recent. In his time, Baldwin was pessimistic about the prospects for police reform. There have been decades of police reform since Baldwin wrote about everyday racialized police violence in Harlem, but as the passages above demonstrate, little has changed. We share Baldwin's pessimism regarding the possibilities and promises of police reform. Like Baldwin, we understand racialized police violence to be a permanent feature of police as we know it. The excuses and explanations for police violence—too many bad apples, too little faith in police—serve only to draw our attention away from where it should be: on the persistent historical fact of racialized police violence against the poor. In the fifty years since Baldwin wrote about police as a lethal occupying army in the Black ghetto, there has been no end to police reform and equally no end to police killing and the routine harassments, humiliations, and fear that constitute policing. Indeed, if anything, police reform has only intensified the policing and caging of the poor and of people of color.

This is a book about the language of police and police reform, both of which come to us in a register we might call copspeak: a language that limits our ability to understand police as anything other than essential, anything other than the guarantor of civilization and the last line of defense against what police call savagery. When we see the world that copspeak describes to us—one forever threatened by disorder and chaos—we have no choice but to trust that police, even in Ferguson, can get better; no option other than to hope that police reform, even in Baltimore, will work; and no alternative than to believe that the police even in its current form—particularly in its current form—is indispensable. And so copspeak promises us police reform. But police reform never ends police violence, because police reform has always and only sought to improve the image of police and to shore up police legitimacy more generally. It has never sought to confront police as the lethal force it is, one charged by the state with managing poverty, patrolling the color line, and ruthlessly protecting establishment and economic interests.[1] When asked by political elites how they could quell the anger in the ghetto, Baldwin reminded them that people in the ghetto knew all too well that police only "protect and serve" the bottom line of developers and real estate speculators. "Are their profits more important than the health of our children?" he asked. But of course this was merely a rhetorical question. The only thing most Black folks hate more than the ghetto, he explained, is police.

Copspeak works because it is convincing to so many. The fear and suspicion that Black and Hispanic and Indigenous and poor and immigrant communities hold for police is matched in the United States by the nearly universal faith and respect held for police by economically secure, mostly white communities. It is to that largely white constituency that police reformers speak in the wake of outrageous police violence. To the furious protesters marching in the streets, police respond with SWAT units and tear gas; to the white communities who nervously watch events unfold on television, they promise better training, an end to overt racial profiling, and more oversight of police. Copspeak is about pacification, not transformation.

When we listen closely, we can hear police admitting all of this. Speaking shortly after her confirmation as US Attorney General in 2015, Loretta Lynch addressed the unrest in Baltimore following the police killing of Freddie Gray. "We have seen brave officers upholding the right to peaceful protest, while also sustaining serious injury during the city's unfortunate foray into violence. And we have watched it all through the prism of one of the most challenging issues of our time: police–community relations." Lynch would return to this theme of police–community relations often in the speeches that followed, a theme her predecessor Eric Holder emphasized as well. The goal of police reform, she said in remarks following her swearing-in ceremony, was to "restore trust and faith, both in our laws and in those of us who enforce them." In other words, the problem is not police violence but the lack of faith some hold for our police officers. It's a familiar depiction of the problem of police violence as always anomalous rather than by design, as always a problem of bad apples rather than institutionalized violence against the poor. As always about you and rarely about police.

According to this view, something might be broken in US policing, but it can be fixed by new reforms. Something has gone wrong in an otherwise fair and democratic system, but new policies and procedures will restore our faith in the police. This view is troubling for the way it normalizes the violence fundamental to police power. The ideology of reform never calls into question the heart of the problem: that in the quest for "good order" the police institution is first and foremost an institution of state-sanctioned violence and police officers are first and foremost violence workers. Most of this violence is not extralegal, but routine and insidious. It was not the jack-booted thug or rogue cop who killed twelve-year-old Tamir Rice, after all, but the friendly neighborhood police officer. Police reform does not challenge police violence; rather, it is the key way through which the state manages and justifies its claim to a monopoly on violence. Policing is not broken. It works exactly as designed.

Understanding Police: Capitalism and Colonialism

Baldwin wrote of the police serving "white business interests," echoing Karl Marx who, writing a century earlier, had identified the centrality of police powers to the birth of capitalism. "Agricultural folk [were] first forcibly expropriated from the soil, driven from their homes, turned into vagabonds, and then whipped, branded and tortured."[2] The peasant became a proletarian at the end of a police nightstick. The role of the police powers in limiting the prospects for the poor was as true in England in the late fifteenth century as it was in Baldwin's Harlem in 1966, and as it is in Ferguson, Missouri today. If capitalism is anything, it is a well-ordered police state. It has always been the job of police to patrol the poor and to be the occupying army in the ghetto.

When we talk about police, in other words, we're talking about capitalism. Capitalism is always on the hunt for resources and markets, yes, and also for control of the laboring poor in Europe, for people to enslave in Africa, and for Indigenous land in the new world. Colonial domination via police power inaugurated an explicitly racial capitalism in which Black, Brown and Indigenous suffering and death served ruling class interests. This book focuses on the historical and contemporary role of police in the United States and, to a lesser degree, places such as Canada and Australia. This focus recognizes that although police emerge from different histories in different places and serve different power relations, there are certain shared realities about police no matter where you are. In settler colonial societies such as the United States, Canada, Australia and New Zealand, for example, police have played a vital role in imposing and defending a mode of production characterized by the theft of Indigenous land and the ongoing repression of Indigenous people.

When we talk about police in the United States and Canada, in other words, we're talking about settler colonialism. As the late Mohawk lawyer and professor Patricia Monture-Angus pointed out, it is law and the police powers that made and makes settler colonialism possible. "Think about everything that First Nations people [in Canada] have survived in this country; the taking of our land, the taking of our children, residential schools, the current criminal justice system, the outlawing of potlaches, sundances, and other ceremonies, and the stripping of Indian women (and other Indian people) of their status. Everything we survived as individual or as Indian peoples. How was all this delivered? The answer is simple: through law."[3]

The routine, everyday details of policing in the United States are written directly into its founding documents. Consider the language of the Second Amendment to the US Constitution. "A well regulated Militia, being necessary to the security of a free State, the right of the people to keep and bear Arms, shall not be infringed." The Second Amendment, which is defended today with patriotic zeal by a predominately white constituency, did not extend the right to bear arms as an abstract idea; rather, it advanced this right as part of a colonial obligation of police and settlers to kill Indigenous people in order to establish and defend an emerging settler state.

Capitalism and colonialism cannot exist without a state willing and able to defend colonial domination, private property, the wage relation, and the ongoing patterns of dispossession that characterize all of these. Ain't no colonialism and ain't no capitalism without cops.

Police: A Field Guide

Despite this, the institution of police appears self-evident and doesn't seem to need specific and rigorous thinking. Discussion of police is often limited to officers in uniform and nothing more. It is not unusual to read books and articles about "law and order" or "crime and punishment" that have very little to say about police. In many valuable texts on prisons and punishment, the police are present, lurking on the page, arresting, harassing, and confining poor people of color. But all too often, the connection between police power and state violence is not directly articulated, and police—as idea, institution and process—remains elusive. One common result is a confused or confusing language surrounding police, where "policing" is conflated with "crime-fighting," or merely "social control" or "law enforcement." According to this logic the police provide security, and who doesn't want that? But policing is too powerful an idea and process to go unexamined. The police are a political idea, a public institution, and a product of sociohistorical forces. This book tackles policing head on by defining its institutional logics and limits, its histories, and its mandates, mythologies, and material realities. It is our attempt to think directly about police and its relationship to racial capitalism. In our view, capitalism not only needs cops; cops are the everyday executives that make the liberal capitalist state possible.

This book therefore refuses to see the world that copspeak describes. What we think we know about police, and how we talk about police, too often comes to us through a register patrolled by police and police reformers. What we should call state rape becomes body cavity search. What we should call a ruthless beating becomes pain compliance. What is racial terror becomes stop and frisk. What looks like an occupation gets called deterrence. When we speak the language of copspeak—of police reform—we see the world as police do. Police reform is the science of police legitimation accomplished through the art of euphemism. Police reform speaks in a language carefully calibrated to limit our ability to understand police as anything other than an equitable force and indispensable institution. He was "armed" and thus his death was justified. She was noncompliant and our use-of-force continuum permitted great violence against her. In all these cases, the language of police sanitizes the fact of everyday humiliation and violence enacted by police. The vocabulary of police reform is a justification machine. *Police: A Field Guide* offers a different vocabulary, one we hope could replace the taken-for-granted definitions that depict a police view of the world.

In this book you will find definitions for nearly one hundred of the most common terms and concepts that describe and explain police. We define concepts such as arrest, patrol, gun, and many more. The view of police that emerges in this book will be unrecognizable to the police chiefs, police reformers and conservative law and order types who generally view police as an essential force for justice, security, and democracy. Our definitions refuse their standard view that police arrest criminals, patrol crime-infested neighborhoods, and use their guns to deter crime and enhance public safety. The definitions offered in this book provide a critical view of police as violence workers in the defense of a racial and propertied order, not as crime fighters who serve and protect.[4]

Police: A Field Guide shares the abolitionist dream of a world beyond walls, cages and armed police. In order to bring that future into the present, we need a different vocabulary of police, one that is free of the copspeak that constrains every conversation about police. *Police: A Field Guide* redefines the terms and concepts that give police momentum. This is not an exhaustive list of entries, but rather a partial list of keywords that, when read together, explain how a language of police reform serves to guarantee a future of police violence and how a redefined language of police might help chart a future free not only of police violence, but also of the police as we currently know it.

The title of this book is thus not a gimmick. Like any other field guide it is based on the premise that what we find in the world is not always self-evident. In the language of police and police reform, police are both the necessary condition for, and a synonym of, civilization.[5] And so any critical view of police risks always drowning in the quicksand of copspeak: He was a threat, so police were justified. It wasn't violence, it was pain compliance. It was police brutality, but police reform will root out the bad apples and put police back on its path to perfection. The truth of police is obscured by the very vocabulary we use to talk about police. The world of police therefore needs a different vocabulary. *Police: A Field Guide* is a study of the language of police and policing. It examines the taken-for-granted language of police, a language we're all forced to speak when we talk about police. Most importantly, *Police: A Field Guide* provides a different way to understand the police nightstick, a different explanation for the police patrol, and a much different definition of police arrest and interrogation than the one police provide. *Police: A Field Guide* explains why Officer Friendly might not be so friendly. Why the Taser might not be the non-lethal alternative police make it out to be. Why police might have more in common with the military than we're led to believe.

Police: A Field Guide, like any other field guide, exposes and demystifies a world that is hidden in plain view. Why won't police oversight stop police violence? What does noncompliance mean in the police lexicon? What might community policing have in common with military counterinsurgency? What do we learn when we take the police uniform, the police badge, and the police dog seriously? What view of police emerges when we refuse the police definition of terms and concepts such as law, security, and order? What happens when we stop seeing the world as police do, as a world populated by threats and emergencies and disorder?

Police: A Field Guide is not an encyclopedia of police and policing. We make no claim to comprehensiveness. This extends to the sites of our analyses. Most of our examples and illustrations focus on the United States. This is a function of our location in the United States, and of our particular interests and experience. The terms and concepts compiled here reflect our own research and thinking on police, influenced by the work of many scholars and activists, and we suspect they will resonate beyond the United States. Readers throughout the world will see similarities between the police prowling these pages and the ones patrolling their streets.

This is also not a dictionary. The entries stand on their own, but when read together they provide a critical theory to understand police and policing. While the book can be read cover to cover, we suggest a different approach. Start by selecting a term or concept at random or based on your own interest. In it you will find other terms and concepts rendered in bold type. This indicates that those terms are defined elsewhere in the book and can be found at the cross-referenced pages. One reader might start with pacification and then read community policing, then ghetto, then broken windows, and so on. Another reader might select law and then read order, deterrence, police helicopter, and so on. In this way, *Police: A Field Guide* is not the same book for every reader. Each reader pursues the line of thought they find most interesting and the connections they find most pressing.

"The world in which people find themselves," James Baldwin wrote, "is not simply a vindictive plot imposed on them from above; it is also the world they have helped to make. They have helped to make, and help to sustain it by sharing the assumptions which hold their world together." When we speak the language of police—copspeak—we risk seeing the world like police, and thus we help to hold that world together. *Police: A Field Guide* offers a tour through the shared assumptions that sustain the police view of the world so that we might abolish it.

Weaponology:
Technologies and
Tactics of Police Violence

Gun

Police are **violence** (96–100) workers. This is true whether they carry a gun or not because violence is a condition of police work. But it is also true that **cops** (219–221) love carrying guns, and in the United States the firearm has become the essential modern police weapon. They carry Glock, Colt, and Ruger handguns, semi-automatic assault rifles, bolt-action shotguns, pump-action shotguns, and flashbang grenade launchers. They carry shoulder-fired weapons that scramble ocular fluid and blind people. They carry **Tasers** (13–16) on one hip, handguns on the other. They pile rifles and shotguns into the trunk of their cruisers. Even when cops aren't shooting their guns, their pistol always remains displayed on the hip, visible to all, sending a message of **security** (86–89) and protection to the good guys while threatening the bad guys with lethal, and legal, state violence.

Cops love shooting their guns. Most people who are killed by police in the United States, more than 1,000 every year, are killed by a cop who fires a gun at them. And cops are very good and very practiced at shooting their guns. Each September since 2010, teams of cops from all over the United States gather in Albuquerque, New Mexico to practice killing people with guns. Over the course of two weeks at the National Police Shooting Championships, what protesters call the "killer cop" competition, they compete against each other in obstacle shooting courses based on "a hypothetical law enforcement encounter" in events with names like "head shots only," which the National Rifle Association (one of the event sponsors) describes as important because police officers need to "incorporate head shots into their training." A scenario called "Accurate, Fast and Fun" evaluates cops for their ability to kill as many people as possible in the shortest amount of time while having the most possible fun. "Drunk Buddies" imagines a scenario in which drunk, knife-wielding men attack police while yelling "kill the cops." Police win if they can kill everyone. Seventy six cops competed in the competition in 2013. At the time more than one-third of them worked at agencies that were or recently had been under federal investigation for human rights violations.[1]

Cops in the United States are heavily armed and this is largely taken for granted. It is true that some—police abolitionists and liberal reformers alike—voice concerns about the troubling implications of police **militarization** (139–142), but by and large the arming of police receives broad support in the United States. The National Rifle Association and other right-wing gun enthusiast groups like to claim that "an armed society is a polite society," which endorses the right of individuals to arm themselves as they see fit, which then justifies more and more powerful police weaponry because of the number of people who arm themselves as they see fit. The irony here is that the Second Amendment, which guarantees a heavily armed population in the United States, was never about the right of individuals to own weapons, but rather was about the need for an armed militia to police Indigenous bodies and control Native land. The Second Amendment was about settler colonialism, not individual liberty.[2] It served to expand the power of the state to control Native land and later, through the **slave patrol** (143–144), to control Black labor. Today it serves to justify the expanded use of arms by police. An armed society is not a polite society; it is a policed society.

The NRA is also not at all interested in arming everyone equally. The NRA and the police have long feared Black gun ownership. This is partly because historically Black gun ownership has often been fueled by the need of Black people to defend themselves against the police and white people with guns.[3] The rate of Black gun ownership often rises in direct response to the racist violence of white supremacy. Thus the state has always sought to disarm Black, Brown, and Native people, not only during chattel slavery and Jim Crow, but also when Ronald Reagan, as governor of California, passed gun control legislation in order to stop the Black Panther Party for Self Defense from arming its members for protection against the police. The police support gun ownership for the white middle and upper class because it is a class understood as de facto police. But this support for gun ownership ends when historically oppressed populations arm themselves.

If you've lived your whole life in the United States, you might be surprised to learn that the use of guns by police has always been, and in some places remains, controversial, not commonplace. Historians of police often point to Robert Peel, an eighteenth-century British politician, as the father of modern police. Peel insisted police should not carry guns, partly to ease the tensions of those suspicious that an armed police **force** (102–104) would be, in effect, a domestic army. Peel is usually invoked by reformers who seek to "disarm" the police. But to limit a discussion of police violence to the problem of shooting deaths risks elevating spectacular police violence—the **SWAT** (135–139) assault and the hail of bullets—over everyday police violence. The shooting deaths might end, but what about the arbitrary harassment, or the racialized targeting, or the **chokeholds** (58–60) and **rough rides** (31–32)? Those will continue as before because police are violence workers.

Throw-Down Weapon

The throw-down weapon, or drop **gun** (10–13), is police slang for an untraceable weapon, usually a gun or a knife, that police officers sometimes carry in addition to their service weapon. If an officer is involved in a shooting with an **unarmed** (257–258) suspect, the officer will plant the throw-down weapon near the victim in order to mislead investigators into declaring the shooting **justified** (238–240). In the late 1990s, an investigation into the Los Angeles Police Department's **CRASH** (128–130) (Community Resources Against Street Hoodlums) unit in its downtown Rampart division revealed that officers routinely planted evidence and used what they called "drop guns" on suspects.[1] Similar investigations have implicated New York Police Department precincts in engaging in the routine use of throw-down weapons, often planting them on suspects in order to make arrests.[2]

Cell phone video of the 2014 police killing of Walter Scott in North Charleston, South Carolina showed **officer** Michael Slager shooting the unarmed Scott in the back, killing him, and then planting an electronic control weapon, commonly known as a stun gun or **Taser** (13–16), near Scott's body. Until the video surfaced and contradicted Slager's claims, the officer said that he had shot and killed Scott because Scott had taken his Taser. In all cases, the use of throw-down weapons demonstrates that police recognize their use of **violence** (96–100) as needing justification and therefore will often try to stack the deck in their favor in order to legitimate their bloodletting.

Taser

A Taser is a handheld, battery-powered conductive energy device, or stun gun, that the police and military use as a "less-than-lethal" weapon. It delivers the electrical potential of 50,000 volts of electrical current into a person's body via electrically charged darts or electrodes attached to wires. Police are trained to fire the darts at a suspect in order to produce total neuromuscular incapacitation. Police departments purchase a version that comes with a "drive stun" mode that allows police to place the weapon directly on a person and drive the electrical current directly into the body. Police call this a **pain compliance** (79–80) tactic, though a number of Department of Justice investigations of police use of Tasers describe this tactic as "street punishment."

A common slang term for a Taser among police and its victims is "cattle prod." The analogy is not coincidental. The first police conductive energy devices were in fact cattle prods. Police began using cattle prods in the 1940s for **crowd** (201–205) control and as an **interrogation** (193–195) tactic. Cattle prods were also used for crowd control in Alabama against civil rights demonstrators, and notorious Chicago police detective Jon Burge used electrical current and cattle prods in interrogation in order to torture confessions out of Black men. The "cattle prod" as police weapon evokes the image of the animal as the object of police interest. The Taser is a cattle prod with the Taser corporate logo embossed on its side.

The physicist who invented the Taser, Jack Cover, was inspired by science fiction novels and the Watts riots of 1965. He recalled that he read a newspaper article "about a man who had harmlessly gotten stuck on an electric fence for three hours . . . the current immobilized his muscles, and I thought, 'Why not convert that into a hand item?'"

The United Nations declared Tasers a tool of torture in 2007. The American Civil Liberties Union has documented a pattern of Taser use by police against children, pregnant women, people who suffer from mental illness or are in mental health crises, and people who fail to "properly" comply while passively resisting police commands. In December of 2009 two Albuquerque, New Mexico police officers fired Tasers in drive-stun mode into the body of an **unarmed** (257–258) man who had refused to comply with police orders and whom they knew had poured gasoline on himself. He burst into flames. The ACLU recorded thirty-one Taser-related deaths in the United States between 2001 and 2008. In 2015 alone the *Washington Post* recorded forty-eight deaths associated with the police use of Tasers.

Tasers are made by Axon, formerly called Taser International, a US-based weapons manufacturer that sells electrical armaments to the military and police, including a number of versions of the Taser handheld stun gun. It claims electrical weapons are a safe, less-than-lethal option for police. The broad adoption of Tasers—more than 15,000 police and military agencies worldwide use them—suggests that police recognize **force** (102–104) as an unresolvable political problem, to which Tasers provide a technical solution. In other words, Tasers depoliticize police **violence** (96–100) and depict it instead as merely a problem of insufficient tools.

A 2012 Amnesty International study found that between 2001 and 2012 more than 500 people had been killed by police in the United States and Canada after being Tasered. In nearly all cases, Tasers were used against unarmed people as a pain compliance tactic. In May of 2011, Waterbury, Connecticut police officer Adrian Sanchez arrested twenty-six-year-old Marcus Brown for acting erratically and failing to comply with officer commands. He handcuffed Brown and placed him in the back of his **patrol** (170–172) car. According to Sanchez, Brown continued to act erratically, so Sanchez opened the door of his squad car and fired his Taser into Brown's chest. Brown died less than an hour later.

Police often claim that the deaths that follow from their use of Tasers are the result of a preexisting condition among victims called Excited Delirium Syndrome. The owners of Axon, the brothers Rick and Tom Smith, have argued that all people killed after being Tasered would have died anyway because of this condition. Police make the same argument and assert that their actions and the use of the Taser during an in-custody death is always the fault of the victim, who, because he or she died, therefore must have suffered from Excited Delirium. Neither the American Medical Association nor the American Psychiatric Association recognizes any such syndrome.

A 2009 study in the *American Journal of Cardiology* concluded that "Taser deployment was associated with a substantial increase in in-custody sudden deaths." A 2011 study by the US Department of Justice concluded, however, that "there is no conclusive medical evidence within the state of current research that indicates a high risk of serious injury or death from the direct or indirect cardiovascular or metabolic effects of short-term [conducted energy device] exposure in healthy, normal, nonstressed, nonintoxicated persons."

Note how the DOJ study defines "less-than-lethal" through a conditional claim: Taser is always less-than-lethal if used against "healthy, normal, nonstressed, nonintoxicated persons." Since a Taser is not lethal for a "normal" or "healthy" person, a Taser cannot be the cause of death. Thus if a person dies after being Tasered by the police, it is only because that person is not "normal" or "healthy." This kind of logic absolves Axon and police of any wrongdoing, and instead blames the victim for their own death.

What is more dangerous, a Taser in the hands of police, or the medico-legal argument about its use that absolves police of responsibility for the dead they leave? Consider again Marcus Brown, who walked into the emergency room of a Waterbury area hospital just after midnight in May 2011 seeking medical assistance. He was upset and agitated. A receptionist refused to admit him and instead called police. Officer Sanchez handcuffed Brown and placed him in the back of a patrol car. Sanchez, who in his report described Brown as agitated and upset, fired his Taser into Brown's chest, an **unarmed** (257–258), restrained man whom Sanchez knew to be stressed and seeking medical assistance. A subsequent Connecticut Division of Criminal Justice **investigation** (175–176) exonerated the officer. The report reads less like an investigation of Sanchez and more like a review of Taser's immutable safety. Since the DOJ study exonerates Axon, Connecticut exonerated Sanchez. "Officer Sanchez could not reasonably believe that his actions were likely to cause serious or lasting physical injury to Mr. Brown" and therefore "the use of [the Taser] cannot be determined to have caused Mr. Brown's death."

This is the warning label found on the boxes in which Taser International ships its stun guns to police:

Tear Gas

Tear gas is a toxic chemical agent that irritates the eyes, nose, throat and lungs of those that come into contact with it. The name tear gas is a misnomer, or better still a euphemism, in that it suggests that exposure merely causes tears in its victims. At a minimum, exposure will result in the uncontrollable emission of tears and mucus from eyes and noses, and will induce violent coughing that could last for hours. At worst it kills its victims.

A variety of chemical agents—CS gas, pepper spray, and others—fall under the general category of tear gas, and nearly all were originally developed for use in World War I. Following the **war** (100–102), the 1925 Geneva Gas Protocol banned the use of all chemical agents, including tear gas, in warfare. The protocol and a follow-up 1993 agreement concluded that tear gas was too dangerous to use in war. Despite the ban, the United States used tear gas in Vietnam. Soldiers fired canisters into tunnels in order to asphyxiate people. In 2007, WikiLeaks released a secret military report that revealed the US military deployed nearly 3,000 chemical weapons in Iraq. The 1925 convention, however, expressly permits the use of chemical agents for "law enforcement including domestic riot control purposes."

Chemical weapons are too dangerous for military use, but not for police use? Military personnel, according to this logic, cannot distinguish between less-than-lethal and lethal gas during warfare, whereas domestic targets of chemical agents can be assured that police will only ever use nonlethal chemical agents. And police use a lot of it. As a theoretically nonlethal weapon, tear gas has come to serve an important reform function. Tear gas produces **order** (83–86) without appearing to cause pain and suffering. CS gas has become among the most common less-than-lethal weapons in the police **crowd** (201–205) control arsenal.

But CS gas is only nonlethal when used under open, ventilated conditions and when exposure is limited to a short duration. But this is never how police use CS or other tear gases. Police do not just use tear gas; they weaponize it. It is used to intimidate, to punish, to inflict pain and suffering, and to torture. A 2012 report on its use by police in Bahrain noted that tear gas was not used for crowd control but to "punish protesters, inflict suffering, and suppress dissent."[1] Among the earliest police uses of tear gas was a "tear gas club," a combination tear gas and **nightstick** (55–58) weapon. With it a **cop** (219–221) could simultaneously strike a person with a billy club while also igniting a small explosive in the shaft that delivered tear gas directly into the face of a victim. One researcher notes, "In the 1920s, Chicago police pioneered the technique of pumping tear gas into small cells. Police would place a box over the prisoner's head and release a canister inside the box. Advances in pumping technology now allow torturers to apply mace, pepper spray, or tear gas directly into keyholes or the mouth or face of prisoners. This technique appeared in Israeli prisons in the 1970s, and spread to American and Canadian prisons in the 1980s, and then Belgium and Taiwan in the 1990s."[2]

Among the first US domestic targets of CS gas were striking West Virginia coal miners. Bayonets and rifles, the usual crowd control tools, left a bloody battlefield behind. CS gas promised to replace the standard punitive police approach with a gentler, more "progressive" one. In a 1921 article advocating the use of gas against workers, police were told that gas "aim[s] at isolating the individual and restoring him to normality."[3] This was a "humane" alternative to dealing with the "mob." Salesmen for tear gas manufacturers would follow headlines for labor disputes and sell tear gas to local police. A Senate subcommittee investigation into industrial-munitions sales found that "between 1933 and 1937, more than $1.25 million [about $21 million today] worth of 'tear and sickening gas' had been purchased in the US 'chiefly during or in anticipation of strikes.'"[4]

Less than lethal, more humane, leaves no mark—none of this is true. In most cases, police, using pressurized grenade launchers, fire weapons-grade CS gas in explosive canisters directly into crowds and into enclosed buildings full of people. The practice occasionally kills victims through blunt-force trauma alone. Most CS gas is released in aerosol form, which causes severe burns and blistering at close range. As a result, in addition to the intended temporary incapacitation of CS exposure that reformers approve of, there are also more severe risks such as pulmonary damage, severe burns, permanent blinding, miscarriage and death. Between 1990 and 1995, at least sixty-one fatalities nationwide—twenty-seven of them in California—were reported following police use of pepper spray on suspects.[5]

The use of tear gas by police is so common that protestors often come prepared by wearing gas masks or face coverings. A common police tactic, used in Seattle at the 1999 World Trade Organization protests and during the 2011 Occupy protests at the University of California, Davis, is to pull off the facemasks of protesters and deliver a form of pepper spray directly to the eyes. When the eyes are exposed at close range, the risks of pepper spray include blindness.

The United States is among the world's largest producers and exporters of tear gas. "Between January 1987 and December 1988, the United States exported $6.5 million worth of tear gas guns, grenades, launchers, and launching cartridges to Israel. Rights groups recorded up to 40 deaths resulting from tear gas during the First Intifada, as well as thousands of cases of illness."[6] US arms manufacturers export tear gas to Israel while Palestinian activists export their experience dealing with chemical weapons back to the United States. In 2014 Palestinian activists trained Black Lives Matter activists in Ferguson, Baltimore and elsewhere how to protect themselves from the threat, as police in Ferguson, Missouri fired tear gas into buildings, directly at protesters, and into crowds that included children during the unrest that followed the police killing of Michael Brown.

Most of the chemical weapons used by state security police in Egypt and Tunisia against Arab Spring protesters were made by a Pennsylvania company called Combined Systems, Inc., a firm that also provides chemical weapons to municipal police departments as well as the Israeli and US militaries. CSI makes a number of different kinds of chemical munitions, flash-bang grenades, various types of grenade launchers and **handcuffs** (20–21). Why would a chemical weapons manufacturer also make handcuffs? Because CSI is in the business of selling order. And order is what police buy from CSI.

Tear gas must be understood as part of a police arsenal intended to produce order. Tear gas, like handcuffs, incapacitates a person. And tear gas, like handcuffs, is a **pain compliance** (79–80) technique that can leave no obvious physical injuries. Through pain and incapacitation, tear gas and handcuffs can appear to magically produce order by pacifying unruly subjects. Thus tear gas is the perfect police weapon because police fear the crowd, the mob, the riot, the collective. Chemical weapons scatter the crowd, and return things to "normal." No more people in the streets making political demands, no more people threatening **private property** (81–83). Just gas and the order it delivers.

Handcuffs

Handcuffs are artifacts of unfreedom. They are a routine sign of the unfreedom built into the very foundation of liberal democracy. They are a means of managing bodies at the point of **arrest** (208–210), of transporting arrestees to the poor house, the jail, or the gallows. Handcuffs have long played an important but overlooked role in the **violence** (96–100) of racial capitalism. The modern police notion of handcuffs enters the English language in the late seventeenth century, the same time police power emerges as a central organizing logic for the administration of the poor and **private property** (81–83). Today's handcuffs are just a shinier and more standardized restraint system than the ropes, rawhides, chains, leg irons, and shackles that were central to both the feudal era and racial capitalism's regimes of settler colonialism and chattel slavery.

Although it might be easy to dismiss handcuffs as just a basic tool, officers are trained in all sorts of methods to restrain subjects with handcuffs, and they are one of the most frequently used weapons in the police arsenal. It might be true that the average police officer will never use his or her **gun** (10–13), but this can't be said for handcuffs.

Handcuffs are used not only for restraint and incapacitation but also for **pain compliance** (79–80). Police scientists have designed handcuffs that shock captives—"stun-cuffs"—or even administer drugs to help incapacitate unruly captives. To be handcuffed is not a pleasant experience, and that's just how police want it. If you are arrested, police will cuff your wrists together tightly behind your back, often for hours. And in the United States, handcuffs are no stranger to police torture and police **rape** (41–43), such as by NYPD officers in 1997 when they sodomized Abner Louima with a broken broomstick. In Chicago, Angel Perez alleged that he was handcuffed to a metal bar in the infamous holding facility known as Homan Square and then sodomized by a metal object, which he believed was the barrel of a cop's handgun.[1] The serial rapist cop Daniel Holtzclaw handcuffed a Black woman to a hospital bed before he raped her. Abraham Joseph, a Texas police officer, handcuffed and then raped an undocumented woman on the trunk of his police cruiser in Houston in 2011.

Perhaps more than any other weapon, handcuffs evoke the ways that **violence** (96–100) is a *condition* of police work, and that the ability to incapacitate bodies is always central to the police project of fabricating **order** (83–86). More specifically, handcuffs signify the individualizing powers of capture and arrest, and it is the handcuff that demonstrates police as the first incarcerators, the first captors. Handcuffs exist on a carceral continuum that includes the back of the police car, the jail, the courthouse, the prison. But as part of this continuum, the handcuff can easily be taken for granted, rarely recognized for its own role in projects of unfreedom.

Handcuffs are so normal, and common, and their use so routine that their insidious role in domination is often ignored. Handcuffs serve the police desire for domination: once handcuffed there is nothing the police can't do to the captive. There is no way around the fact that handcuffs are a form of bodily and psychological domination. To be handcuffed is to be controlled, violently subjected to the prospect of violence delivered in more extreme ways—beaten by a nightstick or raped by the barrel of a gun. Incapacitation opens the very real possibility of extreme degradation and torture. Once a cop handcuffs a subject, that subject is now completely at the mercy of the state and its agents. Perhaps this is why cops themselves frequently complain, and comically so, about being "handcuffed" by **laws** (90–93) and the courts. It is an admission that police are supposed to always be in a dominant, and dominating, position.

K-9

The snarling police dog, a German Shepherd or Belgian Malinois, lays bare the predatory animus of police. The police dog offers the starkest example of policing as a **pursuit** (200–201), a chase, a hunt, transforming humans into prey. The police dog trained to attack is among the most normalized features of every major police department, with little attention paid to this animalized form of police terror.

Police dogs are an extension of watch and guard dogs. The thousands of dogs that assist officers on **patrol** (170–172) are trained to "sniff out" contraband like drugs or explosives and also to engage in "criminal apprehension" by biting fleeing or noncompliant subjects. Through what cops call "bite work," police weaponize the dog and literally animalize police **violence** (96–100). Nearly every day in the United States a police dog chases and bites a person. Their prey are often suspects but this count also includes bystanders bitten by "accident." These are brutal, bloody attacks; the wounds inflicted by a trained attack K-9 are intended to be debilitating and disfiguring. Victims often require prosthetics and surgery and suffer through long, painful recoveries. Victims often describe the panicked moment of attack by a dog's powerful jaws and piercing teeth as like being eaten alive, literally devoured by the state.

Trevon Robinson, a fifteen-year-old Black teenager, was severely bitten by a police dog in the Los Angeles area in the early 1990s. "I said, 'Please, please get the dog off me.' I was crying . . . Sometimes I have a dream of a dog attacking me . . . I wake up and my heart is beating so fast I can't go back to sleep." A seventeen-year-old girl spoke of a similar psycho-political experience of animalized state violence: "I was scared to death. I thought it was going to rip me apart."[1]

Police dogs first appeared in the United States in the early 1900s, with New York City among the first places to experiment in the use of dogs. In this early stage, the police dog patrolled nighttime cities and police administrators and journalists claimed the dog struck terror in the hearts of vagrants and prowlers. Their fundamental task, however, has never been **crime** (93–96) fighting, but the protection of **private property** (81–83) and the policing of surplus populations. The police dog makes sense as a technique of police terror only when understood within the context of the class **war** (100–102) police wage on behalf of the bourgeoisie.

By the late 1950s and 1960s, at the height of the Black freedom struggle, city councils and police administrators throughout the United States turned to the dog to pacify Black and Brown insurgency. It was during this period that "Canine Corps," as they were often called, first proliferated across the country. Those advocating for the introduction of dogs to the police **force** (102–104) saw in trained dogs, especially German Shepherds but also Doberman Pinschers and Rottweilers, a powerful new weapon, a potent **crowd** (201–205) control method, a terrifying means to deter and apprehend "criminals" and, perhaps most importantly, a new and menacing way to patrol the **ghetto** (183–184) and white business districts. The greatest utility of the police dog was its ability to instill fear, what police referred to as the dog's "psychological effect."

For many Black folks the police dog is nothing other than a weapon of anti-Black state terror. The images of K-9s set loose on Black civil rights protesters during the 1960s remain some of the most enduring and terrifying of the era. Although this terror is usually thought of as primarily a Southern phenomenon, the police dog was used frequently against Black crowds and people in Northern cities too. Police dogs attacked and bit Black men, women, and children, echoing the historical terror of the notorious Cuban Bloodhounds trained to hunt down runaway slaves. Ultimately, the use of dogs for crowd control proved too controversial, and patrol and "criminal apprehension" became the primary accepted use of dogs.

The police dog enshrines in police a snarling brutality and savage violence that defies any claim to professed "enlightened" standards. But this is not how police see it. The dog is always described by police as a reform measure, and as a more "efficient" and "humane" tactic of policing. This eventually became most clear with the introduction of the drug or bomb "sniffer dogs" in the late 1960s and early 1970s. Here the dog was, and still is today, framed as a highly scientific tool that greatly enhanced the **searching** (163–165) powers of police, despite the fact that sniffer dogs have been shown to produce "false alerts" quite frequently. We also know that these dogs are highly influenced by the perceptions and actions of their human handlers, and there is growing evidence demonstrating racial discrimination in drug sniffs.

But forget its terror and its racist and classist history, we're told. The sniffer dog fights the **war** (100–102) on drugs and the patrol dog fights the war on crime. And the animal comes to us not as the snarling beast but the friendly pet. The police dog, cops say, is "colorblind" and heralds a "post-racial" era in policing. An enormous police dog industry reinforces this view through magazines, conferences, training organizations, and public relations experts. Meanwhile police continue to use the police dog in highly racialized ways. Indeed, the historical anti-Black terror of the police dog was evoked in Ferguson when police used them to hold back crowds protesting the police killing of Michael Brown. Every person a police dog has bit in Ferguson, Missouri has been Black.

There is something about the police dog that plays off of a primordial human fear: the animal terror of being hunted down and devoured. This is what the police dog teaches us. Despite its own claims to civility, the police power is a predatory power. Malcolm X once said that "police dogs and police clubs" provided the proof that the "American white man" was "one of the most cruel beasts that has ever taken people into captivity." He referred to police officers as a "two-legged dog." It is in the growling police dog that the brutal image of police emerges most clearly, and in the bloody wounds and torn flesh of their victims that the point of the police power comes so clearly into focus. There is no better contemporary example than the famous phrase popularized by a cartoon police dog, McGruff the Crime Dog, in the 1980s: "Take a bite out of crime!" Police, after all, is a beast.

Racial Profiling

Racial profiling refers to the practice among police of choosing whom to **search** (163–165), whom to **stop and frisk** (27–31) and whom to **arrest** (208–210) based on race. It is discriminatory because it bases police practice on a person's perceived race, ethnicity, religion or national origin, rather than on evidence or suspicion of criminal activity. Racial profiling is a common practice among police, and though they deny it, it is often the primary factor when police consider who to stop, who to search or who to detain. According to New York ACLU stop and frisk data, nine out of ten of the more than 650,000 people who were stopped and frisked by New York City police in 2011 were innocent of any suspected crimes. And more than 91 percent of all the people police stopped were people of color.

Police disguise their racial profiling in a number of ways. The legal concept of **reasonable suspicion** (255–257) provides cover for much of the racial profiling that police practice. Reasonable suspicion requires that police establish specific and articulable facts based on rational inferences that a person is engaged in or involved in criminal activity before they conduct a stop and frisk. So instead of stopping people based on race, police claim they stop people because those people were in a **crime**-infested (93–96) neighborhood, or because they made **furtive movements** (236–238).

Predictive policing (178–179) provides additional cover for the practice of racial profiling. Predictive policing, also known as data-driven or intelligence-led policing, is the practice of collecting demographic and crime data and using that data to predict criminal "hot spots" and "future crimes." Predictive policing tells us that stop and frisk is based on computer algorithms, not racial bias, and thus as a practice is not discriminatory. It serves to make police appear objective and therefore scientific, rather than biased and therefore discriminatory.

Anti–police **violence** (96–100) activists and organizations have used the overwhelming evidence of racial profiling by police to argue that the higher rates of arrest and police violence in communities of color have little to do with crime and disorder and everything to do with racialized policing and the **disproportionate** (232–235) targeting of poor communities of color by police. This is an important critique that has helped to shine light on the practice of racial profiling as an example of the racialized nature of policing.

There is, however, an often unseen political pitfall in the critique of racial profiling when it is centered in struggles against police violence and racist police practices. For one, it risks depicting the problem as one related to a particular practice—stop and frisk for example—that can be isolated, critiqued and, hopefully, reformed. If only we could prove that police racially profile people, we might then be able to convince or force police to quit the practice of racially profiling people, the argument goes. When offered this way, racial profiling portrays racialized policing not as systemic or fundamental to police power, but rather as an isolated and specific issue that can be rectified. This is critique in a liberal register, consistent with establishment notions of **police reform** (155–160) that refuse to see police as an inherently racist institution.

When offered as a liberal critique of police, racial profiling transforms racism or white supremacy into a kind of idiosyncrasy of police that absolutely limits, rather than expands, the horizon of the anti–police violence struggle. Racialized police violence is the rule, not the exception. Reforms that propose to weed out racist cops or train the racism out of cops will always serve in the end to justify rather than end future racialized police violence. After all, the reformists will remind us, now that reforms have been implemented and cops have been professionalized, that racism has been filtered out of them and their practices. And so racism can't possibly have anything to do with their violence.

This is not to say that radical movements to end police violence secretly wish to expand police power (although it is very literally the goal of some reformist efforts). Rather it is to say that too much is at stake to risk falling into the "realist" or "pragmatic" trap represented by concepts such as racial profiling. "On so many occasions when the protest movements made public statements they expressed an understanding of police violence as the rule of the day and not as a shocking exception. However, when it came time to formulate practical proposals to change the fundamental nature of policing, all they could come up with concretely were more oversight committees, litigation, and civilian review boards ('with teeth'), none of which lived up to the collective intuition about what the police were actually doing . . . the language of alternatives and the terms of relevance are constantly dragged into the political discourse they seek to oppose, namely, that the system works and is capable of reform."[1]

A critique of police that relies on racial profiling is much like a critique that complains about **police brutality** (207–208), which views the problem of police violence as one of *excessive* police violence. We demand an end to police brutality, and if we win we'll get cops who fire fewer bullets at people, and who kill with a **Taser** (13–16) instead of a **gun** (10–13). If we demand an end to racial profiling and win that fight we'll get cops with endless diversity training who kill fewer Black people with a **chokehold** (58–60), who kill fewer adolescent boys and girls of color, and who maybe **rape** (41–43) fewer women than before.

Stop and Frisk

Stop and frisk is a police practice in which officers stop, question and frisk pedestrians or motorists who police suspect of criminal activity. They stop, question, frisk and, often, **search** (163–165). The practice is a central part of **broken windows** (186–189) policing, a theory first elaborated by James Wilson and George Kelling in their 1982 *Atlantic Monthly* article that proposed a zero tolerance policy on minor "quality of life" offenses. Wilson and Kelling urged police to take "informal or extralegal steps to help protect what the neighborhood had decided was the appropriate level of public **order** (83–86)." Their theory imagined that disorder came from a breakdown in normative, middle-class values. Consider how they described it:

> A stable neighborhood of families who care for their homes, mind each other's children, and confidently frown on unwanted intruders can change, in a few years or even a few months, to an inhospitable and frightening jungle. A piece of property is abandoned, weeds grow up, a window is smashed. Adults stop scolding rowdy children; the children, emboldened, become more rowdy. Families move out, unattached adults move in. Teenagers gather in front of the corner store. The merchant asks them to move; they refuse. Fights occur. Litter accumulates. People start drinking in front of the grocery; in time, an inebriate slumps to the sidewalk and is allowed to sleep it off. Pedestrians are approached by panhandlers.[1]

Police, according to Wilson and Kelling, should treat panhandlers and loiterers with zero tolerance. They admitted that the "steps" they proposed—arbitrary search and constant harassment—had no legal merit. But they claimed to know what the neighborhood wanted and thus depicted the issue as a pressing moral problem that only police could solve. Neighborhoods, they concluded, wanted police to remove "panhandlers, drunks, addicts, rowdy teenagers, prostitutes, loiterers, the mentally disturbed."[2] The courts might throw out the **arrest** (208–210), but the arrest would clear the street. And even when the stop and frisk doesn't produce an arrest, it puts "them" on notice. Some "drunks and derelicts," according to Wilson and Kelling, "knew their place," but others didn't.[3] The people who didn't know their place were not the "decent folk" who deserved police protection. Instead they were loiterers or "people who broke the informal rules" and they should be "arrested for vagrancy."[4] Broken windows is about nostalgia for an imagined past and it is also about fear—the fear Wilson and Kelling claim that "decent folk" suffer when police don't keep order in their neighborhoods, and, more importantly, the fear that Wilson and Kelling want police to impose on the "drunks and derelicts" through constant stop and frisk searches.

Stop and frisk is thus not about **crime** (93–96) fighting, it is about putting people in their place. Former Boston, New York and Los Angeles police chief William Bratton became Wilson and Kelling's most prominent acolyte, popularizing stop and frisk at police departments throughout the United States and abroad. Under Bratton, stop and frisk is how police harass, almost exclusively, poor Black or Latino residents. When stop and frisk ends in arrest, it is often for minor offenses such as loitering, trespassing, disorderly conduct, failure to obey, disturbing the peace, jaywalking, **vagrancy** (189–193), or graffiti. But more importantly, stop and frisk rarely results in arrest. The point of stop and frisk, as Wilson and Kelling admitted, is not about fighting crime. It is about *suppressing* crime through constant surveillance, intelligence gathering, searching, questioning, and frisking. Bratton, like Wilson and Kelling, celebrate the "order" that results from stop and frisk—an order they consider a restoration of quality of life. And if we take Bratton at his word, we can only conclude that to police "quality of life," since stop and frisk zeroes in on poor Black and Latino communities, is something constantly under **threat** (222–223) by the very presence of people of color. Stop and frisk is thus a method to impose racialized inequality through fear and intimidation.

Under Bratton, the NYPD flooded Black and Latino neighborhoods with cops who engaged in aggressive stop and frisk practices. The judge in *Floyd et al. v. NYC*, a lawsuit filed by community groups that sought to stop NYPD's stop and frisk practices, agreed that the practice was racially motivated and designed to intimidate. "The NYPD's practice of making stops that lack individualized reasonable suspicion has been so pervasive and persistent as to become not only a part of the NYPD's standard operating procedure, but a fact of daily life in some New York City neighborhoods." And those neighborhoods, the court was quick to point out, are predominately Black and Latino, and the people for whom stop and frisk is part of daily life are nearly universally poor people of color. One NYPD officer, for example, stopped and frisked 120 people during the third quarter of 2009, and every single person was Black.

New York City might get most of the attention when considering stop and frisk policing, but the practice is built into the architecture of policing everywhere. Stop and frisk as it is practiced today is a more recent version of what police have called a *Terry* stop. According to the 1968 Supreme Court decision *Terry v. Ohio*, a police officer can stop, question and frisk a person without first securing a search warrant as long as that stop is based on "specific and articulable facts." The *Terry* frisk is mainly used against Black and Latino populations, but stop and frisk is always at play whenever police pull someone over because the unaccountable **discretion** (176–178) extended to police means there is always a reason to conduct a search, and "specific and articulable facts" can always be invented after the fact.

The Baltimore Police Department saw stop and frisk as a way of "striking fear into loiterers city-wide."[5] In a city of 620,000 people, BPD officers "make several hundred thousand pedestrian stops per year." Nearly all of these stops happen in poor, Black neighborhoods. "One African-American man was stopped 34 times . . . in the Central and Western Districts alone, and several hundred residents were stopped at least 10 times. Countless individuals—including Freddie Gray—were stopped multiple times in the same week without being charged with a crime." During one three-year period, BPD officers made 1.5 stops per resident in Baltimore's poorest neighborhoods, where they arrested more than 750 people on a charge of being "rogue or vagabond" and another 650 for "playing cards." These are tactics that Wilson and Kelling called "order-maintenance" and that the BPD described as "corner clearing." Without any evidence or suspicion of wrongdoing, cops would stop and frisk young Black men and order them off the street. We "do not treat criminals like citizens," one BPD sergeant told the US Department of Justice, demonstrating the extent to which stop and frisk is premised on **racial profiling** (24–27) and the criminalization of Blackness.[6]

Some officers with the Baltimore Police Department refer to the stop and frisk patrol as working the "VCR detail"—the "violation of civil rights" detail. But it is more than a civil rights violation. The point of stop and frisk is to use fear to impose order. As Didier Fassin showed, stop and frisk imposes "a pure power relationship that functions as a recall to order—not to public order, which is not under threat by youngsters quietly conversing on a bench or joyfully playing soccer, but to a social order, which is one of inequality (between the police and the youth) and injustice (with regard to the **law** (90–93) and simply to dignity) that has to be impressed in the body."[7] The point is to humiliate a target population, in other words, with constant stops and harassment.

Stop and frisk, and broken windows policing more generally, is part of what police call **community policing** (122–123). As the experience in Baltimore and New York described above makes clear, community policing defines the community in very narrow terms. Community, in other words, is never meant to be *inclusive*; rather, it is always *exclusive* in nature. Through stop and frisk, police seek to "take back" the city from the poor and people of color and give it to the wealthy and white. When officers use stop and frisk to "clear the corner," they also clear the way for increased development and new urban investment. In short, stop and frisk makes **gentrification** (184–186) possible. Stop and frisk is always about imposing a moral and racialized order of patriarchal capitalism on the poor in the city. Loitering means you're not buying, panhandling means you're not making a wage, drinking means you're not home with a family, streetwalking means you're not serving a husband. So fuck you! You know the drill. Hands against the wall and spread your legs. This is not your city.

Rough Ride

The police make an **arrest** (208–210). They **handcuff** (20–21) a suspect and place the suspect in the back of a police van. The van is hot. It has metal seats. The seats are slick and the corners are sharp. The walls are metal and have no padding. The police do not secure the suspect with a seatbelt. The **cop** (219–221) behind the wheel drives erratically and at high speeds. The van stops often and suddenly. The victim literally bounces off the metal walls and emerges from the van bloodied and unconscious, sometimes with a severed spine and broken bones. This is a rough ride.

It's April 12, 2015 and witnesses see four Baltimore police officers dragging a screaming Freddie Gray toward a police van. Police handcuff his arms behind his back and bind his legs in irons. They throw him in the back of the van. It is a metal box, a cage on wheels. They are on their way to Central Booking, but they never arrive. Instead they take Gray on a rough ride through West Baltimore streets. Nearly an hour after his arrest, the van arrives at the Western District station. Gray is unresponsive, his spine is severed and his larynx is crushed. Blood covers the metal walls and drips from the seat belts that hang unused. Medics arrive and transport Gray to shock trauma where he dies a week later from his injuries.

Now change the name from Freddie Gray to Dondi Johnson Sr. In November 2005 Baltimore police arrest Johnson for what they say is **public** (252–255) urination. They cuff his arms behind his back and throw him in the back of a police van. He arrives, like Gray, with a severed spine. He survives, like Gray, only to die later from his injuries.

In Philadelphia the police and their victims call it a nickel ride. Philadelphia police arrest Gino Thompson in April of 1994. They cuff him and place him in the back of a police van. As with Gray and Johnson, police do not use the seat belt and they drive erratically. The metal walls deliver a ruthless beating, over and over again, until the trauma severs Thompson's spinal cord, paralyzing him from the waist down.

In the media coverage that followed Gray's brutal homicide, the common practice of the rough ride came under scrutiny. Newspapers explained the practice as a form of street justice in which officers punish suspects who "give them lip" or "resist" their commands.

We might be tempted to place the rough ride alongside a suite of dehumanizing police practices such as the **chokehold** (58–60), but we would only be partly right. The rough ride does not just dehumanize, it fully objectifies its victims. It demonstrates the total domination of police power over the human body. It renders its victims objects; mere payload. "You feel like a piece of cargo," said twenty-seven-year-old Christine Abbot, who survived a Baltimore police rough ride in 2012. "You don't feel human."[1]

The *New York Times* described the rough ride as a police "ritual." The Mollen Commission, which investigated NYPD, called it a "bonding ritual that strengthened loyalty and the code of silence." They are content to limit their analysis to the merely descriptive. And indeed the rough ride is so common and so constant as to nearly constitute a police ceremony. But the idea of police **violence** (96–100) as a ritual, as something that serves a ceremonial purpose, opens up an unexpected line of thinking. We should ask what it means about police when we say that the severing of a person's spine serves a ceremonial function. Or that breaking a person's body forms the foundation of police camaraderie and loyalty. It is to say that violence is not a ritual of police, but rather that violence constitutes police. At the heart of police power we find a lethal obligation, red in tooth and claw.

Body Cavity Search

A body cavity search is the manual internal inspection of the body cavities by police officers and jail or prison guards. While a strip **search** (163–165) is limited to the visual inspection by police of a person's unclothed body and body cavities, a body cavity search includes also the forced penetration of body cavities by a police officer, usually during or following an arrest or upon entry to a prison or jail facility. Another word to describe this practice is **rape** (41–43), or more specifically, state rape. Understanding the body cavity search as state rape amends Max Weber's argument regarding the state's monopoly on violence. Weber argued that the state reserves for itself the right to use **violence** (96–100) as part of its exclusive policing power. The body cavity search demonstrates that the state reserves for itself a monopoly on sexual violence as well.

The body cavity search is legally sanctioned sexual violence by the state. It is a practice similar in every respect to criminal sexual penetration as defined in **law** (90–93) by every US state criminal code: the unwanted penetration of a body part or an object into oral, genital or anal openings.

Unlike perpetrators of criminal sexual penetration, however, the police who conduct body cavity searches are not subject to **arrest** (208–210) and are not charged with felony rape. Instead the practice is sanctioned by the US Supreme Court and routinely practiced at every level of law enforcement and in every jail and prison facility in the United States.

Police and the courts defend the practice as a necessary tool to enhance **public** (252–255) safety and **security** (86–89). Its victims describe it as a tactic of state terror designed to control and humiliate. In the late 1970s, an investigation by a Chicago TV station revealed that the Chicago Police Department routinely conducted strip and body cavity searches of women in station houses throughout the city following misdemeanor arrests and even minor traffic violations.[1]

In *Bell v. Wolfish* (1979), the US Supreme Court, in a 6–3 vote, defended the practice and concluded that body cavity searches do not constitute a violation of the Fourth Amendment freedom from unreasonable search and seizure. In other words, the court found that the unwanted, invasive penetration of a person's vaginal or anal cavity by a police officer or jail guard is analogous, in legal terms, to the search by police of a person's car or private residence. The ruling overturned a lower court's decision and created a new and lower legal standard for conducting body cavity searches. A police officer can search your car or private residence, or even your pockets, if the officer can first establish probable cause or **reasonable suspicion** (255–257) that a **crime** (93–96) has been committed. The decision in *Bell v. Wolfish*, however, concluded that no such cause or suspicion was required for an officer to conduct an anal or genital search. The decision provided legal sanction for the practice of body cavity search as a routine part of everyday policing. Justice Thurgood Marshall, who called body cavity searches "one of the most grievous offenses against personal dignity and common decency," did not join the majority. In his dissenting opinion he pointed to evidence "that these searches engendered among detainees fears of sexual assault," and "were the occasion for actual threats of physical abuse by guards."

Critical scholars of police include the body cavity search in a continuum of police sexual violence that includes other forms of coerced sexual violence, such as police officers arresting women and offering to drop charges in return for specific sex acts. As feminist scholars point out, sexual violence against women is often committed by those who women turn to for protection from sexual violence. Thus the legal sanctioning of police rape in the form of the body cavity search reflects a profound institutional indifference to sexual violence against women in all its forms.

No-Knock Warrant

Let's start with a hypothetical. A **cop** (219–221) calls a judge. "I need a warrant." The judge asks the cop, "do you have probable cause?" The cop says, "Yes, absolutely. We have an anonymous tip." Or maybe he says, "we have a confidential informant." The judge asks if police consider the tip reliable. "Yes, absolutely," says the cop. The judge asks if police consider the informant trustworthy. "Sure," says the cop, "our CI gives us reliable info," and in saying these words the cop officially meets the legal standard for probable cause. The judge consents to the petition and tells the cop she'll sign the search warrant. "Great," says the cop, "Oh, and also—I almost forgot—we need an exception to the knock-and-announce rule." This usually takes around thirty seconds.

The Fourth Amendment to the US Constitution prohibits police from conducting unreasonable searches and seizures but establishes an exception by giving police access to court-issued warrants to conduct searches and to seize people and property. In theory, the exception does not absolve police from the requirement that they first "knock and announce" before executing a search warrant in order to give the resident a chance to open the door.

This standard applied until a Madison, Wisconsin cop named Pharo disguised himself as a maintenance man and knocked on Steiney Richards's hotel room door just before 4 a.m. on New Year's Day, 1992. The 1986 Anti-Drug Abuse Act provided a limited exception to the knock-and-announce rule—cops could now request a no-knock warrant or a sneak-and-peek warrant. Madison police requested a no-knock but a judge rejected the request. Cops hate rules when applied to police (see **accountability**, 160–162), so they lied to Richards and violated the knock-and-announce rule. "Who is it?" Richards asked. "Maintenance," Pharo replied. The security chain remained attached as Richards cracked the door. He saw police and closed the door. Pharo and the other cops broke down the door and arrested Richards on drug charges. Lawyers for Richards petitioned the court to exclude the evidence police collected because they did so in violation of a court order. The court refused. The case made it all the way to the Supreme Court in 1997, where the Justices, in the language of copspeak, unanimously agreed that "today's drug culture" constituted "exigent circumstances" that permitted a broad exception to the knock rule.[1] Judges approved fewer than 2,000 no-knock warrants per year in the mid-1980s. After Richards, the number ballooned and by 2010 judges approved more than 60,000 no-knock warrants.[2]

Back to the hypothetical. The cop asks the judge for an exception to the knock-and-announce rule. The informant, the cop tells the judge, says there are exigent circumstances. The cop had never used the word "exigent" before becoming a cop, but Richards established this as a magic word when it comes to warrants. The judge permits the no-knock warrant, and the cop is pleased. He tells his sergeant as they drive to serve the warrant. The sergeant replies, "I guess, but it doesn't really matter." Richards gave police exigent circumstances, but a subsequent ruling really opened the flood gates. It doesn't matter whether cops have a knock-and-announce warrant or a no-knock warrant. If a judge rejects a no-knock request, cops just knock really quietly, like Albuquerque police have been known to do, and then lie to the court and say they didn't; or cops just announce their presence with a whisper and then lie to the court and say they yelled it (see **testilying**, 218–219). Or they break down the door *while* announcing their presence. The other cop says, "Really?" The Sergeant says, "Yep. We can thank Scalia for that." Actually, they can thank Booker Hudson, but Hudson doesn't want their thanks.

Booker Hudson sat in a chair in his living room on August 27, 1998, which he doesn't do anymore because he's in jail now. Detroit police arrived that day with a search warrant. They knocked softly on the door so Hudson wouldn't hear them. They did not announce their presence. They turned the handle on the door and found it unlocked, so they entered. They arrested Hudson on drug and gun charges. His lawyers petitioned the court to exclude evidence collected by police because police violated the knock-and-announce rule. An illegal **search** (163–165) cannot produce legal evidence, they told the court, referencing the exclusionary rule. The trial judge agreed, but the Michigan Court of Appeals reversed the ruling. Hudson was convicted at trial and incarcerated. The case came before the US Supreme Court in 2006 where Scalia, writing for the majority, determined that while police are legally obligated to knock and announce, any failure to do so does not exclude evidence collected in the search from any subsequent trial. The ruling transformed the Fourth Amendment into the Fourth Suggestion. The purpose of the knock-and-announce rule, wrote Scalia, is not designed to protect the public from unreasonable search and seizure. The courts express their concern for officer safety by expanding the conditions under which police can use violence. This is the logic of the knock-and-announce rule; it protects police from **the public** (252–255) by unleashing police on the public.[3]

Scalia's Hudson ruling relied on the same handwringing, cop-speak logic on display with the **Ferguson effect** (235–236). Hudson relied on the old cop canard that strict legal standards and procedural rules should never be applied to police in advance of a police action because it robs police of **discretion** (176–178). If the choice is between following procedural rules or doing nothing, cops will do nothing. The logic at work in Hudson placed speculation and hypotheticals ahead of fact. Like a carnival savant, Scalia claimed to know the future. In the future, cops are always in harm's way, and the courts are always flooded by defense petitions to apply the exclusionary rule to every police violation of the Fourth Amendment. Throwing out evidence collected during an illegal search would risk "setting the guilty free and the dangerous at large," wrote Scalia. His opinion defended the Fourth Amendment by further gutting it.

Back to our hypothetical. The cop doesn't know that Hudson v. Michigan erased the distinction between knock-and-announce warrants and no-knock warrants because most cops don't know the law. His sergeant explains it to him. "They're all no-knock warrants now," says the sergeant to the cop. None of this entered into the debate over no-knock warrants that raged in 2020 after Louisville police murdered Breonna Taylor in her bed during the execution of a no-knock warrant. Louisville banned no-knock warrants after police killed Taylor, joining Florida, Oregon, Virginia, and scores of other cities and states, but the ban does nothing. It doesn't bring Taylor back to life and it won't stop the next execution. It forces no change in actual, on-the-ground, police actions. The Constitution requires that police secure a court issued warrant to search and seize and establishes standards to evaluate the conditions under which they may do so, but legislation and the courts have largely erased these requirements.

Our hypothetical comes to an end. The sergeant and cop arrive at the scene. Texts go out to tactical officers on call, **SWAT** (135–139), **K-9** (22–24), and specialized units specific to our hypothetical department.

Some officers assemble at the station house, others meet at the address of the raid. Some come late. Some bring their own weapons. A woman sleeps in her bed next to her boyfriend while outside, in the dark, heavily armed men prepare to storm her home. The Judge who signed the execution warrant sleeps soundly in her bed. "Expect resistance," the sergeant tells the cops. Snipers take up position. Flash bang grenades at the ready. The great machinery of police **violence** (96–100) lurches into action.

Curfew

A curfew is a form of incarceration. It is the police regulation and control of the movements of members of a population through the restriction of time and space. The policing of curfew is always underwritten by **force** (102–104) and **violence** (96–100). Like round-ups, **K-9** (22–24) police dogs, and **police helicopters** (70–73), curfews impose limits on the time and space of, usually, the poor. Often referred to as a "lockdown," a curfew is at once a police ordinance and a carceral formation. It transforms both **public** (252–255) and private spaces into spaces of captivity, with the choice: disobey and be captured by police; obey and become a prisoner in your own home. A curfew seeks to purify a particular public space through threats of detention and **arrest** (208–210), while simultaneously transforming private living quarters into makeshift holding cells.

Curfews emerge out of a profound ruling class fear of working class revolt, not simply disorder. The word originally meant to "cover fire," which comes from the medieval European practice of ringing church bells to designate the time at which residents were required to extinguish their outdoor fires and return to their homes. With cramped wooden living quarters, fires posed a grave threat to local towns and villages. But curfews were not merely about accidental fires. They were also aimed at the political fires of insurgency and revolution. Curfews have long "served the interests of the ruling class to avoid having groups of peasants and townspeople congregating in taverns, and later, coffee shops" where they might be plotting rebellions and revolutions.[1] The etymology points to the animus of ruling-class power. Curfews are counterinsurgency. They are the *normalization* of **emergency** (223–224) powers in liberal democracies, a key weapon for policing workers, the unwaged, rebels, and those yet able to work, like youth. Modern life is life under curfew.

In the United States, the curfew is among the first legal measures authorities turn to when policing crises, unrest, and general disorders of "**crime**" (93–96) and "delinquency." For instance, in 1703 the city of Boston created a curfew for Blacks and Native Americans, largely as a means of preventing revolt and insurgency.[2] Alongside **slave patrols** (143–144) and **vagrancy** (189–193) ordinances, the curfew was an important tool authorities used to police slaves, and sometimes poor whites, in routine, everyday ways. The curfew was also the key way that white planters restricted opportunities for slaves to organize and socialize after dark, for fear of slave uprisings. Curfews were a common feature of the post-slavery Black Codes, and often worked in tandem with vagrancy laws to control the movement of recently freed slaves. Likewise, the "Sundown Towns" of Jim Crow America were white towns premised on the very notion of a curfew, but only for Black people. They excluded Blacks, especially at night, and would post signs that read "Nigger, Don't Let the Sun Set On Your Back."[3] The curfew was still in use a century later as a way to police riots and protests related to the civil rights and anti-war movements in the 1960s.

US counterinsurgency documents describe the curfew as one of many "populace control" measures conforming to the "rule of **law**." (90–93) Curfews played a role in the recent US wars against Iraq and Afghanistan, and were used in the war zones of World War II and Vietnam, as well as domestically, such as in facilitating the internment of Japanese Americans.

Curfew arrests made up the majority of arrests (42 percent) in the LA riots in 1992, and in the Cincinnati riots in 2001—both of which were in direct response to police violence against Black men. The curfew was used extensively in the "Battle of Seattle" in 1999 and against the Occupy Wall Street protests in 2011, as well as in New Orleans in the aftermath of Hurricane Katrina. Curfews were used to quell the Baltimore and Ferguson protests and riots in the aftermath of the police killings of Michael Brown in August 2014 and of Freddie Gray the following April.

But the curfew has long been used as a routine measure of structuring the everyday lives of the racialized poor, especially young people. Many US cities and communities have youth curfew ordinances for the summer months, or even year-round, which give police wide **discretion** (176–178) to stop virtually anyone who looks under age and is in public after a specified time. Curfews that target youth also target the entire family. Parents are held responsible and can be deemed legally unfit if their children are caught out during a curfew. For example, when Baltimore enacted its emergency curfew to police the uprisings of 2015, critics pointed out that Baltimore already had on its books a year-round curfew for youth under fourteen, which penalized parents $50 for the first citation and subsequently fined them up to $300 or led to jail. Curfews are about more than just the policing of public space—they necessarily police morality and family, too.

The curfew is a mainstay of contemporary political power, but its effectiveness as crime control is by and large unsupported. Research since the mid-1990s has demonstrated that juvenile curfews, for instance, do very little to actually suppress crime and delinquency. "What is certain," according to sociologist Loïc Wacquant, "is that these curfews significantly increase chances of incarceration for the young residents of poor urban areas," with police commonly arresting for curfew violations rather than other forms of violations.[4]

Whether in response to a crisis or targeting "delinquency," the curfew always seeks to *produce* a specific *kind* of space by actively policing what *types* of people and behaviors are allowed to move in and across that space. This is what Don Mitchell means by the "annihilation of space by law," which "is unavoidably (if still only potentially) the annihilation of *people*" because the curfew is not merely a prohibition against unwanted behaviors, but a prohibition against specific types of unwanted people.[5]

For someone other than cops and legal authorities to be out legally during a curfew they must prove they are not only an adult, but also a worker. This is stated directly in most curfew laws: unless going to and from a place of legitimate employment, you are not granted legal permission to be out past a certain time. The age threshold for youth curfews is usually premised on the legal age requirement for employment. The curfew dances to the rhythms of capitalism.

The curfew is an anti-public policy. It demands that all of us, at all times, justify our public existence by proving our status as workers. It demands we all just stay home, isolated from a nighttime social life outside of the bourgeois family, preparing for the next day of work—and if you are to be out, you better be buying something or working for a wage. It is the ruling class's hatred of any mode of being that doesn't make them a buck. The curfew is the ruling class distrust for all the parts of our lives that aren't yet subsumed by the laws of capitalist labor and the wages of work.

Policing is itself a kind of endless curfew. The logic of curfew animates the **traffic stop** (73–75) and **stop and frisk** (27–31), and the police **patrol** (170–172) as much as the **slave patrol** (143–144). The spirit of the curfew is present in the policing of suspicious persons who are supposedly out of place, and whenever the cop says "Hey, you there" or asks "Where are you going?" or "What are you doing here?" Wherever there are cops, the **force** (102–104) of the curfew is mobilized, even when a curfew hasn't been formally declared. To the defenders of **order** (83–86), there are always fires that need covering because there is always disorder lurking in the populace, threatening to burn the system down.

Rape

Rape is a key method and mode of police **violence** (96–100), a form of terror that emerges out of the routine operation of police power. Rape by **cop** (219–221) or attempted rape by cop, usually called sexual misconduct by police, is the second most common complaint lodged against police by victims of police violence, after complaints about the unjustified use of force. Rape by cop is therefore not an aberration but rather is set into motion by the legal authority that animates police power. This is because police power is a patriarchal power. The **security** (86–89) state, including police, is animated by a masculine logic that seeks to call domination, in all its forms, protection. As Andrea J Ritchie states, "When we begin to understand that police are a significant source of violence against women and LGBTQ people of color—even as they are promoted as our protectors—we must question whether countering police violence is really a question of dealing with a few '**bad apples**' (224–227) or problematic policies."[1]

Police sexual violence, and especially rape by cop, is configured by longer histories of rape and sexual conquest as weapons of settler colonialism and chattel slavery. Under chattel slavery, Black people were deemed legal property (see **no humans involved**, 240–242), and Black women and children were subjected to rape, forced pregnancies, and other forms of sexual violence. The police rape of Black and Brown women today not only belongs to this history, but is directly structured by it, as their bodies are essentially rendered property of the state when in police custody. Similarly, rape has been a central settler colonial weapon of disciplining and dominating Indigenous women and children, and it isn't a surprise that cops have been implicated in the murders and disappearances of Indigenous women, as the Murdered and Missing Indigenous Women (MMIW) movement in Canada has helped to make visible (see also **starlight tour**, 46–48).

At least in the United States, Oklahoma City cop Daniel Holtzclaw is perhaps the most famous of all police rapists, ultimately found guilty in late 2015 of multiple counts of rape, forcible sodomy, and sexual battery. All of his victims were Black women. To hunt his prey (see **pursuit**, 200–201), Holtzclaw used the basic tools and methods of all **patrol** (170–172) officers: running background checks on police databases as a way to locate people who have criminal histories. Holtzclaw would then exploit this knowledge by coercing women into performing sexual acts on him. This highlights a key feature of rape by cop: the least powerful in society are often targeted the most since they have fewer options for legal recourse, and this is only exacerbated when victims have to turn to the very institution that employs the person causing them injury. If Holtzclaw's case presents an anomaly it is that he was actually investigated and caught by police, charged and tried by a prosecutor, and convicted by a jury. We know that most cops who rape or engage in other acts of sexual violence don't get caught, much less prosecuted and convicted.

Police sexual terror in the United States usually isn't framed by officials, media, and many commentators as political terror; instead, rape by cop is considered a form of individual terror and an isolated example of police criminality. Certainly there are cultural elements at play in police violence, including police sexual violence. But this point should not obscure the structural relations of patriarchal domination codified in the juridico-political dynamics of police power. When a cop commits a rape, in clear violation of **law** (90–93), and hence commits a **crime** (93–96), it is the fact that he is a police officer—a state agent certified by law—that establishes a relation of dominance in the first place. Cops not only have more power than their subjects, but this imbalance of power is institutionalized, legally sanctioned, and codified by a **badge** (106–110) and a **gun** (10–13). Thinking of police sexual violence as an abuse of power, and hence something that can be fixed by changing police culture and tweaking policy and adding more laws to the books, obscures the point: cops don't abuse their power when engaging in police sexual violence; they merely use their discretionary powers granted them by law. Police are agents of the state and thus the pattern and practice of rape by cop must be understood as a form of political terror. This becomes all the more apparent when we recognize that most of the victims of police sexual violence are from historically oppressed populations.

There is little if anything that is in place, or could be put in place, that could significantly prevent police officers from using their legal power to commit rape so long as policing exists as it has always existed. This is why referring to this violence as "sexual misconduct" is misleading, as this phrase too quickly pathologizes and fetishizes technicalities, all the while refusing to stare the real problem in the face. As long as we have cops and capitalism, we'll have Officer Hotlzclaws.

Lynching

To lynch is to put to death, usually by hanging, without a trial. From the beginning of chattel slavery to the present day, the lynching of Black people in the United States has most often been described as an extralegal punishment meted out by whites against Black people charged with a variety of crimes—often the supposed **rape** (41–43) of a white woman. But the practice had nothing to do with **crime** (93–96) and everything to do with white supremacy. Lynching has served as a central tactic of racial control by white economic and political interests in the United States. Historically, the answer to Black economic independence has always been white terror.

The journalist Ida B. Wells, among the most prolific chroniclers of late-nineteenth-century lynching in the United States, argued that white economic elites, under the guise of Black criminality, used lynching as a way to suppress Black political power and punish Black economic competition. White business owners would often hire off-duty police and sheriff's deputies (see **rent-a-cop**, 144–146) to attack or intimidate Black shopkeepers or owners and then lynch those who defended themselves. And white-owned newspapers would celebrate white **violence** (96–100) by inventing "horrendous" crimes of those lynched.

And the "lynching localities," as Wells called US cities, were organized around "lynch laws" enforced by white police. Her use of the phrase "lynch law" was meant to demonstrate the ways in which the lynching of Black people by whites should not be understood as extralegal but rather as fundamental to the US legal system, a system designed to limit the horizon of Black life. In other words, **law** (90–93) and police made, and make, lynching possible. Police lynched Black people, allowed the lynching of Black people, or ignored the lynching of Black people. Wells chronicled the pattern not as one isolated by geography or history, but rather as a fact of Black life. In an 1893 article Wells explained that "over a thousand black men, women and children have been thus sacrificed the past ten years. Masks have long since been thrown aside and the lynchings of the present day take place in broad daylight. The sheriffs, police, and state officials stand by and see the work done well."[1] And it was work that continued even after the death of the Black men and women they lynched. As Ruth Wilson Gilmore explains, "One favourite pastime of lynchers was to empty their Winchesters into the victim's dead body, to watch the bullets destroy whatever human form remained after burning, cutting, tying, dragging, flaying, disemboweling, dismembering had, in Ida B. Wells' words, 'hurled men [and women] into eternity on supposition.'"[2] This nineteenth-century pattern continued into the mid twentieth century as "sheriffs or deputies participated in roughly half of all lynchings between 1930 and 1933."[3]

Lynching "was public torture, and both press and posse elites encouraged 'everybody-white' to get in on the fun. Mobs thrilled to participate in the victim's slow death, to hear agonized cries for pity and smell roasting human flesh, to shoot the dead to smithereens, to keep body parts—ears, penises, breasts, testicles, charred bones—as souvenirs, and to read detailed descriptions of torture in the newspapers."[4] Wells explained that police and white-owned newspapers invented the **threat** (222–223) of Black criminality in order to give cover to the racist violence of the nineteenth-century lynching of Black people. White-owned newspapers thrilled in giving the gory details of lynching. The history of policing the **ghetto** (183–184) is a history of lynching.

This history explains why social justice activists and critics of police violence call the police killings of Black men and women a form of lynching. Their point is to draw attention to the way police **violence** (96–100), like lynching before it, seeks to constrain Black life through terror. To be clear, the point is not that police violence is wrong only *because it is a form of lynching*; rather, police violence serves the interests of class and race domination that is premised on the idea that Black life is a threat to white life, and thus that white violence is the only solution to a presumed Black "criminality." "These rhetorical features," according to Bryan Wagner, "are commonly shared between the discourse on lynching and the discourse on police."[5]

And the similarities between lynching and police violence extend beyond discourse. Like under the **slave patrol** (143–144), Black life and Black communities are under constant police surveillance, and this surveillance and its material practices—slave passes checked by the slave patrol or **stop and frisk** (27–31) enacted by police—discipline Black people. Police and sheriff's deputies took an active role in the lynching of Black people or stood passively by during lynch mob actions. There was nothing extralegal about lynching. It was part of the job of the police, and we are reminded of this with each exoneration following the police killing of a Black person.

The terror of lynching defined the Jim Crow south, but also the US Southwest. The Texas Rangers lynched hundreds, possibly thousands, of Mexicans and Mexican Americans in the early twentieth century. It wasn't only racial animus that explains why police participated in the lynching of Black and Mexican-American people. Lynching was lawmaking. The history of lynching in other words is not just a history of racial terror, it is a history of US lawmaking and law enforcement.

Starlight Tour

Welcome to Saskatoon, Canada, home of the Starlight Tour, where Indigenous people make up 15 percent of the population, but more than 70 percent of the prison population. Where two-thirds of Indigenous people live in poverty. Where Native people make up half of all people the Saskatoon Police Service arrest and comprise all of the passengers police take on their terrifying Starlight Tours. The Starlight Tour, a phrase coined by Saskatoon police, finds its cognate in the **rough ride** (31–32) common in the United States. These are forms of "street justice" in which police officers single out and target individuals for punishment. Police detain and **handcuff** (20–21) an individual on a minor infraction and then take them for a ride. The rough ride ends with the bloodied body of a helpless victim. The Starlight Tour ends in a frozen field, far from town, on a cold winter night, where police abandon their victims.

Starlight Tours produce gruesome deaths. They require an explanation and police are happy to provide one. These Native men and women are drunk, they say. Police **arrest** (208–210), incarcerate, and release them over and over again. This frustrates police. They hate the paperwork. During an official inquiry in 2003, police admitted to the practice. The Tour is intended to teach them a lesson. So men and women are abandoned at night outside the city. It is a regular practice in Saskatoon. Sometimes those they abandon make it back to town. Sometimes they don't. On a cold November night in 1990, Jason Roy saw the bloodied face of his seventeen-year-old friend, Neil Stonechild, pressed against the inside back window of a Saskatoon police service cruiser. His frozen body was found the next morning. In January 2000, two more men, Rodney Naistus and Lawrence Wegner, were found frozen to death miles from Saskatoon. Their deaths are known as the Saskatoon Freezing Deaths.

This police explanation is a revealing one. How can they justify a violent practice against a people who have done nothing to police, if not by blaming those people? They are marked as outcasts and so police ask: *Is it not our job to cast them out?* Police place a murderous violence at the center of police power. They admit that the practice happens, and they are forced to admit that sometimes those they abandon die, but it is **justified** (238–240) by affirming an essential pathology (they're poor, uneducated, criminal, and drunk). The Indigenous life is thus the proper object of police power and Indigenous death is the result of this interest.

There is another explanation. A Starlight Tour begins with a hunt and a capture. And here we find a contemporary version of a much older practice. What was in Africa a hunt for slaves, or in Europe a police hunt for the vagabond poor, in the settler colonies was a hunt for Natives. In settler societies such as Canada, the United States and Australia, police emerge first as a power unleashed on Indigenous people in order to produce and enforce a colonial society based on the spatial exclusion of Native people and the dispossession of Native land. It is a logic of elimination. Policing in settler societies serves to reinforce this arrangement, and this is still true today. This is why police in US cities with large Indigenous populations frequently tell Native people to "go back to the reservation."

Consider the language of the euphemism. The first reference in Starlight Tour is to the night sky. It is not the lights of the city, but the night sky of the frozen prairie. Indigenous men and women are to be banished from the city to the frozen prairie. This is the tour they must take. So the momentum of colonial police power rushes along a track leading always to the spatial exclusion of Indigenous people. And what does it mean to call it a tour? The use of the word "tour" makes clear that it is routine, the practice is understood as unexceptional, the presence of Indigenous people on the "tour" is volitional, and that ultimately for everyone else it is educational. The lesson is not for Indigenous people alone. Police give them a tour in which their own death is prefigured. It is a tour from the city to frozen fields, from life to death. And they must die because it is meant as a specifically colonial tour, one from savagery (Native life) to civilization (Native death).

The Starlight Tour focuses our attention on the abandonment—Native men and women left to die in a frozen landscape—but before we consider the abandonment we should consider the capture. The police are a hunting power: the all-points-bulletin, the manhunt, the raid, the dragnet, the chase, the **pursuit** (200–201).[1] And the prey for this hunt is never arbitrary: the "illegal alien," the homeless person, the Native. Thus the Starlight Tour should not be understood as a practice based on what Indigenous people have done, but rather on what they are. The **crime** (93–96) is *being* Indigenous, and in settler society the Native is the subject that should not exist, a living reminder—an accusation—of the crime of colonial dispossession. They are hunted, captured and abandoned. It would be easy to understand this as an example of the Indigenous person abandoned by law, of their rights abandoned by the settler state. But this view misses the point of abandonment. A Starlight Tour is an exile, but those left by police to die are not exiled from law; rather colonial **law** (90–93) and order is made through their abandonment.

They are hunted, captured, banished, killed. These are the principles of settler colonialism, and of police.

Flashlight

The police flashlight illuminates everything but its own purpose. It might seem like a minor police technology, but it is significant for its practical and theatrical powers. The police flashlight is among the most commonly used police technologies. It illuminates the inside of a vehicle by a traffic **cop** (219–221) during a stop. It provides light when questioning a suspect or witness at night. It searches a dark alley or building. In the most literal of ways the police flashlight demonstrates that a central task of policing is making the invisible visible, the illegible legible. The police flashlight belongs to a larger family of police illumination, such as spotlights or thermal imagers on **police helicopters** (70–73) as well as the police cruiser headlights that help illuminate a **traffic stop** (73–75). Moreover, this desire for luminosity or legibility can be observed in all sorts of other police measures, such as surveillance tactics like stakeouts, wiretaps, CCTV, and even **interrogations** (193–195), **searches** (163–165), and **stop and frisks** (27–31).

But if the modern police flashlight is read in symbolic terms, this routine apparatus points us to the gothic mythology animating police power: the police as the radiating light of civilization that overcomes the darkness of barbarism. Indeed, the police project of fabricating **order** (83–86) has long imagined itself as a **war** (100–102) of light against darkness, good against evil. Which is also to say police see themselves as always under attack by the forces of darkness. What all of this suggests though is that the problem of darkness, which the police flashlight is intended to solve, is at once mythological and material, theatrical and spatial. This is represented in the films and novels of the police gothic, where the agents of order are in **pursuit** (200–201) of the enemies of order through shadowy streets and alleys and dark buildings and rough tenements, usually under the midnight sky. The police, then, are always working in the literal and figurative shadows and hence always resorting to illuminating technologies and theatrical tools as a guiding light in the war against forces of darkness.

The mythological trope of darkness was first materialized in police practice in eighteenth- and nineteenth-century Europe, when police required that people carry candles and lanterns and install streetlights in order to illuminate themselves between sunset and sunrise. This practice was also used in the United States with "lantern laws" intended to illuminate the Black bodies of chattel slaves. Indeed, the proletariat understood street lighting as a police technology. Street lights were among the first objects destroyed by the **crowd** (201–205) in rebellions, in which protesters recreated darkness as a key tactic of insurgency and revolution. The police flashlight, however mundane or normalized today, belongs to this political history, a history that casts illumination itself as a weapon of the powerful.[1]

Police luminosity has always been tethered to political violence. The police flashlight doubles as a multi-use police weapon, not merely an ad hoc, impromptu baton but an organized component of police power. Though it varies from department to department, the police flashlight is often considered a legitimate police weapon. Indeed, the organized nature of the flashlight as weapon is perhaps best observed in the gun-mounted flashlight that helps officers better illuminate targets in their **gun** (10–13) sights, or the police flashlight that doubles as a **Taser** (13–16) stun gun. **Rent-a-cop** (144–146) companies often train officers to use the flashlight as a tactical self-defense weapon, as well as to fire their weapons holding either a regular police flashlight or the gun-mounted version. One of the newest variations on the police flashlight is the "tactical strobe light," a handheld flashlight with a strobe light function designed to psychologically disorient and visually confuse.

There are plenty of examples of the flashlight-as-weapon, such as the 1992 Detroit beating of Malice Green, who was killed due to "blunt force trauma" from fourteen strikes of an officer's flashlight. Or the 2011 killing of Kelly Thomas, a homeless schizophrenic man in Fullerton, California who was beaten to death by police with flashlights. Or in the brutal choking death by a cop of thirty-nine-year-old Jonathan Sanders. Or the gruesome choking death of an Alabama teenager in 2013, in which police shoved the butt of a flashlight down the boy's throat while looking for contraband. The political history of the police flashlight suggests that illumination itself is a weapon of the powerful, and police vision a genus of police violence.

Rubber Bullets

"We do not use rubber bullets," says a Minneapolis Police Department spokesperson. "We use 40 mm less-lethal foam marking rounds." Here is a classic example of copspeak, or the police use of semantics to obscure a most fundamental **violence** (96–100). Our spokesperson is merely attempting to transform the embodied **force** (102–104) of police—the kind that terrorizes, bruises, rapes, maims, and kills—into a technicality about language and terminology.

Sponge bullets. Foam rounds. Baton rounds. Sponge grenades. Bean bag rounds. Plastic rounds. All different but related terms for munitions that fall under the category of "kinetic impact projectiles," an industry euphemism for "less lethal" bullets, which is its own euphemism. The most common delivery method is a specialized grenade launcher, although some of these munitions can be fired out of shotguns, rifles, and pistols.

Rubber bullets are not rubber bullets. They consist of a hard core, like wood or plastic and sometimes even metal or steel, covered in a softer outer tip or shell made of rubber, foam, or sponge. Police everywhere in the world use these munitions in **crowd** (201–205) control as a method of **pain compliance** (79–80). Police reformers love rubber bullets and other so-called less-lethal weapons because they claim they constitute a more humane approach to riot control, but in practice rubber bullets constitute the weaponization of humanitarian reason. Less-lethal weapons like rubber bullets serve a specific political purpose: the belief that it renders more acceptable what is at heart an inhuman violence.

The rubber bullet exemplifies what Jasbir Puar calls the right to maim, a logic more complementary than opposed to the right to kill. On the surface, the right to maim appears more humanitarian than the right to kill because it appears to place limits on police violence. It appears to recognize a victim's humanity and impose a level of restraint on police based on that recognition. "Shooting to maim in order not to kill," writes Puar, "might appear as minor relief given the proclivity to shoot to kill." On the ground, the right to maim aims to debilitate entire populations by targeting practices aimed to incapacitate, disable, and maim its victims. Despite the humanitarian window-dressing, the right to maim is a logic of brute violence, a rationality designed to justify and perpetuate relations of domination by producing perpetual conditions of debilitation and disability within larger structures of inequality, dispossession, and exploitation.[1]

The murky, early history of less-lethal munitions only partly disguises the development of rubber bullets as a maiming technology. Some trace the history to the 1880s, when Singapore police would break off the ends of broom handles, load the shards into their guns, and fire at protestors in order to maim, rather than kill, people. Whose definition of humane does this meet? As early as the 1920s, ammunition manufacturers began experimenting with various kinds of less-lethal rounds as a way to expand their market by helping authorities enforce Prohibition laws. One such round was a "shotgun shell, with a brass case and a paper front, loaded with bird shot (dozens of tiny BBs used in hunting birds)." What sort of firearm would shoot these rounds? The Thompson machine **gun** (10–13), more infamously known as the Tommy Gun, but also known by more menacing names, such as the Annihilator, Trench Broom, Chicago submachine gun, and Street Sweeper. Unsurprisingly, angry crowds and protestors were the primary targets.[2]

Imperial powers used their colonies as laboratories, where they experimented and perfected these kinetic munitions of **pacification** (89–90). In the 1960s colonial British forces used wooden bullets against pro-communist protesters in Hong Kong. They called these rounds "baton rounds," a name that references and mimics the blunt force trauma of a police baton or **nightstick** (55–58)—a historical detail that exposes the lie in the benevolent rhetoric surrounding the rubber bullet. To this day, rubber bullets are frequently referred to as baton rounds.

We find the first use of rubber bullets, in a strict technical sense, by the British Army in the 1970s as a weapon to disperse and disable rock-throwing protesters in Northern Ireland. It didn't take long for the use of this missile-looking rubber round, about 6 inches in length, to stir controversy. In a four-year period, the British fired fifty thousand rubber rounds at Irish protestors. The British weapons were notoriously inaccurate and known to ricochet unpredictably off pavement and buildings, and this inaccuracy and other uncontrollable and unpredictable features of the rubber bullet remain true today.[3]

A flashpoint moment in the use of rubber bullets in the United States came during the Rodney King uprisings in 1992 when police found a tactical advantage in the very unpredictability of the rubber bullet. The Los Angeles Police Department deployed what they called "knee-knockers," a singular rubber bullet projectile that police shot at the ground. The collision with the ground split the projectile into five bouncing bullets that ricocheted indiscriminately into the crowd. As a journalist pointed out, "Such a design ensures that it's impossible to target one problematic individual in a crowd, let alone target any specific part of their body. Knee knockers were indiscriminate pain bombs. And the police loved them." Soon after, in 1995, the Department of Defense established the Joint Non-Lethal Weapons Directorate, a program created to develop and experiment with so-called less-lethal munitions. The directorate developed a number of weapons, including the sponge grenade, which has been described as resembling a NERF toy if NERF toys were sinister and painful. The directorate monetized its work and licensed the sponge grenade to private arms manufacturers, who today make and sell it to police agencies around the world.[4]

Police claims notwithstanding, rubber bullets, like Tasers (13–16), are in fact dangerous and deadly. One significant medical study tracked injuries from kinetic impact munitions between 1990 and 2017. Researchers found that "these projectiles caused significant morbidity and mortality during the past 27 years." Police killed at least fifty-three people with these so-called less-lethal munitions and permanently disabled 300 people.[5] Subsequent studies confirmed these findings and explain why the Physicians for Human Rights have called for a total ban on the use of rubber bullets and their kinetic kin.

"It felt like something sharp entered my body really fast" is how photojournalist Andre Mercharles described the pain after Minneapolis police shot him in the leg with a rubber bullet, only to then shoot him again with a rubber bullet the following day. "It's like the officers were thinking. *These people are not humans; they're animals . . . And we're just going to be trigger-happy and keep shooting.*"[6] In May 2020 while covering the George Floyd uprisings, a

Minneapolis cop shot a freelance journalist, Linda Tirado, in the eye with "foam marking rounds," permanently blinding Tirado. "It exploded my eyeball, which has now been patched back together . . . My vision is gone no matter what it winds up looking like scar wise."[7]

Rubber bullets produce horrific eye injuries, many resulting in blindness, a more common result than police and their spokespersons admit. "I don't know why, they do seem to directly hit people's eyes [a lot]," says Michelle Heisler, a doctor and director of Physicians for Human Rights. "It hits your eye and ruptures the eyeball, or the globe . . . basically, your eyeball explodes." In the mass uprisings in Chile in 2019 and 2020, eye injuries from rubber bullets became so common that eye bandages became a galvanizing symbol of protest. A National Institute of Human Rights study found that rubber bullets injured nearly 2,000 people in Chile, including 268 eye injuries. The people who suffer these eye injuries are actually lucky, says Heisler. The eye socket offers police the clearest path to the brain, which might help explain the frequency of the injury. In other words, these wounds do not constitute unintended consequences and Tirado and other victims are lucky that police didn't succeed in killing them.

Police and their apologists like to suggest that these weapons offer a safe alternative to lethal weapons and that better training or improved weapon design will make the weapons somehow more humane. This is the typical copspeak of **police reform** (155–160), the idea that police can somehow be perfected. The history and use of rubber bullets offer no evidence to sustain such a claim. "These technologies are always evolving, but the core problems aren't resolved," admits the head of the Security Policy Reform Institute. "Regardless of whether you put a little sponge on top, it's still inaccurate, and it can still cause severe damage from the sheer impact."[8]

The same can be said about police, more generally. The rubber bullet, in other words, offers a metaphor to understand police. Rubber bullets merely provide a semblance of humanitarian cover, offering up a dishonest image of a kinder, gentler police face. In practice, the rubber bullet reveals the inhumanity of police, the cruel, gleeful desire to inflict pain on anyone standing in its way to enforce the racialized regime of **private property** (81–83). There is no humanity in the choice to kill or maim, there is only police.

Nightstick

The police nightstick, also known as a truncheon, a billy club, or a baton, is among the most terrifying weapons and enduring symbols of police **violence** (96–100). The nightstick is the ruthless and vicious tool of police power. Its primary purpose has always been to bloody and bludgeon a suspect into compliance. But it is more than a tool of blunt force trauma to the head, torso, arms, or legs. It is also a means of **pain compliance** (79–80), as police use the nightstick to **force** (102–104) submission by beating and choking suspects, or pinning them to a wall (see **chokehold**, 58–60). And it is also a tool of sexual terror when police forcibly sodomize subjects with the nightstick (see **rape**, 41–43).

The nightstick is a weapon of overt political repression, inflicting violence against those participating in organized rebellions and uprisings, from the 1886 Haymarket Massacre, to the 1937 Memorial Day Massacre, to the 1965 March on Selma, to the protests at the 1968 Democratic National Convention. More recently, cops used the baton against protestors in the countless uprisings associated with the Black Lives Matter movement and the Standing Rock Sioux Tribe struggle against the Dakota Access Pipeline expansion in North Dakota.

Forget juries and judges. The nightstick is the quintessential symbol of "street justice." From the police perspective, the streets and alleys are the courtroom, and the **cop** (219–221) the only jury and judge that matters. This sentiment is most famously characterized by Alexander "Clubber" Williams, the notorious nineteenth-century New York cop known for his fondness for terrorizing subjects with his truncheon: "There is more law in the end of a policeman's nightstick than in a decision of the Supreme Court," he famously said.[1] The police, he made clear, operate according to their own **law** (90–93)—the police laws of **discretion** (176–178) that grant cops the power to act against the unruly, disobedient, and impolite. But still the organized terror of the Billy Club is not necessarily wielded against the law, as if its brutality is somehow exceptional and outside the supposed civility of legal scripture. As Karl Marx reminds us, "club law is also law."

The very tactical design of the nightstick—a simple hard piece of wood or metal baton designed to beat and bludgeon—makes clear that this weapon is not about reducing "**crime**," (93–96) but is instead a tactical option to force the "unruly" and "disorderly," or the "assholes" that question police authority, into being obedient, docile, and polite subjects.

"Street justice" is a euphemism for racist state terror. It is by swinging their nightstick that cops police the color lines and property lines of racial capitalism. This is why cops have called the nightstick the "nigger be good stick," displaying for all to see the racist animus of the police power in the most terrifying of ways. We do not lack for examples of police clubbing people of color. Among the most well known was the beating of Rodney King by seven white LAPD officers. The beating of King is often credited with ushering in significant reforms around the police use of batons or nightsticks. And now the nightstick is cloaked in the mythology of **police reform** (141–143), a narrative of "progress" that claims the nightstick is either "banished" from policing, or its use significantly reduced, or the training improved.

This discourse is premised on a simplistic binary between the barbaric past and a more "civilized" present. As Los Angeles police Deputy Chief Bill Murphy said, "Back then, it was pulling out a baton and whacking people . . . After that video played that night, no one hardly ever used the baton. It was banished. It became a symbol."[2] The symbol of racist terror now repackaged as "hygienic" or a "less-than-lethal" weapon. It stands now alongside the **Taser** (13–16), maiming and killing more efficiently. The *Los Angeles Times* reported that in 1990 the LAPD used the baton 741 times, but in 2015 *only* 54 times. Here we can see how this language of reform has little interest in actually challenging the police monopoly of violence, but is only concerned with creating the distinction between "good" and "bad" police violence via a logic of "proportionality" and "quantity." But the fact remains that across the United States the police nightstick, often now called the "collapsible baton" or the "sap" or "blackjack," is still one of the most routine tools of racist state violence. And what does their reform matter anyway, when even where it's banished the **flashlight** (48–50) remains in the arsenal of police power and has always served the same purpose as the nightstick?

In September 2015, a Stockton, California cop clubbed a sixteen-year-old Black male jaywalker in the face multiple times with his nightstick. As the officer approached the teen for allegedly attempting to cross the road illegally, the teen told the arresting officer to "get the fuck off me!" Here we see the racist animus of the baton merging with the police demand for complete compliance, total obedience. And it was this failure to fully comply with the officer, police claimed, that **justified** (238–240) the officer using his baton to force the Black teen down on his back. The teen defended himself by grabbing the nightstick in order to stop the blows. The officer yelled "stop resisting," which police often do whether anyone is resisting or not, and began striking his victim in the face multiple times. Eventually, more officers arrived, only to throw the Black youth on the ground before putting him in handcuffs and a police car. A police spokesperson stated afterward as a video of the violence circulated online, "If everyone would just learn to comply with the lawful orders from police officers and not try to hold or grab any of our weapons, force would never have to be used."[3]

The crack of the nightstick is always preceded by the threat of the nightstick. A Baltimore officer stated that city officers twirl their wooden sticks from the rawhide loop handle as a means of intimidation: "Criminals don't like to see us twirl the stick. I have heard that twirling the stick is intimidating. It's supposed to be intimidating. It's a stick."[4] If you've ever been to a protest cleared by "riot police" recall the sound of frontline police knocking their batons on their large shields in a loud rhythm to intimidate protesters. In 1947 the *Baltimore Sun* reminded its readers of the limits of possible reforms targeting the use of the nightstick: "After all, telling a policeman not to swing his espantoon [nightstick] would be like asking a happy man not to whistle."[5]

The nightstick exposes the visceral, callous, and base violence at the heart of police. As Clubber Williams made clear, behind all police power is the bloody end of the nightstick. Even when policing is said to be many things at once, such as increasingly "community oriented" and "friendly" with digitized **predictive policing** (178–179) and crime mapping, the presence of the nightstick, twirling in the hands of **the beat** (172–174) cop, reminds us that blunt force trauma will *always* be central to police power, no matter how "friendly" and "reformed" it claims to be.

Chokehold

Strangulation, asphyxiation, choking—these have long been mainstays of cops whether in liberal democratic or totalitarian regimes.[1] Robbing the breath of someone held in state custody—detained, arrested, interrogated, imprisoned—is a central mode of police control and coercion. A vast catalog of strangulation and asphyxiation techniques has been designed, used, criticized, abandoned, and reformed over the years.

The chokehold is both the most common police strangulation method and, in the United States, one of the most controversial. The chokehold that slowly squeezed the life out of Eric Garner on a New York street in 2014 is no longer the most recent, probably safe to say not the most well-known now either after George Floyd? At least since the late 1970s and early 1980s, the Los Angeles and New York police departments used and **justified** (238–240) chokehold techniques, while at the same time banning and sanctioning some versions of the technique. In a five-year period in the 1980s, LAPD officers killed sixteen people with a chokehold, and fourteen of these deaths were of Black people. The LAPD chief at the time, Daryl Gates, even went so far as to say that "some Blacks" were more susceptible to death by chokehold due to the biological makeup of their arteries compared to "normal people," and then banned the practice. But following the beating of Rodney King, Gates commissioned a study on the reintroduction of the chokehold, arguing that reviving the chokehold as **pain compliance** (79–80) would limit the use of the **nightstick** (55–58).[2] Police offered the chokehold as **police reform** (155–160), as something that makes police **violence** (96–100) more "humane," "less lethal," and so more hygienic.

Police have various terms to euphemistically describe an acceptable chokehold, such as "carotid control hold" or "vascular restraint." Police depict the problem of the chokehold as a problem of training. It is deemed excessive by police to force someone unconscious by placing direct pressure or **force** (102–104) against a subject's windpipe, but it is acceptable to cut off blood flow by applying pressure to the carotid artery. But tell this to the person being strangled, for whom the distinction between acceptable and unacceptable chokeholds means very little.

And the chokehold is not the only way that police strangle and asphyxiate people. Strangulation and choking have long been an **interrogation** (193–195) tactic used to force a confession. The first federal investigation of police practices, the 1931 Wickersham Commission, investigated various police methods, including waterboarding, in which cops pour water slowly down a person's nostrils in order to simulate a drowning in order to force a confession. Police did not invent this tactic, but it and other forms of drowning techniques have long been part of the police project.

Cops also choke suspects or detainees with their neckties or scarves. As neckties became less common, police improvised and found other methods to rob someone of their breath. One of the most common ways police choke people echoes the torture of prisoners by the US military at Abu Ghraib prison in Iraq. Called "bagging" or the "dry submarine," a **cop** (219–221) puts a plastic bag or cloth sack over a detainee's head while sealing the bottom. This became a popular practice among Chicago and New Orleans police in the 1970s and '80s.

Police reformers claim bagging is no longer common police practice. But it hasn't disappeared, only morphed into a different form. Police now place "spit hoods" over suspects' heads in order to prevent them from spitting on or biting officers. Police officials insist the hoods, made of mesh or heavy canvas, are not designed to suffocate or asphyxiate suspects, but Jack Marden would disagree if he could. When Midland County, Michigan police arrested the fifty-six-year-old Marden on a felony assault warrant, they alleged he became aggressive with police and demonstrated erratic behavior, such as stripping down naked and yelling incoherently. Police eventually restrained Marden by hitting him in the head, tying him to a chair, and strapping a spit hood over his head. Marden eventually died, and a lawsuit alleges that police killed him by suffocation.

Police describe the spit hood as a humane alternative to force. It is, in other words, a gentler method of restraint than the nightsticks, **Tasers** (13–16) or fists that would otherwise be used. But the result is often the same: terror and death. In addition, police routinely use what are called EDP bags, an acronym for "emotionally disturbed person." Police use them to totally restrain subjects by zipping them up into a full-body container. Some versions cover the whole body including the head. It is no accident that this technology of police reform looks a lot like a body bag for the dead.

Lapel Camera

Lapel cameras, a type of body-worn camera that police wear on their lapels or attach to their **uniform** (141–143), are designed to capture video and audio of police–community interactions. Since 2014, they have become the sine qua non of **police reform** (155–160), particularly by reformers who celebrate the lapel camera for the way they claim that it disciplines police. On its surface it is a convincing argument. Lapel cameras appear to check police authority. It has been through the release of videos of the police killing of Walter Scott and so many others that anti–police violence activists have organized protests and forced some reforms on police departments. The lapel camera video of the March 2014 Albuquerque police killing of James Boyd, a video that Albuquerque police chief Gordon Eden at the time defended as a depiction of legal homicide, sparked **public** (252–255) outrage that led to months of protests and the eventual indictment of two police officers.

But before we celebrate the end of police **violence** (96–100) let's remember that Axon, the manufacturer of the most common stun gun used by police, **Taser** (13–16), also manufactures the most common lapel cameras for police. Since its rollout in 2008, it has been marketed as a way to record citizen misconduct against police and thus to protect police from **police brutality** (207–208) complaints, not as a tool to protect people from police violence. And lapel camera videos of police shootings have been cited as important evidence in the exoneration of police officers in fatal encounters. How can lapel cameras both serve the goals of anti-police violence activists and, at the same time, the interests of police? The short answer is that it cannot. The lapel camera mostly serves the interests of police.

Remember that body-worn cameras are tools organized, controlled and deployed by police. How should they be used? When should they be used? Where should they be used? These are all questions answered exclusively by police. Any police reform demand that includes a call for all police to wear body cameras is a call to invest total oversight authority of police with police. This is a version of **police oversight** (146–149) consistent with police claims that only police can police the police. But even if there were independent control over police body cameras and the videos they capture, we'd still be captive to the police view of the world. To watch lapel camera footage is to see the world through cops' eyes. To elevate its importance as a reform measure is to anoint the police perspective as the most legitimate perspective.

The lapel camera does not stop police violence. It witnesses it. It offers only the promise, always unfulfilled, of future restraint. The lapel camera doesn't stop the violence; it watches it, records it. It cannot in any way prevent police violence because the very premise of recording the violence requires that what is caught on camera not be stopped, cannot be stopped. It can only be viewed.

When we understand the lapel camera this way, and as part of the larger police surveillance apparatus, a different view of its purpose emerges. It is of a piece with CCTV cameras (closed circuit television cameras), ankle monitors, red light cameras, dashboard cameras, drones, and more. It monitors, records, registers. It is among the tools designed not to check police power, but to extend it; to maximize and intensify its reach; to overcome the physical limits of the **cop** (219–221) walking **the beat** (172–174), or driving the police cruiser, or flying the **police helicopter** (70–73). Surveillance allows police to be everywhere without being anywhere.

Lapel cameras are part of a logic of **order** (83–86) that recognizes the limits of **force** (102–104) to produce that order. Where once the violence of the state produced order—the public flogging or hanging, or shaming—we now find a power augmented by constant surveillance. The goal of this power, according to Michel Foucault, is to produce obedient subjects. And so at best we cannot confirm whether or not we are under surveillance. Power is visible, but not verifiable. You are seen, but you do not see. Through the "eye of power" we are made visible—to police, to the boss, to the teacher, to the doctor—and that visibility renders us "knowable." This is not solely a punitive power. Police surveillance has a disciplinary effect. Police fabricate order by the threat of force but also through the lens of a lapel camera, or the eye of a drone, or the searchlight of a police helicopter. This surveillance seeks a different power relation. No longer does it rely only an external force applied to bodies—a **nightstick** (55–58) crack to the skull—but also now it is present always in the body of the subject. We behave ourselves, in other words. We are disciplined. Violence or surveillance is not just a means to enforce forms of authority and control, but the source of progress itself. The obedient subject of panoptic power is the productive worker, the well-behaved student, the law-abiding citizen. And, yes, the productive cop too. The cop who properly enforces **broken windows** (186–189) policing. The cop who **stops and frisks** (27–31). The cop who barks commands and justifies their force, and has the video to prove it. "Is it surprising," asks Foucault "that prisons resemble factories, schools, barracks, hospitals, which all resemble prisons?"[1] The lapel camera makes all the world a cop world.

Data Center

Stewart Brand, the founder of the *Whole Earth Catalog*, a DIY-oriented, hacker-inspired, counterculture magazine started in the 1960s, told a room full of hackers in 1984 that "information wants to be free." The phrase became a slogan for the hackers and cyberpunks who despise the commercialization of the Internet. Brand believed in the transformative power of technology and based the prospects for human technoliberation on the struggle between those who want all information freely available and those who seek to collect it, aggregate it, put it behind a paywall, and monetize it.

Brand saw the Internet like Martin Luther saw the printing press: Finally! A technology with the capacity to destroy an older, repressive **order** (83–86) by democratizing information and thus knowledge. Religious authorities (in Luther's case) and information gatekeepers (in Brand's case) controlled access to information and filtered all knowledge through the prism of their own social and class position in order to benefit them personally and as a class to the detriment of the social good.

Not all hackers share Brand's technoenthusiasm. Aaron Swartz, for one. Swartz co-founded Reddit, co-developed the news feed format RSS, and was an early member of Creative Commons, a nonprofit organization that developed an alternative copyright format for intellectual property. Creative Commons offered what some call copy*left*, a copyright format based on free use and public domain for artists and creators who want an alternative to the commercialization and control of information by profiteers. Information might want to be free, but someone first has to set it free.

Swartz wrote the *Guerilla Open Access Manifesto* in 2008, and in it he updated and revised Brand's technosloganeering. Information doesn't want to be free. That's technogibberish. "Information is power," Swartz wrote, "but like all power, there are those who want to keep it for themselves." Brand offered an apolitical enthusiasm for the power of technology. Swartz knew technology as just another mode of political struggle. Those with privileged access to information, "students, librarians, scientists . . . You get to feed at this banquet of knowledge," he wrote, "while the rest of the world is locked out. But you need not—indeed, morally, you cannot—keep this privilege for yourselves. You have a duty to share it with the world." Those without the privilege of access "have been sneaking through holes and climbing over fences, liberating the information." Now it's your turn.

Police use different words to describe the setting free of information. Those words are "stealing or piracy," as Swartz acknowledged. No matter, he concluded. "There is no justice in following unjust laws." He concluded the manifesto by listing various and specific ways to set information free, all of which constituted violations of property law. This included his command to "download scientific journals and upload them to file sharing networks," which was precisely what he was doing over the holiday break on the campus of Massachusetts Institute of Technology in January 2010. According to a criminal complaint, an MIT researcher called police and complained that "someone had entered [a] restricted room and connected a laptop and external hard drive directly to a networking switch" and then hid the equipment under a box and left the door unlocked. The researcher told police that the laptop was "illegally downloading scientific periodicals from JSTOR," a private database of academic journals sold to universities via subscription. Scholars conduct research for the common good at public and private universities. They publish that research in academic journals owned by private companies. Those private companies then package those journals into databases and sell subscriptions to those databases to the same universities where those professors and graduate students who wrote the articles work.

Police set a trap for Swartz. They installed a camera and watched Swartz enter the closet three times over the course of a few days in early January, each time swapping one hard drive for another. On his third visit, at 2:11 p.m. on January 6, 2010, Swartz left the closet with the laptop and the hard drive. Police followed him and arrested him near campus (see **Arrest**, 208–210). Federal prosecutors charged Swartz with wire fraud and various violations of the Computer Fraud and Abuse Act. Swartz refused a plea deal that would have sent him to jail for six months but would have required that he admit to breaking the **law** (90–93). Facing thirty-five years in prison and a $1 million fine but refusing to abandon the moral obligation he described in his manifesto, Swartz committed suicide in his Brooklyn apartment on January 11, 2013. "Information is power. But like all power, there are those who want to keep it for themselves." And those people have police and prisons.

To Swartz's alternative to Brand's slogan, we could add another. *Information is power. But like all power, there are those who want to sell it to, and steal it from, police.* Everything cops do and everything the police powers entail requires the use, collection, and analysis of enormous amounts of information. Police are not good at doing this and as a result, with the help of the venture capitalist wing of the CIA, In-Q-Tel, rely on a police-military security industry of shady private vendors that control and monetize police surveillance data gathering, storage, and analysis. If you're in jail, it's likely that a for-profit police vendor managed and profited from the information that police used to put you there.

Many municipal police departments run their data collection and analysis efforts in what they call Real Time Crime Centers (RTCC). These centers, which look like low-rent NASA control rooms, coordinate the many databases and data collection and data-driven activities of police. From RTCCs, police monitor their **jurisdiction** (104–106) in real time through networked camera systems that link their small, municipal camera networks with larger private camera networks of banks, retailers, and even private residences. They route FBI and Department of Homeland Security (DHS) databases through RTCCs. They monitor social media; collect images, videos, and license plate numbers; listen in on phone calls; and hack into mobile phones.

To do this, police purchase devices and software from private vendors. In return the private vendors upload and aggregate all the information that police gather with those devices. Like JSTOR, these vendors then sell subscriptions to the databases of police-generated information back to the same police who collected the information. In other words, private companies in the techno-police surveillance industry are not in the business police think they're in; they're in the business of aggregating and monetizing data collected by cops.

Cops are the cartel drug mules of the surveillance and **security** (86–89) industry, an industry that sells to police cheap technology packaged with Trojan horse software. There is no evidence the microphone networks that ShotSpotter sells to police to listen for gunshots reduce gun crime. A company called Cellebrite sells police expensive phone hacking devices called Universal Forensic Extraction Devices that allow police to physically hack into computers and mobile phones. Cellebrite servers hold the data that police extract. Snaptrends and the CIA-funded Geofeedia sold software to police departments that allowed RTCCs to target, monitor, and geolocate individual social media users. Facebook and Twitter banned the companies after investigative journalists discovered that the two companies violated privacy rules. The software auto-uploaded all data that police gather to private servers. The CEO of Snaptrends, Eric Klasson, changed the name of the company in June 2020 to Pandemic Insights and announced plans to monetize police data that his firm aggregated for commercial clients.

Hundreds of police departments make subscription payments to a company called Vigilant Solutions and in return get surface-and/or cruiser-mounted automated license plate readers that harvest and geocode license plate numbers. Vigilant sells readers to private firms as well and all of its devices upload data to Vigilant's proprietary, national database of license plate numbers that includes data on more than two billion license plates. Stingray sells police devices that mimic cell phone towers so that police can eaves-drop on phone calls and Stingray can upload the data.

When police upload data to private servers, hackers steal the data. Sometimes the hackers work with or for the US government, such as the bulk data gathering operations of the National Security Agency (NSA). According to documents released by Edward Snowden in 2013, the NSA deployed a data capture and analysis tool known as BOUNDLESS INFORMANT to hack scores of servers in North America and extract billions of pieces of intelligence from various US computer server networks. Most of the targeted servers held troves of data collected by or for police.

Among the servers targeted by the NSA was one codenamed WAXTITAN. The server, owned by a Texas company, hosted data from a police vendor called Netsential. In June 2020, Distributed Denial of Secrets, a data transparency collective, released 269 giga-bytes of police data that hackers who claimed to be affiliated with the group Anonymous extracted from Netsential servers. The hack came in retaliation for the police murders of Breonna Taylor and George Floyd and during the brutal, federal crackdown on Black Lives Matter protestors during May and June 2020. Known as Blue-Leaks, the hack included information from hundreds of police departments and state-run DHS Fusion Centers, which are state-level data center clearing houses that coordinate data analysis and distribution among police and other public agencies.[1]

The hack revealed that the many vendors of police surveillance technology had help converting police into their data mules. Years ago, large, national retailers, with Target Corporation in the lead, developed public–private information gathering partnerships with municipal police departments in order to convert police into retail security appendages. The result has been to blur the line between public police and private-sector **asset protection officers** (118–122). Police hail these as cost-effective "retail partnerships." But what do they know? They're the mark.

Nearly every police agency, local or federal, relies on information held by corporate or private security firms. Some police rely on information purchased from data aggregating companies such as ChoicePoint, which maintains enormous databases of information tailored for public and private-sector clients. The Department of Homeland Security developed its network of "fusion centers" in order to serve as a public sector data center. The BlueLeaks documents revealed the extent to which police work in tandem with (or more accurately, on behalf of) private firms to pursue largely secret, and fully privatized, information gathering operations. It's not for nothing the NSA and Anonymous both targeted Netsential.

Target Corporation launched its "Safe City" program in 2003, a retail anti-shoplifting partnership with police. Target seeded police departments all over the country with small grants that police used to create large, citywide retail, banking, real estate, and housing/lodging data-gathering operations. Every police department that created a Safe City program hired Netsential, a small firm run by the spouse of an FBI agent, to create a website and host its data. Most of the data are collected or captured by networked cameras, store security, hotel clerks, apartment managers, neighborhood associations, and bank tellers.[2]

Among the largest retail partnerships in the United States is one created by the Albuquerque Police Department (APD). Target gave APD $100,000 in 2006, which APD used to expand the Albuquerque

Retail Assets Protection Association (ARAPA). Police hired Netsential to create Community Oriented Notification Network Enforcement Communication Technology (CONNECT), which coordinates data gathering, analysis, and data management for ARAPA. On its CONNECT website Albuquerque celebrates the program as "an interactive tool which links law enforcement to community partners to communicate about crime and public safety issues occurring in Albuquerque." Local security executives from Walmart and Target, where police make 60 percent of all their shoplifting arrests in Albuquerque, control the partnership. They recruit members and vet those who apply to ARAPA and request access to CONNECT data, including police agents from dozens of different local, regional, and national agencies.

Police officials describe ARAPA as small in scale—a few hundred retailers—with a focus on retail and property crime only. They claim that only a small team of APD investigators have access to ARAPA data, along with a small list of mostly local law enforcement agencies, including the local sheriff, US postal inspectors, and the District Attorney. But according to BlueLeaks documents, ARAPA and its website portal CONNECT entail much more than retail and property crime. The membership roster includes or included thousands of private residents, business organizations, neighborhood association block captains, apartment managers, hotel clerks, bank tellers, pawnshop owners, and more, all of whom upload information—often license plate numbers, photos, or surveillance video using facial recognition software, and more—to Netsential's website. The BlueLeaks hack included internal ARAPA documents and these demonstrate the operation has always been about gathering information that police would have required a warrant to collect. To get around legal limits to data gathering, APD encouraged ARAPA members to upload any and all information to CONNECT, including photos, tips, video, and any information on any activity that members deemed "suspicious."

The BlueLeaks hack included a roster for ARAPA, which contradicts APD's claim that the program is limited in scope and focus. More than 2,600 authorized users have uploaded data from among more than a dozen different data gathering operations since 2006. In addition to bank tellers, hotel clerks, apartment managers, neighborhood block captains, college professors, and local pastors uploading data via CONNECT, police recruited the office manager at a substance abuse treatment facility and a consultant registered in New Mexico as a government relations lobbyist. Nearly a third of the names on the list are local, state, or federal law enforcement officers, including hundreds of officers from agencies with no clear role in retail crime enforcement in Albuquerque.

The City of Albuquerque, a sanctuary city, claims it refuses to cooperate with federal immigration police, but it shares ARAPA data with federal immigration police who use the information to hunt migrants. The leak demonstrated that APD does not limit law enforcement access to the database to a small group of police. More than a thousand cops have or had access, including special agents for the US Forest Service, intelligence coordinators and agents from the Drug Enforcement Agency's New Mexico High Intensity Drug Trafficking Area, multiple special agents from the Department of Homeland Security's Immigration and Customs Enforcement, intelligence research specialists from DHS Homeland Securities Investigations, DHS Customs and Border Patrol agents, and detectives and investigators with the 377 Security Forces Squadron from Kirtland Air Force Base.

When Minneapolis police murdered George Floyd, protestors confronted police and Target Corporation. First they burned down the Third Precinct police station. Then they destroyed the Lake Street Target store around the corner. The destruction of Target was no accident. Some media outlets described it as a looting, but protestors had something else in mind. They knew Target cultivates a close relationship with Minneapolis police. They knew Target hires hundreds of former FBI agents and local police. They knew Target runs two forensics labs that rival every federal or state criminalistics labs. They knew, despite official denials, that Target uses the Lake Street store to "experiment" with surveillance technologies, including automated facial recognition. They knew that nearly every shoplifting arrest that Minneapolis police make in that neighborhood happen at the Target store. So they chanted and posted online, "Loot every Target," while they destroyed the Target.

Somewhere in a nondescript building in suburban Texas, a web hosting company's server farm holds your complete digital profile—your geocoded photo, your address, your arrest record, your license plate number, your social media posts, a transcript of a phone call you made. Police routinely mine the data, private vendors seek ever more ways to monetize it, **rent-a-cops** (144–146) guard it. Stewart Brand claimed that "Information wants to be free." Aaron Swartz knew that someone's got to set it free first.

Time to sneak through corporate holes; time to climb over the police fences; time to hack the servers; time to set the data free.

Police Helicopter

According to the Bureau of Justice Statistics, more than 200 police departments in the US engage in aerial law enforcement through the use of helicopters and, to a lesser degree, fixed-wing aircraft. The Los Angeles Police Department's air support division is the world's largest municipal police aviation department, with nearly 100 officers and 19 helicopters, and operates out of the largest heliport in the United States. Combined with the 18 helicopters of the Los Angeles County Sheriff's Department Aero Bureau, the skies above Los Angeles are never without police helicopters.

The pivotal moment for the police helicopter as a routine form of police urban **patrol** (170–172) came in 1966 in Lakewood, California, a suburb of Los Angeles. "Project Sky Knight," funded by the National Crime Commission, and conceived by Los Angeles County Sheriff Peter J. Pitchess, proposed the helicopter as a means of continuous, constant aerial patrol. Pitchess, who used helicopters first during the 1965 Watts riot, sought to extend the helicopter's potential for permanent police patrol. A promotional video for Project Sky Knight described the helicopter as "bad news for bad guys," while explaining that the experiment "takes its name of the knight of old, whose vow was to protect the weak, and pursue the wicked. But all too often the bad guys got away."

Project Sky Knight was celebrated by the media, which called the helicopter the "Heavenly Prowl Car." Today Airbus markets its helicopters as a "force multiplier" to police departments worldwide. Their sales materials describe its use: "In Europe, when crowds or demonstrations grow unruly, helicopters discreetly ferry crowd-control police into position so as to avoid provoking **violence** (96–100) that might put ground personnel at risk." More than 2,000 police helicopters prowl the skies over US cities. If we consider the tactical helicopters operated by US police departments as a unit, it is larger than every military on earth except for the fleets maintained by the United States, China and Russia.

Police helicopters are loud and visible and serve as a constant reminder of the ubiquity and reach of police power. That reach usually extends specifically to what police call "**crime** (93–96) infested" neighborhoods (see **CRASH**, 128–130). But air power obliterates any useful distinction between suspect and bystander, target and non-target. As one LA journalist wrote in 1992, "Hearing LAPD helicopters circle overhead is a nightly phenomenon over much of the Los Angeles basin, even in middle-class neighborhoods like my own . . . Their circular flight patterns have a way of making people feel as if they're smack in the center of a crime drama."

Police explain that this "nightly phenomenon" of police "in the air" supports the work of police "on the ground." They use helicopters to quickly locate and track fleeing suspects, for example. But nearly all police departments claim aerial patrols serve first and foremost as a deterrent. According to the Institute for Police Studies, police helicopters "contribute to a significant deterrent effect." The Chicago Police Department claims its helicopter operations "enhance the capabilities of first responders through the deterrence and prevention of crime."

What does it mean for police to invoke **deterrence** (228–231) as a way to explain the purpose of aerial policing? Deterrence has long been a guiding logic of police power, and patrol strategies specifically. The introduction of the police helicopter promised to revolutionize the police powers of deterrence through the nearly magical powers of total mobility and swift punishment. Police power is positioned as omnipresent, "all-seeing," and able to stop crime before it happens (see **predictive policing**, 178–179).

Deterrence theory is also at the heart of military strategy and engagement. The theory of deterrence proposes confronting a **threat** (222–223) with the permanent presence of intimidating and overwhelming power with the promise of punishment, swift and severe. This requires not just air power but air superiority. "Whoever controls the air," according to a 1995 Air Force study, "generally controls the surface." Air power is the permanent presence of coercion and intimidation. It "produces physical and psychological shock."[1] This is deterrence.

The constant sound of police helicopters hovering over South Central Los Angeles underscores nearly every scene of director John Singleton's 1991 film *Boyz n the Hood*. The ominous sound of helicopters and sirens is the film's soundtrack. And the helicopter's thermal imagers and 1,000,000-watt searchlights turn night into day (see **flashlight**, 48–50). Singleton depicts a South Central Los Angeles where police power occupies everyday life, peering into windows and drowning out conversations. The film's costar, Ice Cube, called police helicopters "**ghetto** birds" (183–184) on his 1993 album "Lethal Injection." That same year hip-hop artist KRS-One, in his song "Sound of da Police," sang "Woop-woop, that's the sound of da police. Woop-woop, that's the sound of da beast." He repeats the word *overseer* over and over again in the song until it sounds like *officer*, connecting the history of slavery and the **slave patrol** (143–144) to police. "The overseer rode around the plantation. The officer is off patrolling all the nation."

Air power serves the same purpose whether in Kosovo, Iraq, or South Central Los Angeles, whether we're talking about a military "no-fly" zone in Iraq after the first Gulf **War** (100–102) or the "no-fly" zone above Ferguson, Missouri after the police killing of Michael Brown. It is the ever-present threat of punishment. Military bombs falling on Iraqi villages or police searchlights landing on Compton streets. A US military drone killing a dozen people in a wedding party in Yemen in 2014 or Philadelphia police dropping bombs from helicopters on Black MOVE activists in 1985, killing eleven people, including five children. "Woop-woop, that's the sound of da police. Woop-woop, that's the sound of da beast."

Traffic Stop

The routine policing of automobility appears so boring and mundane that it is easy to miss how fundamental traffic enforcement and the traffic stop is to the police project. Despite the less prestigious status of traffic duty compared to, say, detective work, it is the most common **patrol** (170–172) activity. Being pulled over by police on traffic duty is a frequent and fundamental experience for millions of people each year. Indeed, according to the Bureau of Justice Statistics, the traffic stop is the most common way people come into contact with police. As sociologist Charles Epps notes, "The police make some eighteen million traffic stops per year in the United States. Nationally, 12 percent of drivers are stopped per year by the police. Among racial minorities the rate is considerably higher: 24 percent or more by some estimates."[1]

In July 2016, Saint Paul, Minnesota police officer Jeronimo Yanez shot and killed thirty-two-year-old Philando Castile during a routine traffic stop. Yanez pulled Castile over, asked for his driver's license and vehicle registration, and then shot Castile in the chest. Yanez claims Castile, who never unbuckled his seatbelt, made **furtive movements** (236–238). In the aftermath, various commentators noted that Castile had been stopped nearly fifty times in fourteen years for minor infractions like broken taillights or failure to signal. Castile's murder evokes a long history of police pulling over Black drivers in racially **disproportionate** (232–235) ways, popularly referred to as "driving while Black," as well as municipalities using traffic enforcement as a fiscal strategy.

Castile's experience illustrates the way traffic enforcement serves as one of the most insidious modes of police power, one in which racialized suspicion animates the politics of unfreedom. The automobile and the roadway have long signified one of the most concrete ways freedom of movement is imagined and practiced. Nevertheless, the liberty and autonomy promised by driving an automobile on the open road is always haunted by the specter of police, especially for people of color. If the automobile makes free movement possible, then the traffic **cop** (219–221) marks its limit.

The traffic stop belongs to a broader logic of policing: the interruption of motion, mobility, and circulation. Getting pulled over by the traffic cop is a forceful prevention of motion in order to interrogate, and also possibly to restrain in **handcuffs** (20–21), detain, **arrest** (208–210), or, like in Castile's case, even kill. As a mode of suspension of the freedom of movement, the traffic stop is by definition a routine loss of liberty at the level of the body, woven into the circuits and rhythms of everyday life. Hence the traffic stop is itself a modality of force whether or not overt acts of violence, such as the killings of Terence Crutcher, Samuel DuBose, and Walter Scott, result from it.

The traffic stop reveals the magnitude and ordinariness of the police manhunt as the traffic cop pursues (see **pursuit**, 200–201) and captures the prey. Here we can also think of the speed trap—the officer hiding in the shadows waiting to pounce on an unsuspecting driver. Despite liberal claims that **reasonable suspicion** (255–257) and probable cause somehow restrain the discretionary powers of the traffic cop, the commonsense wisdom of the street—that they can pull you over for anything—is the real truth. The near-carte blanche powers of police **discretion** (176–178) find their fullest expression in the traffic stop. Broken taillights. Swerved. Failed to signal. Headlight out. Over the speed limit. Under the speed limit. Leaving a known **crime** (93–96) area. Windows too dark. Didn't stop at the stop sign. Fit the description. Before he was shot eight times in the back, Walter Scott was first stopped for a broken brake light. Before dying in a Texas jail cell in 2014, Sandra Bland was stopped for failing to signal a lane change.

Police in Albuquerque, New Mexico pulled over Andrew Lopez in 2009 for having dim headlights and no taillights. Officers later claimed that his car was involved in an incident involving a handgun, despite the fact that the car's make, model and color did not match the vehicle involved in the incident. A frightened Lopez attempted to run from the scene. This is how an April 2014 US Department of Justice investigation report of the Albuquerque police department described the traffic stop: "When Lopez reached a fence and began to turn, the officer shot at Lopez three times. One of the shots struck Lopez, causing a nonlethal bullet wound. Lopez fell to the ground and lay motionless on his back. The officer [Justin Montgomery] walked around the truck and fired a fourth shot into Lopez's chest, piercing his lung and heart and causing his death. Lopez was **unarmed** (257–258). The officer fired the fourth and final shot when Lopez was not pointing anything at officers and while he lay on his back already wounded."[2]

Beware, the state demands your obedience during the traffic stop. The entire sequence of the good traffic stop is structured by the state expectation of complete obedience to police authority. Sirens and lights are behind you, and you are expected to pull over immediately. Then you are told to turn off the engine and put both hands clearly in view on the steering wheel. You must always be courteous, and always let the officer do the talking. Be polite. "Yes, officer." "No, officer." "Thank you, officer." Don't ask questions or talk back or challenge the cop's understanding of the encounter. It is a rehearsal of and for domination. If you break out of the polite decorum by asking questions, acting the smart ass, slow in response to what is commanded, or if you make any movement the officer later calls "furtive," well, the full **force** (102–104) of the state can make itself known. And sometimes, *even when you do exactly as you are told*, as Philando Castile did, *you still might end up dead*.

Checkpoint

Police and military units use checkpoints to disrupt the movement and circulation of automotive traffic in order to conduct random searches of vehicles and motorists. A police checkpoint is similar to a **patrol** (170–172). But while a patrol places police in constant motion, whether in police cruisers, **helicopters** (70–73), on bicycles or on foot, so as to impose **order** (83–86) within a **jurisdiction** (104–106), a checkpoint interrupts the constant motion of all non-police vehicles at a particular location.

Though checkpoints are usually associated with sobriety checks, border patrol checkpoints are more common. Border police stop vehicles in order to check the immigration status of motorists. Permanent vehicle border checkpoints along and near the US border with Mexico in the US Southwest are part of a complex of anti-mobility police and military technologies and techniques that include fences, sensors, cameras, drones, watercraft, and heavily armed foot and vehicle patrols—not to mention anti-immigrant vigilantes—that make the US border with Mexico a deadly and "densely militarized space."[1] But border facilities extend beyond permanent checkpoints at or near international borders, including also temporary, random checkpoints often conducted by non-immigration police seemingly unrelated to international borders. Since 2008 as part of various federal programs, US immigration police require that local and state police agencies throughout the United States expand the checkpoint power of the border patrol. Random checkpoints everywhere have been one expression of this expansion, which scholars have shown has focused on Latino neighborhoods in patterns that established a "climate of terror" among immigrant communities.[2]

Checkpoints are often associated with boundaries of access and exit, but the police checkpoint demonstrates the limits of this thinking. The checkpoint erases boundaries and borders and replaces these instead with the police, which everywhere sees borders that need enforcing and people that need stopping. The checkpoint arrests mobility and circulation. "Stop. Show me your papers." It demands constant registration and expects total obedience. As such it is a versatile technology. It conjures images of a police state, at the same time that it presents itself as routine, unspectacular and everyday. Courts have routinely sided with police and have expanded the authority of police to conduct random stops without warrants and without **reasonable suspicion** (255–257) at both permanent and temporary checkpoints.[3]

The checkpoint, like the **traffic stop** (73–75) more generally, might appear as a routine function of police, but it is an expression of generalized police suspicion focused routinely on communities of color. The roadblock has long been a key tactic in controlling the movement of Black people in the US South. The **slave patrol** (143–144) controlled the movement of Black people through the frequent use of roadblocks. The Ku Klux Klan used roadblocks to enforce Jim Crow segregation. In the aftermath of Hurricane

Katrina, police in Gretna, Louisiana set up a roadblock on the Crescent City bridge that linked the city with New Orleans. They fired warning shots at Black people who were trying to flee the flooding in New Orleans.[4] White vigilantes in nearby Algiers Point did the same. "Patrolling in pick-up trucks and staffing roadblocks, they stopped and turned back Black people trying to cross through the Algiers Point neighborhood, harassed and intimidated Blacks who lived nearby, and sometimes, it seems, just shot people without warning."[5] If checkpoints enforce borders, then historically the checkpoint enforces a racial border. The police checkpoint is among the most routine and everyday police practices, as is the fear and insecurity it instills.

Sound

Sound is stimulus. What we call sound is the human brain's perception of an acoustic wave generated by an audio vibration. This acoustic wave, like police, can travel through nearly anything, can penetrate nearly everything. Frequency is measured in units of hertz (Hz), which describes the repeating pattern of a given vibration. A common police siren measures 1800 Hz, which means that police sirens produce thirty repeating audio signals each second, which places the police siren on a spectrum with acoustic vibrations designed to induce pain, panic, and terror (see **pain compliance**, 79–80). Weaponized acoustic waves calibrated to induce pain, panic, and terror, while invisible to the human eye and at some frequencies inaudible to the human ear, inflict damage to eyesight, internal organs, and central nervous system function, among other terrifying physical and psychological injuries.

Sound is a weapon. The Israeli Occupation Forces fire sound bombs. In September 2005, beginning each night at midnight and continuing until dawn, the Israeli air force sent dozens of low-flying jets into Gaza. The jets produced sonic booms when they broke the sound barrier and the shockwaves rolled through Gaza like so many Merkava tanks, damaging buildings, shattering windows and leaving people "shaking inside." One man described it as like being "in the middle of a bomb." Children suffered hearing loss. The number of admissions to cardiac care units doubled. Miscarriages spiked by 40 percent.[1]

Sound, once weaponized, converts your head into a bomb. The British used squawk boxes—a weapon designed to detonate inside a person's inner ear. According to denied reports, the British Ministry of Defense developed a weapon in 1973 for use in Northern Ireland that generated audio signals at two separate sound frequencies that merged into a third frequency in the inner ear of its victims. Some fainted, others got nauseous. The victims weren't in the bomb, the bomb was in them.[2]

Sound terrifies. The Louisville, Kentucky, police department uses sound cannons. In late May 2020, during the protests that followed the police murder of Breonna Taylor, Louisville police, like police departments in Portland and New York (among so many others) used handheld or truck-mounted weapons known as long-range acoustic devices (LRADs) that sent 160-plus decibel (dB) "deterrent tones" at frequencies more than ten times that of police sirens, capable of reaching protestors ten football fields away (see **deterrence**, 228–231). "It sounded like they set off a bomb," one protestor said. In laboratory tests of LRADs, rats suffered organ damage when exposed to sound at 180 dB. An audio engineer in New York subjected to an LRAD attack during protests following the police murder of George Floyd called the LRAD a weapon of terror.

Sound, like all police weapons, terrorizes and maims. Police kill or maim with **guns** (10–13), rifles, and shotguns. They maim or kill with **Tasers** (13–16), **tear gas** (17–20), and **rubber bullets** (50–55). They terrorize with 160 dB sound cannons, 1800 Hz sirens, and flash bang grenades that explode at 170 dB.

Cops even weaponize the absence of sound through the **no-knock warrant** (34–38). The control and weaponization of sound and its absence offers police and the military a nearly unlimited arsenal. Cops use sound to fuck with your head. Police and the military use white noise at high frequency for long periods of time during an **interrogation** (193–195) in order to extract false confessions; or through the use of intense, inaudible, low-frequency infrasounds that seem to come from nowhere and everywhere all at once and induce auditory hallucinations; or through the cumulative injury of constant, loud music; or the maddening drip, drip, drip that the blindfolded subject of police torture endures. There's no escape from the sounds of police violence. Even if you break out of the interrogation room in one piece, the police sound of dread will follow you—the constant siren wail of the police cruiser, the roar of the **police helicopter** (70–73), the mobile police surveillance unit barking orders, the infrasonic acoustic **gun** (10–13) pointed at you.

These are the vibrations of **order** (83–86), the soundtrack to capitalist life delivered in the frequency of police and military occupation.

Pain Compliance

Pain is the adjective that clarifies police power. According to Samera Esmeir, the criminal justice system is "unfathomable without pain."[1] Without pain, police have no authority. The police inflict pain and are the sole authority to relieve it, and this serves the same legitimating purpose at the heart of criminal justice. **Law** (90–93), Esmeir argues, "openly sanctions the infliction of regulated pain."[2] Law endorses the pain police impose.

Pain is instrumental to another purpose: compliance. Police use pain to modify behavior. Pain makes noncompliant subjects compliant. For police, pain is depicted as a discrete tool or technique administered on "noncompliant" subjects. The police threaten and produce suffering and therefore produce the suffering subject, a subject who does not exist outside this relation. Only a sufferer can be the proper subject of police power. And only police can measure suffering; only police can determine compliance or **noncompliance** (245–246). It is equally the job of police to impose pain as it is to measure its effectiveness. And since, to police, pain is always effective at creating compliant subjects, pain is not present if compliance is not achieved.

Consider what this implies. Police claim the power to administer pain in order to create suffering, and also claim the power to unerringly interpret another's suffering. It implies that police have secret knowledge of another's consciousness. But we know from the case of Eric Garner and many others that this is not true. Pain compliance is a phrase that describes a host of specific tactics that police use to inflict pain. These include the use of pepper spray and **Tasers** (13–16), the hog-tying of suspects and the hyperflexing of their joints, and in the case of Garner, the **chokehold** (58–60). Eric Garner died in a chokehold while saying, over and over again, "I can't breathe." The officer did not loosen the chokehold because it was the police officer, not the subject of pain compliance, who measures pain. It is not an accident that the police defended the use of the chokehold against Garner, in part, by claiming that he died from complications related to asthma, not the police chokehold.

The power relation brought to life by pain compliance is a relation that excludes all others. "Whatever pain achieves," according to Elaine Scarry, "it achieves in part through its unsharability."[3] There is only a sufferer who suffers and a **cop** (219–221) who administers pain, who measures pain, and who determines when pain culminates in compliance. Pain to the police is progressive. It produces a preferred outcome. But to believe this is to be in the thrall of the instrumental logic of police. If police power is about **order** (83–86), and the compliance that pain produces marks what police consider orderly, then pain is that which makes the world orderly.[4] An orderly world, legible to police, destroyed for Eric Garner.

The Oath:
Core Values of Police

Private Property

Private property does not merely describe a relation between an owner and a thing. It is a social relation—the right to exclude—shot through with violence. If I take food from a grocery store, drive a car off a dealer's lot, or move into your spare bedroom, and I do it without permission, without paying, and, most importantly, *without* punishment or fear of punishment, then we cannot say food and cars and spare bedrooms are private property. Without the enforcement of an exclusive claim there is no private property. Private property is therefore always based on **force** (102–104), which is to say that there is no private property without **violence** (96–100).

The capitalist state defends private property rights. "The first and chief design of every system of government," according to Adam Smith, "is to maintain justice: to prevent the members of society from encroaching on one another's property, or seizing what is not their own. The design here is to give each one the secure and peaceable possession of his own property."[1] Justice, in other words, is found in the realm of property. The state's use of violence to enforce property relations is how capitalism defends what it considers just. To speak of enforcement is to speak of police. Property is thus a form of police violence. In Smith's day, the word "police" referred to an expansive authority to regulate commerce and property. The section titled "Police" in his *Lectures on Jurisprudence* explained the general principles of law and government as the domain of police. "The objects of police," according to Smith, "are the cheapness of commodities, public security and cleanliness."[2] In particular "whatever regulations are made with respect to the trade, commerce, agriculture, manufactures of the country are considered as belonging to the police."³ The point of all this property policing is to produce "liberty"—freedom from coercion, freedom from violence, freedom to pursue one's fullest potential. The irony, of course, is that the freedom from coercion and violence that capitalism promises is a freedom delivered at the end of a cop's **nightstick** (55–58). The "invisible hand of the market" is attached to the strong arm of the **law** (90–93).

Private property, established through force, has transformed the world we live in. And it was and is the job of police to **patrol** (170–172) the landscapes of private property, to enforce these boundaries and barriers, walls and enclosures. Thus property might best be understood as a police category. Police **arrest** (208–210) the trespasser, evict the squatter, and foreclose on the jobless homeowner. Encroachment on private property is a threat to capitalist **order** (83–86), and it is police who manage this **threat** (222–223).

Private property *requires* violence. Consider the law of adverse possession, for example. The owner of real property—a suburban house or a city lot or a rural pasture—is required to announce and sustain an exclusive claim to property through a variety of acts—paying taxes, erecting fences and "no trespassing" signs, mailing eviction notices to renters who are in arrears, making improvements, and more. These are all performances of an ongoing, exclusive claim. If an owner does not perform these acts, another may do so and claim ownership. Violence too is among the required performances of property. The state of Florida's Justifiable Use of Force Statute, also known as Stand Your Ground, describes violence as among property's rights. If a person has "a reasonable fear of imminent peril of death or great bodily harm," the law permits the use of lethal force, but only if an aggressor "had unlawfully and forcibly entered a dwelling, residence, or occupied vehicle." The law, however, forbids the use of lethal violence in that same circumstance if the aggressor "has the right to be in or is a lawful resident of the dwelling, residence, or vehicle, such as an owner, lessee, or titleholder." In other words, as far as the law is concerned, the authority of the state to sanction the use of violence exists only in the context of a property relation. *People* do not have an unalloyed right to kill, but *property owners* do.

Property relations are violent relations, and property has always been a racialized category. Historically, the law has elevated the property claims made by white people. Consider the history of the **slave patrol** (143–144) in the Virginias and Carolinas, for example. We should understand the work of the slave patrol as a defense of whiteness as an exclusive property claim—a property claim that extended over Black life. And what happens when the oppressed rise up and riot in challenge to the privileges and whiteness of property? The elite fear the destruction of their property, yes, but even more they fear the destruction of the social relations that make private property possible. And so they fear a world without police.

Order

At first glance it may seem that **crime** (93–96) and **law** (90–93) are the categories that best explain police. After all, police officers enforce the law, and police officers investigate crime and criminals. When we think of police, we often think of police in **uniform** (141–143) making an **arrest** (208–210), or we think of a **cop** (219–221) conducting an **investigation** (175–176), collecting evidence at a crime scene. But policing is not about crime **deterrence** (228–231), and the police are more than the sum of individual cops. It is through the concept of order we can best make sense of the concept of police. The central mandate of police has always been "good order" and always in the broadest sense possible. And this means that policing is about more than merely crime, but also what the criminologists James Q. Wilson and George L. Kelling refer to as quality of life.[1]

Spend just a few minutes reading Wilson and Kelling's seminal 1982 essay **"Broken Windows"** (186–189) to be reminded of the police imperative of order. For their admirers, Wilson and Kelling inaugurated a new era of quality of life policing that, their promoters say, drove down crime and brought new promise to the "crime-infested" inner city. But in truth it merely repackaged a much older imperative of policing as first and foremost about controlling the poor. Consider a vignette from their essay in which they depict the poor as an eternal **threat** (222–223) to good order and police as a bulwark against that disorder:

The people on the street were primarily black; the officer who walked the street was white. The people were made up of "regulars" and "strangers." Regulars included both "decent folk" and some drunks and derelicts who were always there but who "knew their place." Strangers were, well, strangers, and viewed suspiciously, sometimes apprehensively. The officer—call him Kelly—knew who the regulars were, and they knew him. As he saw his job, he was to keep an eye on strangers, and make certain that the disreputable regulars observed some informal but widely understood rules. Drunks and addicts could sit on the stoops, but could not lie down. People could drink on side streets, but not at the main intersection. Bottles had to be in paper bags. Talking to, bothering, or begging from people waiting at the bus stop was strictly forbidden. If a dispute erupted between a businessman and a customer, the businessman was assumed to be right, especially if the customer was a stranger. If a stranger loitered, Kelly would ask him if he had any means of support and what his business was; if he gave unsatisfactory answers, he was sent on his way. Persons who broke the informal rules, especially those who bothered people waiting at bus stops, were arrested for **vagrancy** (189–193). Noisy teenagers were told to keep quiet.[2]

Wilson and Kelling ignore the question of race except, as in the first line of the passage above, to imply that it doesn't matter. But the order that police impose on the poor—how to behave, how to punish, who belongs and who must be banished—is always also a racial order. The imperative for bourgeois order contains a "white supremacist desire for surveilling, policing, caging and (preemptively) socially liquidating" the poor and people of color.[3] This intensified targeting of the poor seeks to build and forever protect an order based on **private property** (81–83). This is policing as and for **gentrification** (184–186).

No violence appears in the story of Kelly the cop that Wilson and Kelling recount. Presumably the white cop just walks a **beat** (172–174) in a Black neighborhood, good-naturedly swinging his **nightstick** (55–58), politely ordering people around. They depict him imposing order without the presence or threat of police **violence** (96–100). Just tell those noisy teenagers to keep quiet and they will. But order requires obedience. What happens when they disobey? Perhaps Wilson and Kelling ignore this question because it is immaterial to the question of police and order. It is not *behavior* that defines disobedience and disorder; it is being poor or being Black that defines disobedience and disorder. This is what happens in the **ghetto** (183–184), where the order police impose comes from what James Baldwin called the "thunder and fire of the billy club."[4] Wilson and Kelling make this argument explicitly. No inference is necessary to understand what they mean. The white cop always assumes the businessman is right and acts accordingly. As Baldwin reminds us, police "are present to keep the Negro in his place and to protect white business interests, and they have no other function."[5]

If police have "no other function" than to "keep the Negro in his place" and "to protect white business interests," what an enormous function it is. Order as racial and class order seeps into every nook and cranny of the state, preoccupies every top cop and county sheriff in the land, and defines every age and era of the police. It was in the service of good order that police **lynched** (43–46) Black men or stood by while white mobs did. It was for good order that white slave-owning society created the **slave patrol** (143–144) as a means to police the movements of Black people on and off the plantation. The mass incarceration of people of color emerged from white fear of the threat of Black criminality to good order, which is just a euphemism for white supremacy. Histories of settler colonialism are always police histories. They are stories of police controlling Indigenous people in the city in order to create and maintain a white order. "Keeping order in public space still largely means mostly non-Indigenous police controlling the movements of Indigenous peoples in city space."[6]

The cops in **uniform** (141–143) realize that the good order they impose sometimes requires terror and "thunder and fire." It is through **community policing** (122–123) that they convince themselves, and seek to convince us, that all this violence is necessary. They hedge their bets that when we see the world through their eyes we'll see enemies of good order, not victims of state violence. But as Walter Benjamin warned, the status quo "is the catastrophe."[7] So refuse to see the world through police eyes. Refuse to see police as heroes patrolling the **thin blue line** (110–112) between civilization and savagery. Refuse to see your **security** (86–89) as a gift police give you. Instead see police as they are: an armed wing of the state out to defend the status quo, out to keep you in your place, out to protect business interests. Nothing more.

Security

Security is the essential police concept. All that police do is **justified** (238–240) in the name of security. Police **patrol** (170–172) the **ghetto** (183–184) in the name of security. Police patrol the middle-class suburb in the name of security. Your captivity by **arrest** (208–210) and **handcuffs** (20–21) comes from the need for security, and its close cousin safety. Security is the reason police shoot armed, and even **unarmed** (257–258), poor people of color. Security is why the **cop** (219–221) has the **gun** (10–13) holstered on the hip in the first place. The **body cavity search** (33–34) that routinely humiliates poor women is always justified with appeals to security. The **K-9** (22–24) is set loose on a fleeing subject because the runaway poses a security **threat** (222–223) to officers or the general **public** (252–255). It is for security that police respond to riots, strikes, or public protests with **Tasers** (13–16), **nightsticks** (55–58) and **tear gas** (17–20).

The fetish of security animates not only the violence work of police, but the mythology and existence of the modern state. According to conventional thinking, liberal democracies such as the United States are not in fact security states because they are built first and foremost on the social contract of individual liberty and the rule of **law** (90–93). That is, what makes a democracy liberal is the precedence that liberty and law take over the absolutist desire for security. Liberty, it is said, is the real foundation of a democratic society and allows for a superior form of government because it actually holds political power accountable while protecting individual freedom via the rule of law. This is not to say that liberal mythology eschews security entirely, just that it has to be balanced with liberty so that ultimately liberty prevails and is kept intact.

The liberal state still must provide security to its citizens, but its obligation is to do this without sacrificing liberty.

This is the classic liberty versus security debate, which usually assumes that liberty is the first principle of liberal democracies and is the reason they are called liberal democracies, not security democracies. But the ideology of security, which is to say the ideology of war (100–102) and police, has always been absolutely fundamental to the rule of law. This is not to say that liberalism's commitment to liberty is a sham. Rather, it is to suggest that maybe "liberalism's central category is not liberty, but security."[1] Security, not liberty, is at the heart of liberal democracy. Karl Marx called security the supreme concept of bourgeois society, and we can point to any issue—from parenting, terrorism, travel, migration, education, homelessness, homemaking, climate change, crime (93–96), or consumerism—and find the imperative of security lurking in official discourse of the problem that confronts the liberal state. These are made by the state and capital into a "security issue," which is also to say a police issue, since security is the central police concept.

Security always trumps liberty. This is not an accident or a distortion of liberal principles, but a principle built into the very architecture of liberal thought. The key here lies in the prerogative power that John Locke described as internal to liberal doctrine. The prerogative, according to Locke, refers to those times when even in a society constituted "of the people, by the people, and for the people" (that is, law), the branch of the executive must retain the prerogative for wide discretionary power (see discretion, 176–178). That is, even in a democratic society ruled by the laws of the people, the state must retain for itself an emergency (223–224) power to decide when, how, and to what extent to protect life, liberty, and private property (81–83). Law, he surmised, is often too slow or cumbersome to address emergencies, accidents, and immediate threats to order, and therefore the right of the state to take swift security measures must always take precedence. The only thing that must be maintained is that the state act in the best interests of the safety of the public (252–255) and the public good. Importantly, Locke's understanding of security was intimately linked with the securing of private property and accumulation within the context of settler colonialism in the Americas.

This precedence of security over all else in liberal democracies is normalized and operationalized in the unlimited discretion that the modern state codifies in law and grants to police. Police is security; police is the normalization of emergency power throughout the entirety of political territory since there is no domestic **jurisdiction** (104–106) where police don't claim prerogative to intervene in the name of security. To see police as a category of security, and not of law, is to insist that police power exists because law, or the liberal state, recognizes its own failures in compelling desired behavior and in responding to unforeseen disorders. This failure of law is why law turns to the prerogative of security, the power of police to restore order. As Walter Benjamin argued, "The 'law' of the police really marks the point at which the state, whether from impotence or because of the immanent connections within any legal system, can no longer guarantee through the legal system the empirical ends that it desires at any price to attain." And so, "the police intervene 'for security reasons' in countless cases where no clear legal situation exists."[2]

Just as almost any foreign policy action has been **justified** (238–240) in the name of national security, so it is that security is the justification for all sorts of domestic policies, regardless of how violent and brutal they might be. The imprisoning of over 2 million mostly poor people, with Black, Brown, and Native people caged at higher rates: this is security. The police killing of over a thousand people a year, almost all of them poor: this is security. And this begs the question about what and who is exactly being secured? The security that animates police might seem like safety from crime. But the law has actually made it clear that police are not obligated to protect individuals. Police, the law says, are really only obligated or mandated to protect **order** (83–86), which is also a way of saying the securing of capitalist property relations. If you aren't a large property owner or part of the upper classes, police don't really care about you or your security and safety. In fact, you are the embodiment of insecurity, of threat, of disorder. You don't need the protection *of* law and order, you need protection *from* law and order. So when cops talk in the language of security, remember: it is not your security they mean.

Pacification

Pacification is not about peace; it is the policy of war-making. Pacification is as much the terror of shock and awe as it is the hearts and minds campaign. To pacify a population—to impose order through coercion and consent—is not limited to military destruction and occupation. Pacification is a police concept, which is to say that pacification is ultimately animated by the logic of **security** (86–89). "Capital and police dream of pacification: a dream of workers available for work, present and correct, their papers in order, their minds and bodies docile, and a dream of accumulation thereby secure from resistance, rebellion or revolt."[1] Pacification dreams of an unruly world populated by disobedient subjects who refuse to go along with the state's vision for order. Pacification does not announce the end of hostilities, but the beginning of compliance-or-else.

Pacification is as fundamental to police as it is to military conquest. And this is to say that the police power and the **war** (100–102) power are not separate and distinct spheres of state power. The police and military pursue pacification with an iron fist and a velvet glove, with coercion and consent. The military drops bombs and builds schools, and both tactics are strategies of pacification. Police use physical tactics—**chokeholds** (58–60), **handcuffs** (20–21), **nightsticks** (55–58)—and, for the same reasons, police use psychological tactics—**community policing** (122–123), **Officer Friendly** (132–135), coffee with a cop. The entire edifice of **broken windows** (186–189) policing is about pacification, built as it is on a simple idea: if you are not polite to police and the interests they protect, you are a **threat** (222–223).

The goal of pacification projects is to produce obedient, docile, and servile subjects. This last one—servility—is important for the way it implies a humiliation at the heart of cop–community relations. Police don't expect obedience; they impose it. The purpose of the **interrogation** (193–195), the **body cavity search** (33–34) and the **stop and frisk** (27–31) is, first and foremost, humiliation. It reminds you that you are helpless before the police powers. Yet police also try to impose obedience through public relations campaigns designed to win the support of the population. Efforts designed to convince you that police are "here to help." To think of police as agents of pacification is to find in all of these police activities a logic of domination and forced obedience.

Pacification is about the fabrication of **order** (83–86), and order-building requires dispossession first and foremost.[2] Pacification serves ongoing settler colonialism by eradicating "existing Indigenous societies while establishing a new society on expropriated land that also erases its colonial past."[3] Pacification is the amnesia that a liberal capitalist order requires. Albuquerque, New Mexico police officers, for example, produce compliance, and thus pacification, with a "knee strike to the head of a defenseless suspect."[4] But this is not recorded in required use-of-force reports as **force** (102–104). Instead police disguise their **violence** (96–100) with words such as "distraction strike" or "distraction technique." In other words, Albuquerque police kick and punch and strike people with **nightsticks** (55–58) and fists and knees until those people are obedient, until those people are pacified. And then those cops walk in parades and hand out stickers to children at the State Fair. And they visit local schools to provide safety lessons where they talk about community–police partnerships as the key to nonviolence. This is pacification.

Police demand that **the public** (252–255) trust the police, but the police don't trust you. If you are someone who thinks critically about **Officer Friendly** (132–135) and his act, or even if you're just not a **cop** (219–221), then you too are a threat who might need to be pacified. The police want to pacify you, but they especially want to pacify the poor, people of color, and Indigenous people. This desire for pacification animates everything that the police do.

Law

This is the story law tells of itself: law describes a body of rules, either formal or customary, imposed on a populace or constituency by an authority, often a religious order or a secular state. These rules are commonly understood to govern the behavior of all, and any violation of prescribed behavior is punished by a penalty. Most importantly law is understood to produce a just **order** (83–86), one based on norms in which punishment follows violation, and all of this serves the goal of equality—we are all equal before the law, in other words. When we submit to law, we submit to an objective authority, rather than to the strongman or the dictator. This is what is meant by the phrase "rule of law": to be ruled by law, not men.

In this story the rule of law acquits itself quite nicely in comparison to the law of the strongman. After all, who would choose to suffer at the whim of the strongman, when all can be equal before the law? But the story law tells of itself, one of justice and righteousness, obscures a dark side. The legal equality law promises is unevenly distributed based on a person or group's location within relations of production. "How noble the law, in its majestic equality, that both the rich and poor are equally prohibited from begging in the streets, sleeping under bridges, and stealing bread!" Here Anatole France's great satire of law points out the cruel absurdity of law's "equality." Law merely reflects the principles and institutions of a given society in its historical context. Thus in a capitalist society organized around **private property** (81–83) and the accumulation of capital, law valorizes private property by criminalizing behaviors that violate private ownership. In other words, theft can only be a **"crime"** (93–96) when law establishes "ownership" as a protected legal standard. "In its very neutrality, law maintains capitalist relations. Law is class law, and it cannot but be so."[1] Law is not discovered, it is made, and made to serve class interests. Thus the rule of law emerges from and constitutes a particular social order.

The standard police view of law posits law as that which resolves the problem of the perpetual disorder that follows from a breakdown in social mores and community order. Police enforce the law by fighting crime in order to "protect and serve." Law, in this view, is depicted as representing an objective good created by shared values and norms. Crime and criminals violate those norms and values. The criminal represents disorder; police defend civilization. But if we understand "crime" as any purposeful act that transgresses lawful behavior, or any behavior that violates an official legal edict, then crime is not an independent condition that preexists disorder and requires police; rather crime and the criminal exist only in relation to law. There is no crime where there is no law, or more accurately, there is no crime where there are no police. Law therefore is a mode of disciplinary power and among its most important effects is that it makes us all subjects before the law, before the police.

It is no accident that the phrase "law and order" is the mantra of police in capitalist society, where criminal law stands in as the central mode of law. Evgeny Pashukanis called criminal law a form of class domination. "The criminal **jurisdiction** (104–106) of the Bourgeois state," he wrote, "is organized class terror."[2] Law, particularly criminal law, in capitalist society, according to Pashukanis, is not about justice. As he argued:

> So-called theories of criminal law which derive the principle of punitive policy from the interest of society as a whole are occupied with the conscious or unconscious distortion of reality. "Society as a whole" exists only in the imagination of these jurists. In fact, we are faced with classes with contradictory, conflicting interests. Every historical system of punitive policy bears the imprint of the class interest of that class which realized it. The feudal lord executed disobedient peasants and city dwellers who rose against his power. The unified cities hanged the robber-knights and destroyed their castles. In the Middle Ages, a man was considered a lawbreaker if he wanted to engage in a trade without joining a guild; the capitalist bourgeoisie, which had barely succeeded in emerging, declared that the desire of workers to join unions was criminal.[3]

And so the criminal deserves **violence** (96–100), and it is through this violence, according to Walter Benjamin, that "the origins of law jut manifestly and fearsomely into existence." Through the state's "exercise of violence over life and death more than in any other legal act, law reaffirms itself."[4] Law is thus a central element in a repressive order, and, according to Nicos Poulantzas, "by issuing rules and passing laws, the State establishes an initial field of injunctions, prohibitions and censorship, and thus institutes the practical terrain and object of violence. Furthermore, law organizes the conditions for physical repression, designating its modalities and structuring the devices by means of which it is exercised. In this sense, law as *the code of organized public violence* is the most routine and insidious institution of legal violence."[5]

Crime

A normative or positivist view of crime considers it an objective depiction of individual, deviant behavior. According to this view the crime rate measures misconduct in a particular place among a particular population. A constructivist view sees crime as a social construction. "Crime" is a measure of social control rather than a description of deviance, and the crime *rate* measures the intensity of that control in a given place on a given population. A constructivist view considers the possibility that a dramatic increase in crime rates is as much a function of improvements in data collection methods as it is in something called lawlessness.

Despite the different understandings of crime by positivist and constructivist interpretations, both generally depict crime as a legal category. One commits a crime when one breaks the **law** (90–93). But this view ignores the role of police in the construction of crime as a category. Law establishes what is unlawful; police decide what is a crime. The police powers of **investigation** (175–176), **interrogation** (193–195) and **arrest** (208–210) constitute the usual way something gets counted as crime. A Baltimore police department sergeant ordered an officer to clear a corner where young Black men were congregating. When the officer asked what crime they were committing, the sergeant replied, "Make something up." When a Baltimore detective was told he made a bad arrest, he explained to another detective, "We don't care about what happens in court. We just care about getting the arrest."[1] The power to define what is or isn't a crime, and who is or isn't a criminal, rests with police alone.

Police unions (150–151) and conservative **law** (90–93) and **order** (83–86) politicians are among the most vocal members of the get-tough-on-crime lobby. They depict crime rates as an objective measure of deviance—always with a focus on street crime and never corporate or white collar crime—and they use this as a rationale for their tough-on-crime positions. The preoccupation among law and order politicians with the problem of crime is often described as a fear of disorder and the crisis that attends that disorder. The solution is to demand "'more than usual law,' to ensure, in a moment of crisis, 'more than usual order,'"[2] to expand the punitive criminal justice system with more mandatory prison sentences, more heavily armed police, more solitary confinement, and more life without parole.

Even if one believes that crime describes deviance, it does not follow that these tough-on-crime proposals solve the problem, unless the problem is not enough people of color in jail. Police of course claim otherwise. **Predictive policing** (178–179) programs such as **CompStat** (180–182), "quality of life" practices such as **broken windows** (186–189) policing, and even tactical units such as **police helicopter** (70–73) divisions, are all among the specific ways police claim to engage in crime **deterrence** (228–231), but this is a theoretical, not an empirical, argument. It imagines that crime rates measure an active criminal world lurking just beyond the reach of police. It assumes that only police, via the **threat** (222–223) of punishment—arrest and incarceration—prevent crime. The police concept of deterrence needs crime rates in order to assume that criminals preexist a crime, and that these criminals-to-be will choose not to commit a crime based on the threat of arrest and incarceration.

Constructivist theories of crime view it as a measure of poverty and inequality. According to this view poverty, not deviance, is the root of crime, and rising crime rates are a measure of the intensity of that inequality. The constructivist view generally rejects zero-tolerance criminal justice reforms and instead proposes social services and alternatives to jail and prison, such as probation and parole, as a fairer and more effective approach to the problem of crime. But this has had the effect of greatly expanding the scope and reach of the criminal justice system. The result has been an explosion in new prison construction in order to cage the increasing numbers of Black and Latino prisoners and thus an expansion of what scholars call the carceral state. What is important to keep in mind, though, is that this was the result of a bipartisan consensus between conservatives and liberals, and even though liberals and conservatives differ regarding the status of crime as something either real or political, both link race to criminality.

Despite these differences, Naomi Murakawa sees a lot in common between the normative and constructivist views of crime when it comes to how both understand the relationship between crime and race. Whereas conservatives historically see Black crime as "a mani-festation of civil rights gone too far," liberals see rising Black crime rates "as indicators that civil rights had not gone far enough." She argues that "rising crime of the 1960s was not uniquely racialized as a conservative strategy to conflate civil rights with black crim-inality; rather, the race 'problem' of the civil rights movement from the 1940s onward was answered with pledges of carceral state devel-opment—from racial liberal and conservative lawmakers alike." In other words, while liberal and conservative views differ regarding the status of "crime" as either *real* or *political*, both link race to criminality. She encourages us to think about "crime politics," rather than crime, as a way to understand the intense criminaliza-tion of Black life in the United States. How else to explain the explosion in the incarceration of Black people over the past forty years? "Between 1926 and 1976, black admission rates to state and federal prisons varied between 81 and 137 admitted per 100,000, and white admission rates varied between 22 and 50 admitted per 100,000 . . . a three-to-one ratio . . . After 1976, however, the black admission rate hit a six-to-one ratio."[3]

Crime is also a gendered category. It is only since 1993 that mari-tal rape has been a crime in all fifty US states. But again, we would be better to focus on police rather than law when considering the crime of **rape** (41–43). "Only a fraction of rapes is reported, the most frequently mentioned reason for nonreporting being fear of the criminal justice system. Women of color fear its racism particularly. Only a fraction of reported rapes is prosecuted. Many rapes are 'unfounded,' an active verb describing the police decision not to believe that a rape happened as reported."[4]

The category of crime serves then as the primary tool for social control and order. Nearly one in ten Black men who are in their twenties are currently in jail, and one in three Black men will be incarcerated at some point in their life. But before they can be locked in cages, they must be arrested by the police. Crime, in other words, is at the **discretion** (176–178) of police, not the rule of law. Crime is a **cop** (219–221) category.

Violence

The power to kill is the power from which all other police powers follow. The police can **arrest** (208–210) you and put you in **handcuffs** (20–21) and take you to jail because they can kill you. Cops can make you move along because they can beat you with a **nightstick** (55–58) or sic a **K-9** (22–24) on you. They can beat you and kill you with legal and political impunity because police claim the ultimate authority— the **discretion** (176–178) to take a life in order to make order. Max Weber famously identified the state as that institution that "claims the monopoly of the legitimate use of physical **force** (102–104) within a given territory," and it is to the police that this violent monopoly is delegated. When we talk about police power we are also talking about state power, and when we talk about police **violence** (96–100) we are always already talking about the legal violence of the administrative state. We are talking about the organized violence that is required for the system of racial capitalism to exist.

Cop (219–221) power is always an executive power that exercises the discretion to use violence or decide against using violence, to kill or to let live. Think of Hobbes's notion of Leviathan and Locke's notion of the sovereign's prerogative to decide who is a **threat** (222–223) and what is an **emergency** (223–224), and see that cops are "petty sovereigns," invested with an unlimited discretion to identify and respond in whatever ways they deem necessary in any given moment.[1] Cops exercise violence routinely and with near legal impunity.

Police are curators in the art of violence. They have a plethora of weapons to help them perform this legal violence. And though police can array this violence however they see fit, it is never exercised equally across a social **order** (83–86). State violence is always more concentrated in spaces of poverty and exclusion such as the **ghetto** (183–184), and against the poor and people of color confined there. It isn't a coincidence that police violence is often framed as disinfecting and sanitizing. Consider the slang cops use when talking about police violence. When they strike someone on the head with a nightstick: "wood shampoo." When they explain why they brought in **SWAT** (135–139): "crime-infested neighborhood." Cops "sweep the streets" and "take out the trash" when they discipline the "savages," "filth," "scum," and "dirtbags" roaming urban space. Police logic is the logic of sanitation, the logic of "polishing" and making "polite" those "dirty" populations that threaten order.

The legal capacity to use violence separates police from all other institutions, since police are legally sanctioned to exercise violence against virtually anyone who is not ostensibly a police officer. But we need to be clear here: violence is not just a right of police work; violence is a *condition* of police work. The work of police therefore is the work of legal violence. Cops are violence workers first and foremost. One of the most influential sociologists of police to make this point, Egon Bittner, argued that "the role of the police is best understood as a mechanism for the distribution of non-negotiably coercive force employed in accordance with the dictates of an intuitive grasp of situational exigencies."[1] Bittner argued that the authority of police to use **force** (102–104) is nearly without restriction, particularly because the use of force comes with no real consequences. The idea of lawful violence is thus meaningless, as police violence stands forever outside legal sanction.

Coercive force structures all police practice. We call police because of their capacity to deploy violence if necessary. Even when an arrest appears to take place with no visible resistance, this encounter is in no way absent of violence but completely structured by it. As legal theorist Robert Cover famously noted, "We don't talk our prisoners to jail."[2] It only appears that the defendant goes along willingly. Violence is always there, and ready to make itself known.

An important implication is that police violence shouldn't be reduced to only those instances where death or outright bodily violence is the result, instances popularly referred to as **police brutality**

(207–208). The point is that police violence is never exceptional, however spectacular and appalling it might be, and that the majority of police violence is routine and ordinary, built into the very mandate of police that makes police such a unique and powerful force in all of our lives, but especially the lives of the poor. Legal violence is the principal dynamic that renders an equal exchange between cop and non-cop an impossibility.[4]

But policing is rarely recognized as violence work. This might be due to your experiences with friendly, respectful and understanding cops. Or maybe you've been a victim of crime or personal violence and police came to your aid. Or maybe you have cops in your family and hence see them as much more than violence workers. But to say that cops are violence workers isn't to narrow the issue to a discussion about individual personalities or particular incidents. To do so would be to reduce a discussion of police violence to **bad apples** (224–227) and legal critiques of intent and reasonableness, which is also the same as speaking in law's language of judges, lawyers and cops. To say that cops are violence workers is to speak about the structural dynamics of policing as both an institution and a sociopolitical process. In addition, the police power endlessly works to disown its violent function, whether through phrases such as "protect and serve," "public safety" and "**security** (86–89)," or the image work of public relations that represents police as friendly and helpful. Even **Officer Friendly** (132–135) is no stranger to violence, because he or she is still a cop for whom violence always remains a condition of employment.

From the police perspective though, they rarely use violence and instead use the word "force" to refer to their violence. The term "violence" is reserved for the non-state, unsanctioned behaviors or actions of anyone who isn't a cop, anyone who defies police authority to dictate any given situation. Yet frequently police and those who protest police violence agree on the definition of police violence as an injurious act against a body defined in relation to professional standards, usually understood as excessive acts that defy legal or institutional guidelines. We should look beyond this definition because it ignores the ways nonlethal police violence, so commonplace and everyday, goes unseen. Researchers, journalists and reformers can spend a lot of time with police and never see cops use violence and therefore miss the ways that even routine policing is experienced by the poor as nothing but constant humiliation and indignity. This too is violence and should be seen as such.

Thinking of cops as violence workers isn't to suggest police share any solidarity or real interests with workers in other sectors. Some on the left have argued that cops should be included within the 99 percent and therefore leftist activists should engage in more friendly, reformist relations with cops so as to ultimately convince them to switch their loyalty away from the 1 percent. However appealing this might seem, it resonates only to the extent that it hinges on an ahistorical, hopeful naiveté untethered to actually existing historical patterns and contemporary conditions. Police violence is most often used against low-wage workers, the surplus populations excluded from a consistent, livable wage, and the activists and movements challenging the status quo.

Police unions (150–151) collectively bargain to be free of independent **police oversight** (146–149) regarding their use of violence, and this means they bargain collectively for the right, as a condition of their employment, to be as violent as they see fit. Police unions collectively bargain to maintain and expand the police capacity to deploy violence in order to protect the racialized status quo of capitalist **private property** (81–83) relations. Cops bargain with the capitalist state, which means the state engages in negotiations over the very question of police violence, and since no police department in the United States submits to independent oversight, this is another way to see that the state always defers to police on the use of violence.

If the police relation is always nonnegotiable and unequal because it is always structured by law's violence, then the problem of police violence is the problem of policing and **law** (90–93) more generally. Yet this is too limited a view, since it gives too much blame to police and not enough blame to capitalism, specifically a neoliberal capitalism that has systematically produced the largest inequality gap between the rich and the poor in history, and frequently through programs like **broken windows** (186–189) policing that unabashedly target the poor, people of color, and the homeless. As Karl Marx famously diagnosed, "capital comes dripping from head to toe, from every pore, with blood and dirt."[3]

Capitalism doesn't exist without cops because cops are the violence workers that fabricate and maintain relations of private property that are fundamental to capitalism. This means that even the overt forms of police violence such as the killing of Kelly Thomas cannot be reduced to repression alone but are actually generative of social **order** (83–86). This is among the most frightening facts of police violence: it is productive. It produces a very specific outcome. The liberal capitalist state requires these deaths because they help to produce the current social order. This also means that those movements of insurgency or resistance, such as those associated with Black Lives Matter or Indigenous struggles like Idle No More understand that they are not merely confronting some isolated issue of the police and police violence but are confronting and contesting the very legitimacy and lifeblood of racial capitalism.

War

Make no mistake: the police are at war, and have always been at war. They wage a war on **crime** (93–96) and a war on drugs and a war on terror, all of which emerged from a war on poverty. Policing is a form of domestic warfare, both in how police talk about policing and in how the state carries it out.[1] The rhetoric of war is thus not a metaphor. It comes from the material realities of manufacturing and reproducing an **order** (83–86) of racial capitalism.

The police project is a war project and this view helps cut through the ideologies of **reform** (155–160) that assume police are ultimately a **force** (102–104) for good and a beacon of civilization. The war power of police is therefore viewed by police as the force that constitutes police. There has never been a "golden age" when police were not at war. We should say that again: there is no golden age of policing where police were actually democratic, nonviolent, and didn't target the poor, people of color, and activists. This is why Black urban communities have long described police as an "occupying army" and the **ghetto** (183–184) as an "internal colony." They use the language of war because policing is war. Life in the ghetto is experienced as violent occupation.

All different factions in this class war recognize it as a war. It is not just poor people of color who draw on the language of war when describing police as an occupying army. When politicians speak of crime and cops, they also speak in the language of war. Lyndon Johnson called for cops to launch "an immediate attack" on crime in 1966. "The front-line soldier in the war on crime is the local law enforcement officer."[2] Bill Clinton reminded Democratic national convention goers in 1992 that "[President Bush] hasn't fought a real war on crime and drugs. I will." And the war they delivered put more cops in poor communities and more people of color in cages. If we include jail, prison, probation and parole, the incarceration rate grew from 780,000 when Johnson launched his attack to 7 million in 2010.[3] And this war was experienced most intensely in minority communities. As Richard Nixon's chief of staff explained, "[President Nixon] emphasized that you have to face the fact that the whole problem is really the blacks. The key is to devise a system that recognizes this while not appearing to."[4] So they offered programs and policies designed to make the war appear civil, humane, and peaceful in order to capture our hearts and minds, programs such as **community policing** (122–123) and **Officer Friendly** (132–135).

There is nothing new about any of this. As Robin Kelley explains, "The position of the police as an occupying army in America's inner cities is not a new phenomenon. It is not a recent manifestation of a post-industrial condition in which the disappearance of jobs in urban areas generated lawlessness and disorder, nor is it the result of the federal government having declared war on drugs, though these things have certainly heightened police–community tensions in urban neighborhoods of color."[5] Police are a crucial part of the perpetual and permanent war that began with Indigenous dispossession and genocide and chattel slavery, historical processes that still very much structure the political and cultural economies of capitalist accumulation at home and abroad.

So there is no need to distinguish between the War on Terror abroad and the War on Crime at home. The police war against crime and drugs is the same war as the War on Terror, and of course the War on Terror is waged domestically by both police and the military. "Drugs help supply the deadly work of terrorists," explained George W. Bush in 2002. "That's so important for people in our country to understand. You know, I'm asked all the time, 'How can I help fight against terror? And what can I do, what can I as a citizen do to defend America?' Well, one thing you can do is not purchase illegal drugs. Make no mistake about it: If you're buying illegal drugs in America, it is likely that money is going to end up in the hands of terrorist organizations."[6] There is no war on crime, drugs, and terror. There is only war against the poor.

And police and war are inseparable, always already together.[7] The agents and officials of the warfare state talk endlessly about police as soldiers, and police power more generally as always engaged in wars, battles, campaigns, raids, and operations. Police departments have long utilized the same technologies and weaponry used in colonization and warfare, speaking to the shared material mandate of militaries and police forces. The **cop** (219–221) *is* a soldier, looks like a soldier, trains like a soldier, and cops have long understood themselves as soldiers and policing as a war against the disobedient assholes and "filth" of the city. Police is a modality of war, just as war is a modality of police power.

Force

Force generally refers to the physical coercion and compulsion police use to impose order. This is called the police use of force. **Cops** (219–221) put their hands on you, strike you with a **nightstick** (55–58), put you in a **chokehold** (58–60), **Taser** (13–16) you, **handcuff** (20–21) and **arrest** (208–210) you, shoot and kill you. But force is also a synonym for police itself—*the police force* describes the police collective. The state delegates its monopoly on legitimate **violence** (96–100) to police, which uses force to impose order. This is police force. What constitutes police, *force*, is also what names it: *the force*.

So force is simultaneously what police do and what they are. But it would be incomplete to limit any definition of force to merely the physical coercion used to impose order, because cops use more than physical coercion. Force, in other words, also refers to a capacity to convince and control, and the power to influence or intimidate. Police speak of the **deterrence** (228–231) effect of **police helicopters** (70–73), and what goes unsaid is the dread the sound delivers as it hovers over "crime-infested" neighborhoods. Police celebrate **community policing** (122–123) as a cop–community collaboration, but its logic rests in an argument about **pacification** (89–90), and thus **order** (83–86), as coming about through both the physical and the psychological. That really nice **Officer Friendly** (132–135) who came to your school to read to your kid made sure she strapped her nightstick, her Taser, and her Glock 22 pistol to her waist. This too is force, the "speak softly but carry a big stick" version.

So perhaps it would be more accurate to say that police use violence through physical coercion, and force through psychological coercion as a means to achieve order. But this would be incomplete as well. After all, both "force" and "violence" as police and many critics of police violence define it, refer to the use of physical coercion, and both, in their generally accepted usage, ignore forms of coercion and compulsion that leave no physical marks.

We are now at the impasse in which police intend us to be. What is the difference between force and violence? We do not have the language to explain it. Indeed if it's true that police have near total **discretion** (176–178) to use force, what objective criteria could possibly define unjustified force, excessive force, or **police brutality** (207–208)? And yet these are the only terms we have available to us—terms that serve ultimately to reinforce the legitimacy of police use of physical and psychological coercion. After all if the problem is excessive force, then force cannot be a problem, and violence is not part of the conversation.

So let's start over and define the difference as police would: force is the use of physical coercion to impose order, whereas violence is the domain of criminals and criminality and is the very thing that police force is arrayed against. Police have total discretion to use force as long as it is not **disproportionate** (232–235)—shooting a handcuffed subject or beating a small child with a nightstick would be the application of disproportionate force and distinguishes excessive force from justified force. To avoid excessive force, police adhere to the **use-of-force continuum** (258–261), which appears to limit where, when, and how police use force. This is the police version of force, and it is taken for granted by police and **criminology** (261–263).

Perhaps the solution then is to reject the police definition of for ce *and* of violence, and to refuse to see the world like police. Let's turn our attention away from police and toward the subjects of the police use of force. And yes, let's pay attention to Chicago Detective Jon Burge's torture victims for example (see **interrogation**, 193–195), but let's not limit our attention to only the sensational cases of police violence. What would happen if we focused our attention on the searing pain of **tear gas** (17–20) or the dull, lingering ache that comes from being **handcuffed** (20–21) behind your back to a wall for hours? What definition of force could we write if we considered the emotional pain an **arrest** (208–210) causes a mother whose parental rights are suddenly in jeopardy, or the financial pain that follows a resisting arrest or a felony battery charge that a **cop** (219–221) slaps on top of a simple misdemeanor just to "teach you a lesson"? How would our view of police use of force change if we paid attention to the fear a police presence generates in immigrant communities, or the terror caused by the sirens and sounds of deterrence? This is not about what is **justified** (238–240). That is a police word. This is about what is inevitable. When we no longer see the world like police, we understand why police describe what they do—*police use of force*—the same way they describe what they are—*the police force*. Because police force is another word for fear and intimidation. Police don't *use* force; police *is* force.

Jurisdiction

The word "jurisdiction" refers to a particular mode or expression of legal authority and its reach. When we speak of jurisdiction, we speak of the exercise of judicial authority over subjects or areas of the **law** (90–93), and the extent and limit of that authority. When applied to the police powers, it nearly always refers to the spatial scope of police authority.

But "the object of police," writes Michel Foucault, "is almost infinite." The liberal state is obsessed with **order** (83–86) and "there is no limit to the objectives of government when it is a question of managing a public power that has to regulate the behavior of subjects."[1] And so here we find the paradox of jurisdiction that does not appear in the **criminology** (261–263) books or the legal dictionaries: what the liberal state claims to limit is in fact limitless; what law says is not permitted (unlimited police powers) is in practice realized. It is jurisdiction that animates the rule of law, and it is the rule of law that promises to restrict the state's reach, to constrain the police powers, but instead it does something quite different. When legal questions arise, jurisdiction prompts us to ask: Who or what can claim authority? Where and what are the limits of this authority? Who must submit? And the answers to these questions chart a liberal route to what the law considers just. As Robert Cover famously pointed out, "all legal interpretation takes place in a field of pain and death."[2]

A defendant is judged and convicted through legal interpretation, then police shackle her and prison guards incarcerate her. The military claims jurisdiction, and a defendant becomes a combatant and disappears.

Now consider the concept of jurisdiction when applied to police. It is limited only by territory. Who can claim authority? Only police. What are the limits of that authority? They are only spatial, only geographical. Who must submit? Everyone within the jurisdictional boundaries. If jurisdiction defines the liberal relationship between justice and truth, the definition of police jurisdiction renders truth a spatial effect of the police powers. Police know no limit to the mode of expression of police powers within jurisdictional space. And we should remember that most of the jurisdictional decisions of the criminal justice system take place in the street, on **the beat** (172–174), not before the court.

Jurisdiction appears to limit the police powers by erecting strict spatial boundaries and, in so doing, obscures the limitless nature of authority within those boundaries. But remember, there is no escaping jurisdiction. You are always a subject of police power. One police jurisdiction always gives way to another police jurisdiction. It is through the concept of jurisdiction that police promise a limit to the police powers while at the same time seizing a total power and grasp over all territory.

How have we allowed this to happen? How have we allowed truth to become an adjunct to justice, justice to be the exclusive domain of legal interpretation, and legal interpretation to be described as a thing called jurisdiction, to be patrolled by police?

The Badge

The police badge is among the most recognizable symbols of police authority. The metallic, glossy badge is an important theatrical prop in melodramatic fantasies of the **thin blue line** (110–112). In the opening credits of *The Blue Knight*, a 1975 film based on former Los Angeles police officer Joseph Wambaugh's novel of the same name, a white, uniformed cop twirls his **nightstick** (55–58) as he stares into

Fasces, emblematic of authority in ancient Rome and fascist Italy, embellish the border of the LAPD badge.

the camera. A series of transpositions take place: red and blue siren lights spin and flash as the words *The Blue Knight* emerge on the screen. Slowly the title dissolves into a large, shiny LAPD police badge. And then the badge morphs into the white male officer as the camera does a wide aerial pan of the big city landscape as it swallows up the cop walking his **beat** (172–174).

The badge is theater, but it is not innocent. Through its theatrics, the badge does important political work by giving symbolic form to police authority. The **gun** (10–13) might be the most basic and lethal of police weapons, but the badge is the emblematic license for legitimate violence. The badge renders the violent work of policing legitimate and **justified** (238–240), but also noble and sacred. The anthropologist Michael Taussig calls the police badge a "magical talisman," the holy artifact that endows the police community with a mystical authority not just earthly and pragmatic, but nearly divine and transcendent.[1] The symbolic theatrics of the badge conjure something similar to a religious conversion. Putting on or taking off the badge, therefore, always constitutes a transformation. It's a symbol of the righteousness of police. Just by wearing a badge, a person is transformed into a police officer. They undergo a transubstantiation. And just as we are supposed to have faith in Christ and his cross, we are commanded to have faith in cops and their badges.

The overwhelming symbolic importance of the badge should tip us off to the inherently fraught nature of police **violence** (96–100): unlike soldierly violence that might take place "over there," police require some window dressing as a means of making their violence at home appear civilized, chivalrous, and noble. This also conjures up a particular historical formation: the colonial history of the sheriff's badge in civilizing the frontier of the Wild West. The frontier was civilized and pacified, we are taught, not just through any old violence, but through the purifying violence behind the constable's badge. Although the lawman, outlaw, and savage all possess guns and other weapons, they don't all wear the badge, and this makes all the difference.

The magical talisman of the cop's badge shrouds the ordinary violence of police in noble, stately robes and chivalrous customs, and by extension confirms the institution of policing as a sacred tradition of civilization. As *The Blue Knight* shows, police mythology frequently narrates the police officer as the modern equivalent of the crusading medieval knight, and the police badge as the contemporary coat of arms. A police website, *The Modern Knight*, explains:

> A police officer wears a shield on the left side of their uniform for a reason. The strong side, predominantly your right hand, is for your weapon. The left side carries the symbol of the knights of old, the protectors of ancient society. The shield represents the modern commitment that law enforcement officers have made as warriors, servants and leaders to "serve and protect." Police officers are modern knights, going to work each day with weapons and armor with a noble cause to protect our society and ensure our welfare.

We don't suffer from a shortage of representations of **cops** (219–221) as noble knight warriors and crusaders. Pay attention on the street and you might see people wearing knight-themed police T-shirts, one of which depicts a knight's helmet with a thin blue line–themed American flag, accompanied by text: "Fate whispers to the warrior you cannot withstand the storm. And the warrior whispers back I am the storm." Another shirt depicts a cross-bearing Crusader knight wielding a sword, with the well-known Psalms verse: "Even though I walk through the valley of the shadow of death I fear no evil." You might find these shirts worn by members of the Blue Knights, a "law enforcement motorcycle club" with over 650 chapters and 90,000 members across twenty-nine countries. No doubt many have read *S.W.A.T.: Blue Knights in Black Armor*, a novel written by a former police officer.

Police as knights figure prominently in "Honor of the Badge," a speech by Springfield, Missouri police chief Paul Williams, published in the *FBI Law Enforcement Bulletin*. In it Williams writes that "today's police officers are modern day knights, and the badge is their shield . . . it is appropriate that during the police academy, analogies to knights are used to highlight training experiences." Like police officers, knights "promised to defend the weak, be courteous to women, be loyal to their king, and serve God at all times."[2]

Williams equates the knightly Code of Chivalry with the Law Enforcement Oath of Honor, and the badge as the majestic artifact of police honor. Indeed, the mystical, sacred powers of the police badge are best seen in the ritual ceremonies of badge-giving and -taking. Recruits take the police oath to "never betray my badge," and then officially become a cop only when granted the badge. In the United States this comes with a gun, the cop's modern day sword. It goes without saying: you can't officially become a cop if you aren't legally, and ceremoniously, granted a badge. The ceremony bestows knighthood on the cop by granting the title of Officer. But the inverse is also true: without a badge, you are not a cop. When you give up or are stripped of your badge and gun, you lose the knightly power to police. This allure of the badge and the gun can also partly explain why impersonating a police officer is taken quite seriously—proper, legitimate cops must be legally authentic, despite the fact that many officers today carry unofficial badges because they can be fined for losing their official ones.

For Taussig the badge becomes the totem of a violent masculinity enshrined within the culture of policing, with the badge as a symbolic stand-in for the phallus. The stripping of the badge is the ritual act of castration or beheading.[3] This might seem comedic—a theater of the absurd—but points to the symbolic, totalizing grip the police badge holds over the bureaucratic, workaday rituals of police. The stripping of the badge ceremony can also be thought of as an inoculation. The police perform a self-critique and sacrifice the **bad apple** (224–227) officers who have violated the apparent noble and honorable police institution. This is a ritual castration and it works to actually legitimate not only the police institution, but the majestic, sacred powers of the sovereign state. In his comments on "ignominy," or dishonor and shame, in *Leviathan*, Thomas Hobbes distinguishes between two types of honor. There is the "Honorable by Nature" such as "Courage, Magnanimity, Strength, Wisdome" and the "Honorable by the Common-Wealth; as Badges, Titles, Offices, or any other singular marke of the

Sovereigns favour." Hobbes claims that Honor by Nature "cannot be taken away by a Law" and hence "the losse of them is not Punishment." But Honor granted by the "Common-Wealth" "may be taken away by publique authority that made them Honorable" and so taking away their "Badges, Titles, and Offices" is punishment by the "Soveraign."[4] The badge, and the mystical authority it possesses, then, is contingent on state permission and approval. The state giveth, and it will taketh away as it pleases, not unlike the exterminating violence police wield against the enemies of the state.

The phrase "behind the badge" is usually invoked as a mode of humanizing the individual police officer—to show that he or she is just a regular person doing a difficult job. Instead of dismissing this phrase as sentimental ideology, we might instead treat it as a cold hard truth: If we peek behind the badge we find no transcendent, mystical, sacred authority; rather, we find political power propped up by material histories of state power and symbolic rituals of pomp and ceremony. Hip-hop group NWA cuts through the theatrical absurdity in their track "Fuck tha Police": "Without a gun and a badge, what do ya got? A sucker in a uniform waiting to get shot." What separates the legitimate from the illegitimate, and the sacred from the profane, is a cheap metal artifact authorized by sovereign command.

Thin Blue Line

It is often said that police represent a thin blue line between good and evil, anarchy and **order** (83–86), civilization and savagery. As one officer writes on a police webforum, "I generally don't think in terms of 'us vs. them,' but the reality is this: there is a thin blue line that seperates [sic] good from evil, order from chaos and safety from fear. Those are the brothers and sisters on the job." Or consider a line from the 2012 Hollywood police film *End of Watch*: "The thin blue line, protecting the prey from the predators, the good from the bad. We are the police." The performative power of the thin blue line, as these quotations suggest, depends on both a promise of order and its near-constant collapse or breakdown, with the "boys in blue" playing the role of a barricade holding back savage hordes.

Make no mistake, the thin blue line is a battle line, which is to say that the thin blue line is a mythology of **war** (100–102). The phrase itself is widely thought to be inspired by a poem about war and soldiers, specifically Rudyard Kipling's "Tommy," which describes British soldiers in the Crimean War (1854) as a "thin red line of heroes when the drums begin to roll." This police war is waged against anyone or anything that police determine exists on the wrong side of the battle line dividing good from evil.

The thin blue line brings into sharp focus not only the logic of war, but also the theatrical power of police, or the ways that policing always entails a dramaturgical politics of storytelling, symbolic exhibition, and melodramatic fantasies of evil enemies and cruel underworlds. Policing can usefully be thought of as a staging of melodramatic battles between conflicting forces, a form of police theatrics that tries to make the authority of the state appear to be a legitimate form of authority.[1] The modern state, as Poulantzas taught, is always engaged in a sort of political theater via "mechanisms of fear," and to this we can add that the thin blue line is one of the liberal state's most insidious mechanisms of fear.

The word "thin" is interesting here for the way it implies an always unstable and uncertain border between good and evil. The story of the thin blue line is a story of society under attack, which is really just another way of saying that the police are also always under attack, whether it be from super-predator criminals, lower class debauchery, irrational mobs, heartless gangs, crazed drug addicts, merciless terrorists, sadistic murderers, child molesters, prostitutes, con artists, graffiti punks, liberals or leftists, or disobedient youth. The police story of the thin blue line is a war story of the line between civilization and savagery always getting thinner, whether by criminality, a general lack of decency in society, or a failure to properly support the police. This mythology also helps to absolve cops who decide to cross the line, as we often see in television dramas when the cop crosses over to the criminal side in the apparent **pursuit** (200–201) of justice. For cops, the thin blue line is understood as permeable and fluid.

Hence police are constantly complaining that they are underfunded, underpaid, understaffed, under-armed, and underappreciated, while simultaneously claiming criminals are only becoming more vicious, more brazen, and better armed with more advanced weapons.

There is a cottage industry of thin blue line products, including T-shirts, hats, stickers, coffee mugs, and a plethora of other commodities depicting a bright blue line. It has also become a common meme on social media sites like Facebook, as officers and their supporters make a blue line flag the primary image for their profile, largely in response to what they perceive as a war against cops associated with the growing Black Lives Matter protests. One recent campaign encouraged police officers and others to change their front porch light bulbs to blue lights in order to proclaim that "Blue Lives Matter." One T-shirt depicts an American flag in black and white tones, except for one of the stripes being a bright police blue, as if to claim that the very existence of the nation is simply impossible or unimaginable without police.

The thin blue line orients so much thinking about police power regardless of politics. The thin blue line claims that order and civilization can't exist without police, because police power *is* the very line— the border or boundary—dividing wickedness from the good life, morality from depravity, and the sacred from the profane. If there are no police, we are told, there will be no civilization, and life itself will devolve back to a Hobbesian state of nature where life is nasty, brutish, and short. If we don't give our undying support to the cops, which is to say if we refuse the police definition of reality (that is, think for ourselves), mass **violence** (96–100) and chaos will inevitably be the only result.

It was partly for this reason that the Black revolutionary George Jackson wrote in *Soledad Brother* that the thin blue line was "patronizing shit."[2] It is patronizing shit for the way it limits the political imagination by claiming that sociality can only exist with a world full of cops. The thin blue line is patronizing shit for the ways it claims police keep the peace while ignoring the role of police in class warfare. It is patronizing shit for the ways it claims to be about protection from violence when it is really about maintaining the violence of **property** (81–83). To recognize the thin blue line as patronizing shit is to refuse the police definition of reality and to instead begin writing our own scripts of abolition.

Professionalization

A popular refrain in police circles is that policing isn't a job, it is a profession. Cops are, or at least should be, consummate police professionals. But what does it mean for a **cop** (81–83) to be a professional? It means that cops shouldn't be amateur, uneducated, corrupt, untrained, and unaccountable bullies with a **badge** (106–110) and a **gun** (10–13). To be professional is to be educated, impartial, efficient, and trained in techno-scientific **crime** (93–96) fighting methods while rigidly adhering to specialized codes of conduct so as to be incorruptible, fair, efficient, objective, and accountable.

When police talk of professionalization they merge concerns over the conduct of individual officers with institutional police structure and culture. The more that policing institutions are professionalized, the more that individual cops will be professionals, the more that democracy will flourish. The story of police professionalization, then, is a story about the reform of the police into a **force** (102–104) of progress. It is a redemptive narrative in which police advocates admit past faults and corruption in order to rescue the police institution as a noble, always improving, inherently democratic and scientific force for good.

Police professionalization is as old as modern police, with the ruling classes justifying the creation of the earliest modern police departments in the name of a skilled, trained, and politically neutral police power constituted by, and in service to, **the public** (252–255). Robert Peel, credited with creating London's first modern police force in 1829, **justified** (238–240) this new apparatus of **law** (90–93) and **order** (83–86) by claiming that a professionalized police institution that adhered to ethical principles would be a significant improvement over past and more disorganized and unethical forms of policing. He also claimed this professional police would be a more legitimate form of domestic governance than the military despite the fact that he modeled the police on the military. Despite these promises, the police were mired in controversies over political corruption, over its inability to fight crime, and for wanton **violence** (96–100). In the United States, a similar process took place, with newly formed professional departments in the mid to late 1800s quickly caught in controversies over violence against immigrants and the poor and for being at the service of political elites.

This history of controversy, corruption, and racialized violence gave rise to more and more calls for professionalization during the Progressive Era (1890–1920). A central focus was the incorporation of new technology, such as the automobile, two-way radios, fingerprinting, and record-keeping systems, among others. This era gave rise to popular figures of **police reform** (155–160) such as Berkeley police chief and author of the 1931 Wickersham Commission on **police brutality** (207–208) August Vollmer, future president Teddy Roosevelt, and director of the FBI, J. Edgar Hoover.

Police professionalization became a key way in which the FBI legitimated its **war** (100–102) on crime beginning in the late 1920s and a way to distance itself from its own controversial past. J. Edgar Hoover, famed top cop, racist, and anti-labor "red hunter," constructed a kind of scientific masculinity at the FBI through all manner of reforms such as "rigorous training, dress regulations, internal inspections, a strict code of conduct, heavy reliance on the acquisition and sorting of information, and a system of uniform investigative procedures."[1] Police were presented now as experts in science and technology rather than the corrupt bullies of a previous era. The lie detector, for example, largely emerged during this time as a more civil and humane means of replacing the brutality of "third degree" **interrogation** (193–195), working to shore up a view of police as closer to technical experts than brutes.

But police professionalization was not confined to the domestic United States, as this movement plays an important role in US imperial projects abroad. In the name of progress, reform, and professionalization, the United States trained and deployed police in countries around the world, a process that only continues today, as with the US training of Iraqi **security** (86–89) forces. This also helps to highlight the ways that police training and nation-building abroad is by no means innocent, as it serves the interests of US political power and capitalism while at once being directly and indirectly implicated in all sorts of atrocities.[2]

The reformist fairy tale of police professionalization is seductive partly because it masquerades as a self-critique while at the same time rescuing the police as a flawed but fundamentally well-intentioned and necessary institution for the public good. Professionalization is a strategy of legitimization, and this has always been its animating compulsion, and it is why this fairy tale has to be recognized as fundamentally political and ideological. Police professionalization is an inoculation in the way that Roland Barthes thought of the term: the admission of a little bit of evil hides a whole lot of evil. This is the ideological structure of liberal and conservative cop history. The police are always getting better, always improving, always reforming for the better. Police, we are told, are always the bastion and fabricator of progress.

Despite the fairy tale of the police march of progress, the terror of police has never disappeared. There's no evidence it's been reduced in any significant way. Police still routinely wreak havoc against the racialized poor. The "third degree" interrogation is still present, even if mainstream commentators want to write this off as merely a case of **bad apples** (224–227) or isolated cases. The professionalization movement has only entrenched the power of police by separating police from **the public** (252–255) through increased bureaucracy and administrative power while further extending the reach of the state into the lives of the public, but especially the poor.

The critical task should not be to make the police more professional, more educated, more skilled, more proficient, but rather to make police, and the order of private property they build and maintain with organized terror, obsolete.

Models of Policing:
How the Police
Are Organized and Defended

Police Gangs

The nearly 10,000 sheriff's deputies of the Los Angeles Sheriff's Department, the largest sheriff's department in the United States, are organized into four patrol divisions and nearly two dozen station houses. They are also organized into secret clubs with names like the Vikings, Jump Out Boys, Regulators, the Posse, and the Grim Reapers. Nearly all of these clubs are comprised of mostly white deputies who **patrol** (170–172) predominately Black and Latino neighborhoods throughout Los Angeles County. Deputies, and even former Sheriff Lee Baca, say they are akin to fraternities that boost morale and improve unit cohesiveness.

US District Judge Terry Hatter, in *Thomas v. County of Los Angeles*, called them "neo-Nazi, white supremacist gang[s]."[1] They falsified **arrest** (208–210) reports, covered up officer misconduct, celebrated **officer-involved shootings** (246–248) (see also **CRASH**, 128–130), and according to a 1992 investigation, engaged in "off-duty criminal activity."

Hatter was referring specifically to the Lynwood station Vikings. In December of 1991, the LA County Board of Supervisors appointed special counsel to investigate the Sheriff's department. The resulting Kolts Report concluded that "groups of deputies have formed associations that harass and brutalize minority residents . . . some deputies at the Department's Lynwood Station associate with the 'Viking' symbol, and appear at least in past times to have engaged in behavior that is brutal and intolerable and is typically associated with street gangs."[2]

The Kolts report referred to the "clubs" as a "malignant" force and described them as "racist deputy gangs." They meet the United States Department of Justice's definition of a "street gang": any group of three or more individuals that adopts a group identity, often through the use of a group name, slogan and shared tattoos, which controls territory through the use of violence and intimidation in order to engage in "criminal activity."

In one court case involving a police killing, the court ordered a deputy to pull down his socks to reveal whether or not he had a tattoo signifying Viking membership. He did, and next to his Viking insignia he'd also tattooed the number 998, police code for officer-involved shooting.[3]

The Vikings routinely engaged in "warrantless, harassing arrests and detentions, incidents of excessive **force** (102–104) and unwarranted physical abuse against **handcuffed** (20–21) and otherwise defenseless detainees (beating, kicking, pushing, striking with **flashlights** (48–50), choking, slamming doors on legs, slapping, shooting to maim); ransacking homes and businesses; incidents of outright torture (**interrogation** (193–195) with stun guns, beating victims into unconsciousness, holding a **gun** (10–13) in a victim's mouth and pulling the trigger on an empty chamber, pushing a victim's head through a squad car window); quick-stop driving to bang a victim's head against the squad car screen [see **rough ride** (31–32)]; and uninhibited expressions of racial animus by deputies, including use of epithets such as 'niggers' and 'wetbacks.'"[4]

Police gangs engage in activities similar to those of street gangs. Both control territory, wear colors, share an emblem, tattoo those colors and insignia onto their bodies, and engage in criminal activity. But membership patterns blur the line between police and criminal street gangs, questioning the notion that there is a distinction between the two. Scores of police departments throughout the United States acknowledge that active street gang members work as officers for local police departments. "Street gangs, prison gangs, and [outlaw motorcycle gangs] all have members and associates who have either gained or attempted to gain employment with law enforcement agencies, correctional facilities, and judiciary/courts across the country."[5] Members of the Aryan Brotherhood work as correctional officers and serve in the military. Active members of the Diablos MC, Gangster Disciples and Latin Kings work for municipal and county law enforcement agencies, and every major street gang in the United States places its members on domestic and international military installations.

Asset Protection Officer

One day, after months of stealing video games at a Target each week and reselling them at a used gaming store—and pocketing $15,000 over a four-month period—the shoplifter's luck ran out. "I got through the first set of doors," the anonymous Reddit poster writes, "and as I went to leave the terminal doors two guys stepped in and addressed me by name and told me to stop." The asset protection officers knew more than just his name. They knew where he lived and whom he lived with and what he drove and what his roommate drove. "They had actually watched my apartment that day and followed me from my doorstep to the store in order to catch me in the act." Target followed him in the store with its sophisticated facial recognition cameras—cameras tied into their database, which knew that he came to the store frequently but never purchased anything. Target tracked him when he left the store, first with its network of in-store surveillance cameras and then with police surveillance cameras linked to the store. Target used the facial recognition to identify him. They used Target's access to police criminal justice databases to find him. And then they staked out his apartment, tailed him until he returned, confronted him at the store, where they interrogated him (see **interrogation**, 193–195), and then handed him over to police along with an investigative file of surveillance photos and videos.

Asset protection officers or specialists, like those at Target, outnumber high school teachers in the United States. We could double the number of middle school teachers and asset protection officers would still outnumber them. We'd need to hire nearly half a million preschool teachers to exceed the number of correctional officers and bailiffs. If we converted all the cops into librarians, the number of librarians would still not exceed the number of private **security** (86–89) guards in the United States.

More than 1.1 million people worked as asset protection officers in the United States in 2019, a job title that includes **rent-a-cops** (144–146) who work for private security firms, loss prevention agents who work directly for retailers, and surveillance agents who work for casinos.[1] When we combine this with the number of correctional officers and bailiffs (462,300); municipal, state, or federal police (813,500); and private detectives and investigators (36,200), more than 2.5 million people worked as either public or private police in 2019.

Make no distinction between public and private police because police make no distinction. Asset protection officers and loss prevention specialists are cops. They work directly with public police. When an alleged shoplifter leaves a store, both private and public cops hunt that person down often in tandem, as a team, communicating by radios or cell phones. And just like public police, asset protection officers care only about **private property** (81–83), not your or anyone's safety. Asset protection officers or loss prevention "store detectives" protect and serve the interests of capital.

A vast majority of public police departments in the United States permit officers to moonlight as private security. Most departments even regulate the private market for public police. The Albuquerque Police Department (APD), for example, maintains a program it calls "Chief's Overtime" in which the department establishes the hourly rate that its customers pay in order to hire off-duty cops. The city subsidizes this rate with public funds in order to pay **officers** (227–228) to work retail security at an hourly rate that, for some, exceeds the pay they receive at APD.

Many asset protection officers, and public police who moonlight as asset protection officers, work for local or national restaurant chains or convenience stores. The most common places to find an asset protection officer, or an off-duty cop moonlighting as one, are the regional or national retailers that often dominate local economies. The industry employed somewhere between 10 and 20 million people in the United States in 2019, depending on which occupations we include in the count.

Any good definition of asset protection officer begins with the retail loss prevention industry, an industry that charges, on average, two million people a year for shoplifting. And a complete discussion of the retail loss prevention industry begins with Target Corporation. We could highlight the role of asset protection officers at Walmart, where a majority of shoplifting arrests occur, but we focus instead on Target, a retailer whose vice president of government affairs calls it "a high-tech company masquerading as a retailer." Target transformed the field of retail loss prevention into an enormous and technologically sophisticated enterprise based on public–private retail partnerships in surveillance and data gathering.

Target hires (lots of) former cops, including former FBI agents, to run its program, which includes an enormous, in-house database of images, videos, license plate numbers, names, and addresses. It hires scientists to staff its two accredited forensics laboratories— laboratories that exceed the capacity and sophistication of nearly all public-sector crime labs. Target's laboratory scientists work with facial recognition software, perform video/image analysis, and conduct latent fingerprint forensics, among other criminalistics techniques and technologies. Target makes all of this available to local and federal police by routinely opening its labs to cops free of charge. Target gives money to police departments to hire more cops; it gives money to counties to hire more prosecutors; it builds remote-controlled video surveillance networks for police.

Target's forensics labs and its sophisticated technology set it apart from other retailers, including Walmart, Walgreens, and Kohl's, which maintain similarly aggressive though less networked loss prevention programs. The primary difference, however, and what sets Target truly apart, is an obscure program it called "Safe City." Target's loss prevention program constitutes the privatization of many public policing activities, such as domestic intelligence gathering and retail crime enforcement, but it might be more accurate to say that Target's Safe City program, from the beginning, has been a program designed to capture, reshape, and refocus public-sector police in the image and interests of Target Corporation.

Target began seeding dozens of cities with Safe City grants beginning in 2004 to "foster partnerships between local police and community members to reduce crime." We know some of the details of the program because Target publicized it relentlessly. The rest we know because of the hacking collective Anonymous, which downloaded 260 gigabytes of police data in June 2020, including information related to Target's various Safe City activities. This is how Safe City worked: Target gave money to police departments, usually between $100,000 and $300,000, and instructed the police to hire a company called Netsential. Netsential charged police an annual subscription fee and in return built a rudimentary web portal for police and retailers to upload and share intelligence and store data. Once up and running, the local Target asset protection officer recruited loss prevention agents from other retailers, along with bank tellers, apartment and restaurant managers, and neighborhood block captains, among others. Each member gained access to the Netsential web portal, where they uploaded images, videos, tips, suspicions, and descriptions of "suspicious" people and also gained access to the same from all the other members uploading intelligence. Next, Target tied its own surveillance camera network, limited as it is to its stores and parking lots, into the local police network of surveillance cameras, which expanded Target's reach to roadways, intersections, public spaces, and buildings and merged all of this with the surveillance camera networks of banks, hotels, private security, and (at least in Albuquerque) private residences with networked doorbell cameras and microphones.

Consider the benefits of retail partnerships to Target. Police gather intelligence and upload it on a website Target paid for and hold it on servers accessible to Target. The asset protection officers from other retailers and private businesses do the same. Target, and other retailers, gain access to an enormous network of public and private surveillance cameras.

Consider the benefits of retail partnerships to police. In sanctuary cities, police are prohibited from sharing intelligence or data with Department of Homeland Security agents of the Immigration and Customs Enforcement (ICE) bureau. Albuquerque, for example, is a sanctuary city and refuses to cooperate with ICE, but the retail partnership begun in 2006 with Target Safe City money provided a way around the prohibition. Albuquerque police give ICE agents access to the public–private database constructed originally by Target, which includes information and intelligence gathered by police and private sector partners. If you live in a sanctuary city, it's only a sanctuary for Target and other big box retailers.

Community Policing

The first thing that nearly all proponents of community policing say about community policing is that there's no definition of community policing. "Community policing remains many things to many people." Or: "Community policing seems always in vogue, yet its essential qualities remain elusive." Or: "Community policing encompasses a variety of philosophical and practical approaches and is still evolving rapidly."[1]

Advocates for community policing claim that it offers a suite of best practices and policies that promote collaboration and partnership with communities as a way to enlist the active support of an entire community in the fabrication of social **order** (83–86). It emerged as a discourse in policing in the 1960s and '70s in response to the civil unrest of the period. Police were among the targets of civil rights protesters and organized labor, which saw police as an institution that defended Jim Crow racism and enforced capitalist wage relations through aggressive strikebreaking. In response, community policing offers a nostalgic image of an imagined past populated by your friendly neighborhood **cop** (219–221) on **the beat** (172–174). This is a nostalgia that seeks to establish the legitimacy of the police powers. And the legitimacy problem for police is about the legitimacy to use **violence** (96–100). Community policing is not about making police friendlier, but rather about making police violence more acceptable.

Community policing is to the police what COIN, or counterinsurgency, is to the military. The final report of President Barack Obama's "Task Force on 21st Century Policing" explains community policing as a way to "help community members see police as allies rather than as an occupying force."[2] The military allusion is not an accident. COIN and community policing seek to legitimize an occupation. They seek to build community trust in order to more effectively impose order. Military officers take tea with tribal elders; police officers play midnight basketball with **ghetto** (183–184) youth. Military planners place forward bases in rebel territory; police brass place police substations in "high **crime**" (93–96) neighborhoods. It is an occupation (the iron fist) masquerading as collaboration (the velvet glove). Community policing and **SWAT** (135–139) are two sides of the same COIN.[3,4]

Red Squads

The term red squad describes any police intelligence unit, usually secret, that uses covert tactics including **violence** (96–100) to target and intimidate political dissidents, most often on the political left. The rise in red squads is frequently traced to the 1886 Chicago Haymarket Square "riot," in which a labor rally following the police killing of several workers turned violent. A bomb exploded at the rally and was followed by gunfire. Seven police officers and four workers were killed. Eight anarchists were arrested and convicted of conspiracy and four were eventually hanged by the state. The four Haymarket martyrs, as they became known to their working class comrades, were considered part of a vast anarchist conspiracy by police. The origins of the first red squad came in the aftermath of Haymarket, when Chicago police "commenced a terror campaign" in which they raided activists' homes, made illegal **arrests** (208–210) by the hundreds, tortured suspects and intimidated witnesses.[1]

Chicago police quickly institutionalized police terror. Every red squad that has followed has borrowed their tactics: target political dissidents, call them terrorists or agitators, use violence and intimidation, deny that secret units exist. The first targets were anarchists and communists in the late nineteenth century (hence the name, *red* squads). In 1919 and 1920, the US Department of Justice raided union and political meetings in thirty cities in two dozen states, arresting thousands of political radicals, and deporting hundreds of people in what are known as the Palmer raids. Those raids served as a prelude to the Federal Bureau of Investigation's various secret counterintelligence programs that began in 1950s and lasted until the 1970s. **COINTELPRO** (130–132), as it was called, targeted civil rights activists. Today the targets also include radical environmental activists, anti-war protesters, and Muslims.

Consider the New York Police Department. Its "bomb squad," which NYPD created in 1914, operated like the red squads in Chicago, Philadelphia, Los Angeles, Detroit, Baltimore, Washington DC, and other major cities. It spied on anarchist groups, infiltrated the Communist Party USA, raided union meetings, tortured suspects, and traded intelligence information with federal agencies such as the FBI, which had its own red squads. By the 1960s, NYPD's Bureau of Special Services (BOSS) focused on Black Power groups, civil rights activists, and radical left organizations. BOSS placed spies in the **ghetto** (183–184) and launched thousands of **investigations** (175–176) of dissident groups. BOSS kept dossiers on liberal politicians it considered political enemies, and its intelligence found its way to secret military units.

NYPD's Intelligence Division and Counter-Terrorism Bureau, created after September 11, 2001, was first led by David Cohen, who came to NYPD from the Central Intelligence Agency where he served as Deputy Director of Operations. Cohen created a series of secret units in the intelligence division, such as the Demographics Unit (which NYPD denied ever existed until an Associated Press investigation proved that it did), and hired analysts (with a preference for those who spoke Farsi, Urdu, and/or Pashto) from the Defense Intelligence Agency and the National Security Agency, among other spy agencies. According to the Associated Press, the Demographics Unit "is at the heart of a police spying program, built with help from the CIA, which assembled databases on where Muslims lived, shopped, worked and prayed. Police infiltrated Muslim student groups, put informants in mosques, monitored sermons and catalogued every Muslim in New York who adopted new, Americanized surnames."[2] At the same time that NYPD was spying on Muslims in New York, it extended its influence abroad. In 2012 the NYPD opened an intelligence division office in Kfar Saba, Israel, where it collects intelligence on Muslim "radicalization." Its agents train with, and are trained by, Israeli intelligence officers.

The punishing tactics of secret red squad police violence are part of everyday police practice at the Chicago Police Department. In the 1970s a secret unit led by Detective Jon Burge, who learned electroshock torture methods while serving in the military police in Vietnam, targeted residents of Chicago's Southside ghettos and tortured confessions out of hundreds of Black men. In the basements of police station houses, Burge and his detectives **handcuffed** (20–21) men to radiators and then burned and beat their bodies and electroshocked their genitalia.[3] The horrors of Burge's red squad continue. The *Guardian* revealed in 2015 that CPD detective Richard Zuley, who as a reserve officer in the military presided over the torture of Mohamedou Ould Slahi at Guantánamo Bay, also commanded the torture of people in Chicago at Homan Square, a secret black site where Chicago police have tortured confessions out of suspects.[4] **Interrogating** (193–195) Slahi in 2003, Zuley used sensory and sleep deprivation, long-term shackling, physical violence, and simulated executions.[5] Zuley used similar tactics in Chicago, where he threatened to kill suspects' families if they didn't confess and left them shackled in dark basements for hours on end.

The history of red squads should not be mistaken as a story of **bad apples** (224–227) and illegal practices. Red squads are considered by police as "elite" units that recruit the "best and the brightest." Red squads thus were not, and are not, fringe units. From their beginnings, the covert intelligence gathering and intimidation tactics of red squads have been part of regular police practice at nearly every major municipal, state and federal police agency.

Red squads are a covertly organized and carefully structured form of police repression unleashed on political enemies of the state. This demonstrates that policing is not just about **crime** (93–96), but also about the targeting of people who challenge the status quo. And since workers and working-class organizations are frequently the target of red squads, it is the status quo of capitalism and wage labor that police protect. Exposing the dirty tricks, secret violence, and everyday repression of the red squad is essential to any radical critique of the police. The logic of the red squad shares the logic of police: **order** (83–86), which is understood as based on

private property (81–83), capital accumulation, and obedience to authority, coming about only through the violent and repressive capacity of the state. Disorder, which to the capitalist state is the racial and economic justice and political dissent that **threatens** (222–223) bourgeois order, must be ruthlessly repressed. There can be no history of police without a history of red squads.

Qualified Immunity

Don't look to the Supreme Court for clarity on the question of qualified immunity, an incoherent legal doctrine derived (no joke) from an Aesop fable and a guy named Ernie.

Ernie Fitzgerald was working as a civilian contractor for the Air Force in the 1960s when he discovered technical problems (plane wings that cracked during flight) and financial irregularities (billions of dollars over budget) in a military contractor's contract to build an intercontinental cargo plane for the Air Force.

Fitzgerald testified before Congress that Lockheed, the military contractor, concealed these issues. Following Fitzgerald's testimony, one of President Richard Nixon's aides wrote a memo recommending the President fire him or (better) "let him bleed, for a while at least." Nixon chose the former, and Fitzgerald filed a number of lawsuits following his firing, including *Harlow v. Fitzgerald*, which named Nixon and two of his aides. The courts concluded, based on precedent, that the President of the United States, along with legislators, judges, and prosecutors, enjoy total protection— absolute immunity—from civil lawsuits related to official acts and conduct (see **discretion**, 176–178) but that all other government officials engaged in duties that require discretionary action receive conditional or qualified immunity. "High officials," the court determined, "require greater protection than those with less complex discretionary responsibilities."

In *Harlow*, the Justices first asked whether there existed a "compensable claim for relief" to alleged constitutional violations by "high officials." In other words, if a government official violates your constitutional rights, you have a right to pursue a legal action for civil damages against that official but only if you lack all other avenues of redress. You can sue a cop for violating your constitutional rights but only if that legal route offers "the only realistic avenue for vindication of constitutional guarantees."

Police violate constitutional rights routinely, so the Court couldn't establish a strictly objective test because a strictly objective test—Did the **cop** (219–221) violate your constitutional rights?— would, in effect, abolish police. So the courts added an escape clause for cops masquerading as a subjective test. A government official must know and respect your constitutional rights and there should exist legal avenues for **accountability** (160–162) when they violate those rights, but constitutional violations don't happen in the abstract. There are subjective elements to take into account. Qualified immunity, the Justices pointed out, "is available only to officials performing discretionary functions," and discretionary actions "almost inevitably are influenced by the decisionmaker's experiences, values, and emotions." This is subjective, not objective, and requires taking into account a cop's state of mind, knowledge of law, intent, extenuating circumstances, and the presence of malice. The courts assumed that this "subjective" test would protect police from lawsuits, but the subjective test didn't turn out to be the escape clause the Supreme Court intended it to be. Lower courts refused to dismiss lawsuits against cops on summary judgement when a cop asserted a subjective claim to immunity. Instead, most lower courts sent the question to juries, which scrutinized "experiences, values, and emotions" at trial.

So, here's what the Justices had before them. Since police violate the Constitution routinely, a strictly objective test would no doubt result in the abolition of police as we know it. The addition of a subjective element, designed to protect police, didn't turn out to actually protect police at all because too many lower courts kept empaneling juries, calling witnesses, and taking depositions instead of dismissing on summary judgment. "It is now clear," the Justices wrote in *Harlow v. Fitzgerald*, "that substantial costs attend the litigation of the subjective good faith of government officials." When questions of "good faith" go to juries, "there often is no clear end to the relevant evidence," the Justices noted, and this "can be peculiarly disruptive of effective government."¹ Who'd want to be a cop if you could be sued for doing your job? (See **Ferguson effect**, 235–236)

This is the problem that *Harlow* fixed. The Justices decided that the subjective test "dampen[ed] the ardor of all but the most resolute, or the most irresponsible [public officials], in the unflinching discharge of their duties." And so it rigged the subjective test in the favor of police. It took back the question of "good faith" from juries and delivered it to judges. Lower courts should no longer send the "good faith" question to juries but instead should dismiss "insubstantial lawsuits" by summary judgement when a cop makes a "properly supported motion for summary judgement." Be firm, the Justices told the lower courts, when you have a plaintiff before your court who just wants to "play dog in a manger."²

The phrase "play dog in a manger" comes from Aesop's short children's story "The Dog in the Manger," in which a dog in a barn growls at hungry cattle, blocking their access to food and rest. The story ends as though written by a cop. "Now the farmer came in. When he saw how the Dog was acting, he seized a stick and drove him out of the stable with many a blow for his selfish behavior."

Isn't law ingenious? It constructed a legal doctrine that shields cops from civil actions in a case about the employment prospects of a guy named Ernie based on a cop-friendly test derived from an obscure Greek fable about a stick-wielding farmer. No joke.

CRASH

Community Resources Against Street Hoodlums, known by its acronym CRASH, was a Los Angeles Police Department "anti-gang" program that operated from 1973 until it was reorganized in 2000. During most of those years, a CRASH unit operated in every LAPD division in the city. Although often described by the media as an "elite" unit, most were comprised of young, inexperienced officers working in nearly autonomous units with limited supervision. CRASH units throughout the city became particularly notorious for their aggressive tactics.

CRASH units were assigned to specific gangs in areas that LAPD defined as "gang infested," where they were given enormous latitude

CRASH

and autonomy. The notorious Rampart division CRASH unit adopted an "anything goes" approach to eradicate what its officers routinely called a gang "infestation." A 2000 Board of Inquiry investigation of Rampart found that the word "infestation" commonly appeared in CRASH **arrest** (208–210) reports. In other words, it was routine practice to **stop and frisk** (27–31) and detain individuals in areas considered "infested" based on the **reasonable suspicion** (255–257) that mere presence in an "infested" neighborhood demonstrated gang membership and activity.[1] Multiple investigations of Rampart concluded that its officers often forged supervisors' signatures on arrest bookings, routinely invented probable cause, regularly booked suspected drug dealers or gang members on false drug or weapons charges, and often planted **throw-down weapons** (13) on **unarmed** (257–258) suspects in order to claim self-defense after police killings (see **officer-involved shooting**, 246–248). And there were many police killings and shootings in Rampart during the mid 1990s, nearly triple the number of shootings in the 1980s. CRASH officers gave themselves tattoos following shootings. They gave each other commemorative plaques. And they celebrated in sports bars far from the "infested" neighborhoods they **patrolled** (170–172).[2]

It's important to consider the use of the word "infested" for what it reveals about the logic of CRASH. An "infestation" refers to an invasion of a particular place by a dangerous and unwanted species. Think rats or cockroaches. It is also a common racially coded term that circulates in large, urban US police departments to describe a perceived **threat** (222–223) to the (white) body politic posed by, usually, a predominately Black or Hispanic community. It is instrumental for the way it rationalizes the practice of violent police power. But the use of the word "infestation" establishes more than just probable cause for campaigns of stop and frisk **racial profiling** (24–27). It amplifies the police imperative to impose **order** (83–86) by drawing an entire population into the orbit of police power; it marks an entire people the "legitimate" target of police **violence** (96–100).

The word "infestation" absolved CRASH of the obligation to first determine if someone was or was not a member of a criminal gang.

Instead it defined CRASH's job as the same as the exterminator. This is the political dream for police that the "gang infested" neighborhood provides. It removes any limit to the police use of **force** (102–104). Disorder in Rampart was defined by the presence of the poor, largely Salvadoran, people living there. And CRASH's job was to bring order. CRASH officers conducted constant raids, frequent arrests and, ultimately, deportations. In the late 1980s, Rampart CRASH, in cooperation with the Immigration and Naturalization Service, arrested hundreds of young Salvadoran men in Rampart, based solely on the fact that they lived in Rampart and were Salvadoran. They turned them over to INS, which deported nearly 200 of those men based only on the fact that LAPD had arrested them for "gang membership."[3] For a short time CRASH represented what we might call a pure expression of police violence: organized for everyone to see and unleashed on an entire people, who lived under total and violent control, by a police force celebrated by reformers, unencumbered by any limits, and beyond the reach of any authority.

COINTELPRO

Between 1956 and 1971 the Federal Bureau of Investigation, under director J. Edgar Hoover, engaged in a wide-ranging program of covert surveillance, intimidation, harassment and infiltration of, largely, social movements and civil rights organizations within the United States. These activities were organized as part of a program known as COINTELPRO, a codename that combined the first letters of "counter intelligence program." According to an investigation in the mid 1970s by the Senate Select Committee to Study Governmental Operations with Respect to Intelligence Activities, also known as the Church Committee, COINTELPRO "was designed to 'disrupt' groups and 'neutralize' individuals deemed to be **threats** (222–223) to domestic security."[1]

While some surveillance activities focused on far-right groups such as the Ku Klux Klan and the American Nazi Party, COINTELPRO was organized specifically to focus on Black and Chicano radical activists and even mainstream civil rights leaders. A who's who of left political and civil rights organizations in the United States became the focus of COINTELPRO. Organizations such as the American Indian Movement, Students for a Democratic Society, and the Black Panther Party came under intense scrutiny, as did leaders such as Martin Luther King Jr., Malcolm X and Reies López Tijerina.

The FBI sent letters to the spouses of civil rights leaders hoping to create domestic conflict that would end marriages and relationships. In order to sow distrust and internal divisions in the social movement groups they targeted, the FBI spread false rumors that activists or members of various gangs were actually police informants. These tactics occasionally worked exactly as planned. In September of 1969, for example, the FBI took credit for conflicts among radical Black activists in San Diego. Following the violent deaths of San Diego Black Panther Party members John Huggins, Bunchy Carter and Sylvester Bell, agents in the FBI's San Diego field office wrote a secret memorandum to Hoover in Washington, DC, uncovered by the Church Committee, which reported that "shootings, beatings and a high degree of unrest continues to prevail in the **ghetto** (183–184) area of Southeast San Diego. Although no specific counterintelligence action can be credited with contributing to this overall situation, it is felt that a substantial amount of the unrest is directly attributable to [COINTELPRO]."[2]

Throughout the fifteen-year period of illegal activities, the FBI used race as a way to sort the activists and groups it considered "subversive." Groups such as the Southern Non-Violent Coordinating Committee, for example, were considered a "domestic threat" because its leaders and members, according to FBI language, fomented "racial discord." The Church Committee uncovered memos Hoover himself wrote that defined race as the central, organizing logic of COINTELPRO. In August of 1964 Hoover wrote to all FBI field agents that "there are clear and unmistakable signs that we are in the midst of a social revolution with the racial movement at its core. The Bureau, in meeting its responsibilities in this area, is an integral part of this revolution."[3] It was through COINTELPRO that the FBI waged its anti–civil rights counterinsurgency. The program focused in particular on civil rights leaders considered "vociferous rabble-rousers." In August of 1967, the FBI ordered of its agents that "an index be compiled of racial agitators and individuals who have demonstrated a potential for fomenting racial discord. It is desired that only individuals of prominence who are of national interest be included in this index."[4]

Once a group or individual was identified by the FBI as a domestic threat, FBI agents often worked closely with local police departments, or **red squads** (123–126), in order to carry out its various programs, including illegal **search** (163–165) and seizures, harassment, false **arrests** (208–210), and to recruit agents provocateurs to infiltrate groups. FBI cooperation with municipal police departments throughout the United States went both ways. Following the reports of police **violence** (96–100) outside the 1968 democratic national convention in Chicago, for example, the FBI, despite being aware of an organized pattern of violence against protesters, conspired to "refute allegations" against the Chicago Police Department and engaged "cooperative" media to "counteract these allegations."[5]

COINTELPRO was a central vehicle through which police, at both the federal and local level, used violence to defend a socio-spatial **order** (83–86) based on white supremacy and the criminalization of the poor. This contradicts one prominent narrative of 1960s civil rights transformation, in which the federal government deserves credit for dismantling officially sanctioned racism in the United States. Through federal legislation such as the 1964 Civil Rights Act, the 1965 Voting Rights Act, the 1968 Fair Housing Act and more, it was the federal government that confronted and undid institutional racism. But if this is true, it is also true that, at the very height of the civil rights movement in the United States, the federal government assembled its police powers in the form of the FBI's COINTELPRO program to organize and use police violence against the very people calling for that transformation.

Officer Friendly

Officer Friendly is an agent of **pacification** (89–90). His "friendship" comes at a price: accept the police definition of reality and mold yourself and your family into ideal police subjects—polite, polished, obedient workers and snitches who never question the racial **order**

(83–86) of capitalist property relations. So don't let cops read to your kids and don't join the police basketball league. "Coffee with a Cop" is not what it sounds like. In short, don't be fooled by Officer Friendly. He is not a genuine figure of goodwill. He is a strategic ploy to pacify you.

The figure of Officer Friendly is a central trope of **community policing** (122–123). Under the guise of community policing, departments have established programs designed to promote the image of good and friendly policing that downplay more overtly aggressive forms of policing, often called police **militarization** (139–142), like **SWAT** (135–139). The cop on foot or bike patrol has long been a key image and tactic of community policers, as these methods allow cops to have more face-to-face, seemingly friendlier interactions with citizens. The creation of "citizen academies" where community members attend educational sessions with police officials to learn about the job of policing is another increasingly common program, to say nothing of the National Crime Prevention Council's cartoon campaign with McGruff the Crime Dog, as well as the well-known DARE program (Drug Abuse Resistance Education).

Many of these efforts focus on promoting positive images of police to young children and teenagers. Officers visit public schools where they play games and read books to students and give out pro-police coloring books. These are tactics designed to remake the image of police into the friend who's got your back. The National Child Safety Council maintains a Friendly Police Program, which they explain as providing "departments with a specific program of materials that explain the vital job members of local Police Departments perform every day to help keep us safe." The NCSC explains that police departments "will find the materials helpful in presenting programs when visiting daycare facilities, preschools, and elementary schools." A twenty-four-page manual, "Our Friendly Police Officers," is "designed to help develop an early awareness and understanding of the many ways the police department protects and aids the community. It helps children develop a healthy perspective of the job of a local law enforcement officer and encourages them to trust and respect their local police officers."[1]

Chicago police along with the Chicago Board of Education started an Officer Friendly program in 1966, paid for by the Sears-Roebuck Company. It was designed to "humanize the police **force**" (102–104) to urban youth. "If we catch them at 5, 6, 7, or 8 years old, we can nip disrespect in the bud," explained one of the founders. "By the time they reach secondary level, they'll think of law enforcement as a good profession to have."[2] Officer Friendly has recently been "resurrected" on Chicago's South Side in Englewood, a place known as a hotspot for **crime** (93–96), **violence** (96–100), and citizens' lack of trust for police. As one officer stated, "With the young kids, they really love the police. Somewhere along the line we are losing these kids."[3]

But despite these efforts to render policing a friendly form of state power, they are in no way innocent and apolitical. Officer Friendly is premised on the goal of getting children accustomed to obeying and respecting the commands of state authority. Officer Friendly hails his subject with a wink and a nod, a smile, and a coloring book, or by giving a lesson in how to catch a fly ball. Officer Friendly is not merely about rendering the cop a friend, but about rendering the cop a parent. This police logic of parental authority can be expressed like this: "We need to discipline you, and you need to respect our discipline, since we keep your best interests at heart."

In the most practical terms, Officer Friendly, as both a specific program and an ideological framing of community policing writ large, is nothing other than a form of counterinsurgency. Counterinsurgency was imagined as a strategy that relied not simply on violence and destruction of enemy forces, but also on implementing more friendly programs designed to gain the consent of the native population, from building schools and roads to passing out candy to local youth.[4] Indeed, it isn't a coincidence that these programs were introduced in the United States at the same time as US military pacification campaigns in Southeast Asia.

What emerges here are the ways that Officer Friendly, and its paradigm of community policing, renders police power as a productive power that works to produce and build a particular social order by consent and not simply by force. This isn't to say that Officer Friendly's pacification strategies don't also rely on **threats** (222–223) and violence; rather, it is to stress the creative ways police work to gain a population's consent and support. It is much easier to be opposed to the violence of the SWAT team and the problems with police militarization, and even the violence of police killing hundreds of poor people every year. But we should not forget the velvet glove strategies that work in tandem with the iron fist by making policing into a social and civic good through all sorts of "image work" and projects for producing obedient, polite citizens.[5]

The tactics of smiling cops reading to school children, coaching baseball teams, or giving out coloring books to youth exist on a continuum with **arrest** (208–210) powers, **nightsticks** (55–58), **Tasers** (13–16), **K-9s** (22–24), **guns** (10–13), and even **SWAT** (135–139). Although there might not be any bloodletting or bruised and battered bodies, Officer Friendly is still an officer whose very authority is premised on the state's monopoly of violence. Officer Friendly is a tactic that obscures its goal: to normalize and humanize the role of this violent monopoly in the racialized production and reproduction of suffering and degradation. Of course, many see through the lies of the benevolent Officer Friendly and reverse its meaning by sarcastically using the term to refer to violent and rude cops. Indeed, Officer Friendly has never existed for the poor and oppressed. Officer Friendly only really exists in liberal, bourgeois ideology (and their neighborhoods). Even when it comes in a smiling, friendly face, police power is never disinterested, never objective, never neutral, and comes always armed with **handcuffs** (20–21) and an arsenal of weapons. Beware of cops reading to your children. Throw away that coloring book.

SWAT

Special Weapons and Tactics, known by its acronym SWAT, is a fairly recent, but increasingly common, development in policing—the creation and use of specially trained and heavily armed military-style units by local, regional and federal police agencies worldwide. These are units generally described, both by their members and critics, as paramilitary in character. The description is accurate because SWAT units train in military tactics—close quarters combat, urban warfare, assault and rescue, and civil unrest—and they use military

equipment when doing so: body armor, high capacity weapons, and armored vehicles. Today nearly every police agency of any size in the United States has a SWAT unit. Nationally, SWATs have a combined deployment rate greater than 45,000 times per year.

The phrase paramilitary, however, implies that police are not quite the same as the military and that the rise of SWAT marks a troubling trend in policing, one often referred to as police **militarization** (139–142). Critics who say police militarization in the United States is a new problem are quick to point to a provision of the National Defense Authorization Act that allows for the transfer of military surplus equipment to local and state police agencies—sniper rifles, **helicopters** (70–73), night vision gear, mine-resistant tanks, body armor, and much more. This is certainly true, but the link between police and military reflected in SWAT goes back much further and reaches much deeper. Mainstream histories of police often ignore the foundational role militia groups and military soldiers played in the establishment of the police.[1] The first police departments in the United States emerged out of the militias and **slave patrols** (143–144) of the eighteenth and nineteenth century. By the 1990s, all branches of the military were actively involved in domestic and international law enforcement, particularly regarding drug laws.[2] Both police and military engage in "hearts and minds" counterinsurgency policing (see **community policing**, 122–123). Many SWAT units receive training from active duty or retired military personnel. Police in Albuquerque, New Mexico, for example, train specialized military units in urban assault tactics. Many police serve also as reserve officers in the military. And nearly all police departments recruit and employ police with former military experience.

The history of SWAT units in the United States is usually traced to former Los Angeles Police Chief Daryl Gates, cited by many as one of the developers and early adopters of SWAT. Gates started the first LAPD SWAT unit in 1966 and called it the Special Weapons *Attack Team*. The name was quickly changed to Special Weapons *and Tactics* in order to steer clear of the obvious connection with military violence.[3] But Gates's preferred name better reflects the intended purpose of SWAT—urban counterinsurgency. The first

SWAT units in the United States began in earnest during the mid to late 1960s, a period of poor people's movements, civil rights struggle and urban unrest in the United States related to Black, Brown and Red liberation struggles.

Where some saw civil rights struggles as a principled confrontation with Jim Crow racism, white supremacy, settler colonialism, and the criminalization of poor people, others, particularly police and **law** (90–93) and **order** (83–86) conservatives, saw increased lawlessness. SWAT was one of the answers to civil rights movement demands for justice (mass incarceration was another). With SWAT units, police agencies could rapidly respond to civil unrest—otherwise known as political protest—with overwhelming displays of **force** (102–104), a tactic the military refers to as the "shock and awe" doctrine. Shock and awe is as much about **pacification** (89–90) as it is about tactics. Thus SWAT is not new but is cut from the same cloth that gave us community policing. SWAT units often look ridiculous, storming peaceful protests with cops clad in Robocop-like body armor riding down city streets in anti-mine tanks or massive armored Bearcats.

The criticism that SWAT represents a departure from the real work of policing is based on two erroneous assumptions or myths. The first is based on a timeline of SWAT as the exemplar of police militarization. SWAT is depicted as coming from a moment, generally traced to the mid 1960s, in which police abandoned community policing and embraced aggressive, military assault–style policing. This type of criticism, based on the periodization of militarization, would be a compelling condemnation of SWAT as the moment police became militarized—*if there ever existed* a kinder, gentler **Officer Friendly** (132–135) who once protected citizens but now has been displaced by kicking-ass-and-taking-names SWAT units, who see only enemy combatants. This view imagines that police do something other than use **violence** (96–100) to enforce **order** (83–86) and ignores the close historical connection between police and military described above.

Second, the idea that police militarization describes all that is wrong with contemporary policing is based on the erroneous view that **police brutality** (207–208) can be traced in part to the growth in aggressive police units such as SWAT, and its reliance on military weaponry and aggressive **search** (163–165) and destroy tactics. This is an argument that tells us SWAT is bad for policing and thus for civil liberties, and Officer Friendly is good for policing and the safety of our communities. Civil libertarians find in SWAT an ominous sign. They worry that the rise of the warrior cop signals a slow descent into a police state. They want their friendly neighborhood cop back. But such a view ignores the fact that it wasn't the jack-booted thug who killed Jamar Clark. It wasn't a police SWAT sniper who gunned down Yvette Smith. It wasn't a body-armor-clad SWAT specialist who **arrested** (208–210) Sandra Bland. And it wasn't a munitions expert who tackled and choked Jonathan Sanders to death. In all cases it was Officer Friendly out on **patrol** (170–172) engaging in community policing and keeping the streets safe.

Militarization

Police militarization has emerged as one of the most common narratives surrounding police **violence** (96–100), usually referring to the introduction of military weaponry, technology, language, and aesthetics into the realm of domestic policing. Most critiques of police militarization rely on the view that police and military are separate institutions with distinct logics and mandates. The military serves the goals of foreign policy, while the police are concerned first and foremost with domestic law enforcement and are accountable to **law** (90–93). But it is more useful to point out the similarities between the police and the military. Both are state apparatuses sanctioned to exercise violence in the name of **security** (86–89) and **order** (83–86), which are often just euphemisms for the protection of **private property** (81–83) and white supremacy. There is a reason that oppressed populations often speak of police and military as one and the same.

The public (252–255) concern today over police militarization in the United States often glosses over the fact that the military and police have never been completely distinct in the first place. Instead police militarization is usually considered a relatively new phenomenon that emerged with new experiments in policing social unrest during the civil rights era, and later extended to the **war** (100–102) on crime and war on drugs. But the interplay between military and police has a much longer history. Police have long adopted military technologies, and militaries have adopted police tactics and strategies. For instance, the **slave patrol** (143–144), as the first form of US policing, grew out of militia and military forces. Similarly, though rarely mentioned, the historical structure of police organizations that emerged during the rise of industrial capitalism was modeled on the military chain of command. Police adopted the form and style (see **police uniform**, 141–143) of the military. Some of the first police administrators had significant military colonial experience, and it was this experience that made them ideal candidates to keep the peace domestically.

What counts as "police militarization"? Some libertarian critics, so concerned about state power infringing on the rights of private property, for example, limit their concern to the most overt displays of military power—tanks, assault rifles and body armor. The use of **K-9** (22–24) police dogs, however, is rarely ever mentioned in critiques of police militarization, despite the long history of dogs used by colonial militaries. Likewise, **community policing** (122–123), often taken as the antithesis of "militarization," grows out of the US military's **pacification** (89–90) and counterinsurgency efforts in Vietnam.

Importantly, some of the most influential police "reformers," such as August Vollmer and O.W. Wilson, served first in the military and "militarized" the police through policies of police **professionalization** (113–115). Militarizing the police has historically been a means of **reforming** (155–160) the police by making police a more organized and efficient domestic institution to deal with order and security, including through the use of coercion and police violence. Today, we see a twisted reversal: calls for the end of police militarization are calls for police reform and professionalization, and these calls are usually unconcerned with challenging the very foundations of police power. These calls to demilitarize police often rely on the myth, either conceptually or historically, of police as a noble institution that has in the past been held accountable and could once again be held accountable in the future. Their proponents cry, "If only the police weren't militarized, they could return to democratic policing!" But we should ask: What democratic history of police can we honestly speak of? What history is there where police and military were not bedfellows? There is something to be said for the fact that even former police administrators and current police officers join forces with civil and free market libertarians to identify the "militarization of police" as a bad thing, and all join in united calls for reform, usually under the rubric of community policing and "hearts and minds" campaigns.

This is not to deny the very real and frightening tactical and strategic implications of the police use of weapons of war. And it is certainly not to deny the importance of efforts to eliminate military weaponry from policing. Rather it is to insist that the military and the police share much more common ground than is recognized in many critiques of police militarization. It therefore cannot, as a political project, confront the unity of racialized state violence. After all, even if we could take the military out of the police, we would still be left with the iron fist and velvet glove of police power.[1]

Police Uniform

You're walking down the street and a **cop** (219–221) yells, "Hey, you there!" You turn around and in turning, according to Louis Althusser, you are interpellated as a subject, you are brought into a power relationship; you are forced to submit to a coercive authority. It is a famous example, but consider what's taken for granted in this story: how did you know it was a cop in the first place? Subjection, according to Althusser, turns on "recognition." The cop recognizes you as a "suspect." You recognize the shouter as a cop. But the shouting police officer goes undescribed in the story. No mention of a **nightstick** (55–58) or a **flashlight** (48–50). No **gun** (10–13) described as pointed at you. He is not running toward you. There are no sirens. It's just a person on the street yelling, "Hey, you there," and you turn and immediately you somehow know that it is a cop and that you are a subject of police authority. But how do you know it's a cop? It must be the uniform—so common and ubiquitous that it goes without mention—that Althusser thinks triggers your recognition of police.

Ice Cube is not so sure. Ice Cube, the hip-hop artist and actor most famous for writing and performing the NWA song "Fuck tha

Police," was once asked if he thought it ironic that he frequently plays police officers on TV and in movies. He responded by saying, "Why is that ironic? That's acting. It would be ironic if I was a real cop."[1]

So here we have a dilemma. The police uniform either does or does not help us locate the real cop. For some, the history of the police uniform leads us directly to the military. Historically police uniforms have resembled military uniforms, and nearly all still do. Like the military, their uniforms include the insignia of their rank— sergeants, captains, and chiefs. The first municipal police officers in New York wore the surplus uniforms of the Union Army following the Civil War. Most police departments in the United States in the 1950s modeled their uniforms on those worn by officers and enlisted men in World War II. But before we conclude that this is all the evidence we need in order to claim that police and military are one and the same, look at what you're wearing right now. Are you wearing a business suit? Is there a trench coat in your closet? Do you wear combat boots and cargo shorts? Do you have a T-shirt or cap in a camouflage pattern? Are there shoulder straps on your members-only jacket? If police are "militarized" then so are we. We find the clothed body, not just the police body, draped in martial signs.

But the uniform of police and the uniform of the street, though apparently similar, are distinct and deserve a different analysis. Roland Barthes reminds us of the "methodological difficulty of linking a history of clothes at any one moment to its sociology." The spit-shined combat boots of a military colonel represent a form of what Barthes calls *dress*, an "organized, formal and normative system that is recognized by society." But the scuffed and soiled combat boots of the punk, however, represent an *act of dressing*, defined as a "personal mode with which the wearer adopts . . . the dress that is proposed to them by their social group. It can have a morphological, psychological or circumstantial meaning, but it is not sociological."[2]

Patrizia Calefato tells us that the police uniform represents a normative system that signals the "guarantee of state power" and serves as the "watershed between order and disorder."[3] The police uniform must be understood as part of a process of uniformity, the production of **order** (83–86). The police uniform draws attention to the body as the proper object of concern in the police fabrication of order. The police body is uniformed to represent order. But the police project requires that someone embody disorder as well. Therefore it is not just the police who must wear a uniform, but disorderly subjects too. The orange jumpsuit of the prisoner is as much a part of uniformity as police adorned with rank and insignia.

The word uniform in the case of police therefore has a double meaning. It refers to *dress* in the way that Barthes intended, but is also a synonym for "ordered" or "orderly." The police project is the fabrication of a *uniform* order, accomplished by a *uniformed* order.

Slave Patrol

From the 1700s to the end of the Civil War, organized groups of slave catchers patrolled Southern cities and rural areas in order to control the movement and behavior of enslaved Black people. These groups were known as slave patrols. As a slave-catching institution, the slave patrol controlled Black life in the service of plantation owners and overseers. Slave patrols assumed every Black person was an escaped slave and every meeting of Black people signified a coming slave insurrection. They **searched** (163–165) lodges, checked papers, and broke up meetings for fear of a rebellion.[1]

Slave patrols enforced slave **laws** (90–93). The Fugitive Slave Act (1793) and other slave laws established the legal foundation for the slave patrols. One slave law ordered patrols to "prevent all caballings amongst negros [sic], by dispersing of them when drumming or playing, and search all negro houses for arms or other offensive weapons."[2] The slave patrol, like police, did not fight **crime** (93–96); it was set up to enforce a social order based on the theft of Black life and labor and the dispossession of Indigenous lands.[3]

The hunting powers of police were first codified in the slave laws and in the practice of the slave patrol. The language that describes the work of police, "patrolling **the beat**" (172–174) for example, is a language borrowed directly from the slave patrol. The police are not a departure from the slave patrol but "a more delicately obscure adaptation of the slave patrols," in which "measures such as **stop-and-frisk** (27–31), **racial profiling** (24–27), or driving while black," offer a contemporary version of police as the slave patrol: police watching, **arresting** (208–210), shooting Black people. The police operate with a hunting logic, a logic first codified in the United States in the slave laws.[4][5]

The slave patrol confronted Black life as property. Slave patrols were known to **rape** (41–43) Black women, and kidnap and sell free Black men and women into slavery. To be subject to the slave patrol was to be already dead. Slaves in French colonies described escape as "stealing one's own corpse."

In some Southern cities, slave patrols persisted well into Reconstruction and Jim Crow and were transformed into municipal police. While it might be inaccurate to draw a direct line from the Southern slave patrol to all contemporary police forces, the slave patrol provided the template for the organization of police more generally. The police share the logic of the slave patrol, in which **violence** (96–100) is used to establish an **order** (83–86) based on the conflation of Blackness and disorder. If we begin with the slave patrol, we end up with police.

Rent-a-Cop

In October of 2014 an off-duty St. Louis police officer moonlighting as a rent-a-cop with a private security firm shot and killed eighteen-year-old VonDerrit Myers Jr. The officer, Jason Flanery, was in his **police uniform** (141–143), wearing his police **badge** (106–110), and **patrolling** (170–172) public streets when he killed Myers with his police **gun** (10–13). In other words, he was doing the work of police. St. Louis, along with New York, Los Angeles and other cities, officially endorses officer moonlighting, and even sets wages and selects approved employers for officers. Flanery looked like a **cop** (219–221) when he killed Myers. Flanery worked as a cop when he killed Myers. But to some, because he was "off duty" at the time he killed Myers, he wasn't a cop. "What happens," asks law professor Elizabeth Joh, "when an officer's private employer has a different idea of 'disorder' than what the public police department does?" This "blurring of the private and public," according to Joh, "raises unique and troubling questions if public police are to be responsive to the communities they serve, and not just to parts of them."[1]

Myers's killing and the "blurring" of the private and public do indeed raise troubling questions, but not exactly the ones Joh asks. It might be true to say that private policing is a commodification of police, but this is not to draw a distinction between public and private police; rather, it is to say that private companies find *use value* in what police do, and are willing to—have long been willing to—pay for it. In other words, Jason Flanery imposed **order** (83–86), whether with the St. Louis police department or a private security company. So rather than asking if public police working for private firms blur the line between public and private, we might consider the possibility that for police there is no distinction between public and private.

As the killing of Myers demonstrated, cops operate the same whether they work for a private firm or a public agency. But despite this, rent-a-cops are usually depicted as distinctly different in form and function from public sector police. This idea that there is a bright line between policing for private interest and policing for "public good" is among the most pernicious myths of policing. And yet it is from the private police that the modern public sector police derive, and the work of public sector police has long mirrored the work of private police.

The rent-a-cop, or security guard, is an armed employee working for a private firm that engages in policing for profit. It finds its modern origins in the late-nineteenth-century union-busting tactics of industrial capitalism—the era of the Pinkerton Detective Agency and other firms—during a time in which the "right" to break strikes was the authority of private firms.[2] What's clear from these origins is that **security** (86–89) and order were defined as anything that served the interests of private industry. Before police worked for the "public good" they broke strikes and busted unions for private interests.

The shift from an emphasis on private security guards to public sector policing in the early twentieth century is often depicted as a Progressive Era commitment to professional policing and the role of the public sector in providing services. But this ignores the fact that the emergence of public sector police departments at the municipal and state level was as much, if not more, a result of demands by private companies that the state pay the Pinkertons to break legs and bust unions. After the Progressive Era, public sector police were paid by local taxpayers to do the same work they did for private interests. What was considered order and security in the Pinkerton Era—the disciplining of what capitalist firms considered an unruly working class—remained, and remains, the same in the era of public sector policing.

But this timeline is not entirely accurate. There has been no post–Progressive Era shift from private to public policing. Private security firms and public sector police both expanded throughout the twentieth century. And from the very beginning, there was little distinction between private and public police. There are more private police patrolling today than at any other time in history. By the 1970s, two-thirds of all police officers were on private payrolls.[3] The nearly 20 million security guards today represent an increase of around 300 percent over the past thirty years.[4] And many of them work as both private and public police. Like Flanery, most wear their uniforms and carry their service weapons while working for private firms contracted by private clients. And they do the same work for corporate employers that they do for police departments. Their "major customers are large-scale organizations who invest in policing for the same reasons they make other investments: to guarantee profits and secure an environment for uninterrupted growth."[5] Police fabricate order, and that order is for sale.

Police Oversight
Police oversight, sometimes called civilian, community, or citizen police oversight, is the idea that police should submit to a local, independent authority of elected or appointed officials who audit or monitor police departments for misconduct including, but not limited to, the use of, and **discretion** (176–178) to use, **force** (102–104).

Contemporary police oversight generally follows one of four models. Some investigate police misconduct only when official complaints have been filed. They make recommendations on discipline to the chief of police or the sheriff, who has final authority to accept or reject those findings and recommendations. Some have no investigative authority whatsoever and instead review police internal affairs **investigations** (175–176) of misconduct and then make recommendations to the chief of police or sheriff, who has final authority to accept or reject the findings and recommendations. Others only hear appeals by complainants whose charges of misconduct have been previously heard and denied by the chief of police or sheriff. But as with the first two, the appeal culminates in a recommendation that can be rejected by the chief of police or the sheriff. Lastly, some are constituted as independent agencies with a director, a board of commissioners and a staff of investigators. Some of these even hold the authority to issue subpoenas and others have the authority to examine and make recommendations regarding specific police policies. But like the other models, their findings and recommendations are advisory only. No police oversight agency or board operating anywhere in the United States has the authority to discipline or fire police officers. In the history of police oversight in Albuquerque, New Mexico, for example, every police chief has rejected every police oversight commission recommendation regarding police misconduct since the formal practice of police oversight by commission began in the late 1990s.

The guarantee that police oversight will hold police accountable even though it hasn't, and that police oversight will resolve the problem of police **violence** (96–100) even though it won't, is among the most frequently claimed and widely believed promises of **police reform** (155–160). Despite the fact that the authors of the May 2015 report issued by President Barack Obama's Task Force on 21st Century Policing concluded that there existed no "strong research evidence that [oversight] works," new or improved police oversight procedures were among the first reforms the US Department of Justice called for following the police killings of James Boyd in Albuquerque, Mike Brown in Ferguson, and Tamir Rice in Cleveland, among many other places and following many other police killings.

This faith in police reform via police oversight as a way to end police violence, despite the failure of police oversight to end police violence, is shared by some anti–police violence activists as well. Campaign Zero, a series of police reform policies proposed in August 2015 by a number of prominent Black Lives Matter activists, put police oversight at the center of its call to "end police violence in America." Their online campaign demanded "effective civilian oversight structures" that included a "Police Commission" with the power to "discipline and dismiss police officers" and a "Civilian Complaints Office" with the power to "interrogate officers . . . where deadly force is used." Campaign Zero's faith in oversight appears at first glance as something altogether different from the reformist models that reserve for police chiefs and sheriffs the authority to discipline police officers. If the "community" holds the power to monitor and discipline police, then police will be held accountable to the "community."

There are three primary reasons, however, why police oversight of existing police will not end police violence. First, even if there had been a Campaign Zero–like model of police oversight in, say, Ferguson, Missouri on August 9, 2014, Mike Brown would still be dead. The only difference would be that a community oversight commission could have used its authority to investigate the actions of Darren Wilson, the officer who shot and killed Mike Brown. That commission might have fired Darren Wilson, the strongest disciplinary action available, whether wielded by a Chief of Police or a community oversight agency. But Darren Wilson is no longer working at the Ferguson police department as it is. And since no police oversight model includes the authority to charge an officer with a **crime** (93–96), the establishment of the kind of police oversight called for by Campaign Zero would have produced the same outcome that happened in Ferguson without oversight.

Second, police oversight is as old as policing itself. The first police departments in the United States submitted to oversight by, usually, a local political boss. This structure served the interests of police and political elites. The lack of transparency and **accountability** (160–162) in the political boss model of oversight gave way in the Progressive Era to supposedly independent police oversight commissions. But these were usually made up of prominent and politically connected businessmen appointed by local mayors—the same political bosses whose political authority over police Progressive Era reformers sought to replace through independent oversight. Contemporary models of oversight limit authority to an advisory capacity but have sought to sever the influence of local mayors or political authorities by providing police oversight agencies with legal representation and budgets and staff that are all independent of local political authority. And despite all these models and reforms, none of them, whether with or without the authority to discipline, or under or free from local political influence, have been able to *hold police accountable* or *end* or even *significantly reduce police violence.*

And lastly, if the goal is to end police violence, a better approach would be to abolish police, or at least reduce police in size and authority, rather than improve police oversight. After all, there is police violence because there are police. Police oversight, unlike abolition, does not reject police violence per se, but only rejects *unjustified* police violence. The goal of any form of public oversight, whether of police or any other government activity, is to improve, not abolish, services and practices. Police oversight thus subscribes to the notion—one shared by conservatives and many liberals—that police are necessary for good **order** (83–86), that cops need to use violence to impose that order, and that police oversight works to *improve* that violence, which means **justified** (238–240) violence. Conservatives are content to let police chiefs provide that oversight, while progressives want that oversight to be "independent." Either way the outcome is the same. So picture the best police chief or police oversight agency you can imagine. Imagine that it (or she) is independent, aggressive, community-minded, and highly critical of the police use of force. And then remember: Mike Brown would still be dead and Darren Wilson would still not be held accountable.

Police Union

Policing is a heavily unionized profession in the United States. Nearly three-quarters of the hundred largest police departments in the United States operate under union contracts. And these unions, like organized labor more generally, advance the shared interests of its members. But unlike other trade unions, the interests of police unions often come into conflict with the interests of other workers.

While policing is among the most unionized professions in the United States, historically it has been a profession most associated with defending racist Jim Crow **laws** (90–93) in the South and the repression of organized labor in the North. Despite this history of anti-unionism, police unions enjoy unique protections. Police unions were exempted from Republican Wisconsin Governor Scott Walker's 2014 union-busting law, which stripped public employees of collective bargaining rights.

Police unionism represents a profound irony. Where trade unions emerged during the industrial revolution to defend the shared interests of workers, modern police unions in the United States emerged in reaction to Civil Rights–era organizing that highlighted the role of police and police **violence** (96–100) in defending racism and segregation.[1] Police unions thus drew on the language of unionism not as a means to stand in solidarity with other workers but rather in order to give credibility to their efforts to protect police officers from **police oversight** (146–149) and the criminal **investigation** (175–176) of officer misconduct.

While there are no national police unions in the United States, the Fraternal Order of Police counts more than 300,000 sworn police officers among its members. The FOP, like local police unions, opposes community police oversight, supports legislation that limits independent investigations of police misconduct, supports tough-on-**crime** (93–96) political candidates, paints any criticism of police as reckless and un-American and, in 2015, despite widespread protests against racialized police violence in the wake of dozens of police killings of **unarmed** (257–258) Black men and women, lobbied Congress to add police officers as a protected category in federal hate crimes legislation, a law subsequently adopted by a number of states.

Through collective bargaining, police unions have transformed police violence into a contractually protected condition of their employment. This has had the effect of expanding the right by police to choose when and where to use violence at the same time that it has limited civilian police oversight or criminal investigation of that use of **force** (102–104) by police.

Dinkheller

The police found Andrew Brannan deep in the Georgia woods hiding in a sleeping bag under a tarp near a ramshackle shed he'd built himself. They arrested him, a jury convicted him, a judge condemned him, his jailers executed him. "I have to tell the truth," he said, just before the state killed him. "I'm certainly glad to be leaving."

Brannan said other things, too, and Dinkheller's dashboard camera captured it all. Such as "Fuck you, goddamn it, here I am. Shoot my fucking ass," which is what he yelled at Laurens County Sheriff's Deputy Kyle Dinkheller after the deputy pulled him over for speeding on a rural Georgia highway on an early January evening in 1998. Next came, "I'm a goddamn Vietnam combat veteran," which he yelled after Dinkheller ordered him to take his hands out of his pockets. Brannan, irate, started yelling, waving his hands around. He ignored Dinkheller's commands and went to his truck where he rummaged around for something while Dinkheller yelled at him to show his hands. Dinkheller drew his **gun** (10–13) just as Brannan pulled an M1 Carbine rifle out of his truck. "Put the gun down," Dinkheller shouted. Then silence. A brief, agonizing standoff. Then Dinkheller fired the first shot, missing Brannan. Brannan returned fire, hitting Dinkheller in the chest. Dinkheller fell, fired again, hitting Brannan in the stomach. But Brannan kept coming despite the wound, and he closed the distance between them just as Dinkheller's cries stopped and his death rattle began. Brannan stood over him and calmly said, "die, fucker," before putting a final bullet through Dinkheller's eye.

They arrested him and put him on trial. The lawyers and the judges and the "witnesses" did the talking then. First the psychologists, who testified about Brannan's post-traumatic stress disorder (PTSD) and his paranoia; who quoted from his five-hundred-page medical file full of psychiatric disorders; who explained to the jury the toll that Vietnam took on Brannan.

The jury heard about the "booby traps and ambushes" Brannan set in Vietnam and all the people he and the men in his platoon killed. They heard about the brutal killing of Brannan's company commander "under circumstances for which Brannan felt responsible." They heard about him coming home to a life of manic depression, bipolar disorder, and PTSD. The psychologists noted that his marriage dissolved in the chaos of his pain and anger. They described to the jury all the jobs he couldn't keep; how he became "a recluse" in those Georgia woods in his ramshackle shed that some called a bunker—what the court would later describe as his "strange and isolated living conditions." Postwar life had become postlife war for Brannan, who would spend most of his time alone living on government checks because the Veterans Affairs declared him "100 percent disabled." He would forget to take his medication. He would argue with strangers in stores. He would frighten people, including the jury, with his "odd nervous laughter."

And then Brannan's mother, whose firstborn died in a plane crash, whose youngest killed himself, whose husband died of cancer, pleaded with the jury for mercy for her son, who was all she had left. Spare me my son, she told the jury, a broken man, yes, but one "who had shown kindness to several widows and a child in the neighborhood." But the jury showed no mercy because law allows for none when a cop is killed.

And then the prosecutors played poor Dinkheller's dashboard camera video to the jury and everyone heard his cries, his screams, and his dying breath. The sounds and images haunted the proceedings thereafter. Dinkheller's widow, Angela, told the jury that he carried her pregnancy test with him in his cruiser that night. He knew I was pregnant before I did, she told the jury during sentencing. Eight months after his death, she gave birth to their second child. The jury convicted Brannan of first-degree murder.

Some were not permitted to hear or to speak during the trial. The prosecutors struck eleven potential jurors from the pool because they were Black. The District Attorney wanted the death penalty and Black jurors, as a rule, overwhelmingly oppose it. The defense did not call any of the men Brannan served with in Vietnam and so the jury didn't learn about "malignant post-Vietnam Stress Syndrome." Didn't find out what America's endless wars do to a person's body and mind. Didn't know what kind of men emerged from the genocide and Agent Orange of Vietnam. The jury condemned Brannan to death by lethal injection.

And then there were the years in which various judges explained why they had to reject Brannan's appeals, why they had to deny his writs of habeas corpus, why **law** (90–93) required that they send him to his death. They explained that they knew of no "consensus discernable" anywhere—not in Georgia, not anywhere in the United States—that would make executing a mentally ill man unconstitutional. We find no "evolving standards of decency" in that regard, they would write, especially for someone with "the mental health evidence Brannan has shown."[1]

Then, slowly, police began mythologizing Dinkheller and weaponizing the video. Every cop in the United States has seen it. First informally, one cop showing it to another. Then, more formally, the video took on a central role in police training. The dashboard camera footage is shown at police academies across the country as a "teaching tool." Just as war, police, and prison converted Brannan into a monster that needed to be killed, police converted Dinkheller into an omen that foretold a violent death. Year after year, police recruits-in-training screen the video, listen to the screams and watch wide-eyed as Brannan kills a cop. And then a police trainer says something like, "this could be you. This could be your violent death."

In a scene in the 2019 cop-made documentary film, *Dinkheller,* the camera lingers on police recruits watching the video during their training. The scene captures the moment the shooting and the screaming begins. At that moment, their eyes widen, their posture stiffens, their expressions turn from concern to horror as Dinkheller's screams turn from cries to a death rattle. The value of the video to police is clear. Dinkheller is a warning, a prophecy. The dangers of policing, according to police trainers, emerge from the unpredictable and hidden dangers that lurk everywhere. Even the simple traffic stop can turn deadly if, like Dinkheller, you're not careful or if you're too trusting. Your job is to survive, and your survival requires active suspicion, hair-trigger aggression, and a make-it-home-to-your-family-no-matter-what mentality.

The Dinkheller film teaches recruits that it's not enough to shoot first, as Dinkheller did. You must dominate every situation, control every movement, automate your use of force and violence. Fuck polite. Your Brannan lurks somewhere out there. You saw it yourself. Don't be the rookie who makes a fatal mistake. Your job is not to be nice and polite; your job is to use **pain compliance** (79–80). You're a cop, remember; you have the legal power to take a human life. Use it.

The sociologist Michael Sierra-Arévalo calls this the "danger imperative" of policing. According to Sierra-Arévalo, police safety exists in an inverse relationship to police violence. The more police use violence, the more police ensure their safety. Dinkheller refused to use violence until it was too late. This danger imperative structures everything that police do because everyone is a potential threat and every moment a possible emergency. Every shift could end in your death. Every motorist might have a gun. It's not us versus them, it's you versus your Brannan. The film's narrator describes the dashboard camera footage as "a warning about deadly hesitation and fear of punishment." The danger imperative in policing includes the idea that good policing occasionally requires bad policing (see **good cop, bad cop**, 195–197). This is why police **accountability** (160–162) will never stop the killing.

The lesson of the Dinkheller video is clear: don't be like Dinkheller. Shoot first, and quickly, and then keep your mouth shut when the other cop does it too. The Dinkheller film offers a master class in copspeak and reinforces what police have always known: only through violence will police find salvation.

Police Reform

Police reform comprises a vast complex of institutions and agencies across the political spectrum that share a narrative of police as an essential if occasionally flawed institution that requires total respect but occasional tinkering. When crises in police legitimacy strike—often in the aftermath of dramatic and popular protests against spectacular or long-standing patterns of racialized police **violence** (96–100) against the poor—the various actors and agencies of police reform mobilize. These include think tanks, such as the Police Executive Research Forum, scores of **criminology** (261–263) and criminal justice departments at institutions of higher education, various federal research divisions, such as the National Institute of Justice and the Civil Rights Division of the US Department of Justice, and prominent law and consulting firms that hire former police chiefs. These police reformists convene special commissions where they conduct **investigations** (175–176) (and come to similar conclusions) and propose solutions (which rarely differ) in "commission reports."

The organizing principle of police reform is the idea that the institution of police is perfectible. This notion of perfectibility depicts police, whether good or bad *today*, as absolutely essential and always on a path of improvement *tomorrow*. Perfectibility includes concepts such as **accountability** (160–162), **police oversight** (146–149), and **professionalization** (113–115). These are police reform's key terms, but they are not terms that call the police institution into question. To hold police accountable is to assume that police as an institution is necessary and required in the first place. Likewise police oversight refuses to examine the police outside a **justified** (238–240)/unjustified binary. The problem is not the police but a public that requires a better understanding of the police project. Police reform, then, is mostly about reforming the public's view of the legitimacy of police.

Reformists want us to know that we may see the problem as inhering in police, but in reality the problem is with us, with our loss of faith. **The public** (252–255) misunderstands police and thus misunderstands the problem. The problem is not police violence, which is systemic and institutional, but rather **police brutality** (207–208), which is temporary and individual. The problem is not police in general, but a few **bad apples** (224–227). The problem is not institutional, in other words, but situational. Reform, as the primary driver of this eternal pursuit of improvement, is always calibrated to restore our faith in police by reminding us of their essential goodness and the very temporariness of any problem. New professionalization standards are proposed and described at "coffee with a **cop**" (219–221) meetings around town. New use of **force** (102–104) policies are written in consultation with police experts and paid consultants and then presented at "community–police forums" to great fanfare. Existing police oversight mechanisms are overhauled and premiered at ribbon-cutting ceremonies held with community stakeholders. All of this heralds a new era in police–community relations.

Reformists always claim that their reform measures herald a new era for police. Reform will demarcate some break from the violence of the past. This is partly why police historians love to talk about police eras through the lens of reform, the effect of which is an ideological rescue of present police from past sins. The politics of police reform are animated by a particular vision of police history. The structure is familiar: in the past, the police were certainly corrupt and violent and racist, but eventually reformists arrived and instituted all sorts of professionalization standards, such as better technology and training and education, and these standards effectively solved the problem. Reformed police thus belong to a different era in policing. This history seeks to interrupt efforts by activists to draw a line from the racialized police violence of the past to the racialized police violence of the present.

But the reforms of one era become the problems of another. And reform is always followed by a new crisis. And each time new problems arise (which of course are really old problems): a cop is caught perjuring himself, for example (see **testilying**, 218–219), or a cop shoots an **unarmed** (257–258) man in the back, or an entire department engages in racialized policing (see **CRASH**, 128–130) or violence against women (see **NHI**, 240–242). When this happens the agents and institutions of reform mobilize again, as though for the first time, and with concerted, collective amnesia, they diagnose the problem as an unfortunate, temporary, and totally unexpected diversion from the path of police perfectibility. It is the diversion and our persistent lack of faith, not the beating or the lying or the killing, that represents the real intractable problem. Thus all problems are always temporary aberrations from the righteous path of policing, and only reform experts—most of whom are former cops—can truly understand and repair this problem. And for all these reasons reform always fails. Cops kill and lie and **rape** (41–43), even **Officer Friendly** (132–135). So the failure of reform to make police perfect is always depicted as a failure of the public to believe in police, not a failure of reform itself. This constitutes police reform's built-in alibi.

One of the most insidious problems of police reform is how police departments that have been subjected to reform measures, usually by a federal consent decree, are actually rewarded for their misconduct. Reform is a windfall of more money from new grants to hire more cops and purchase more weaponry, technology, training and education.

Police reform often limits its proposals to the panacea of technology—what we might refer to as technological liberalism—as a way to resolve police misconduct or police brutality.[1] Better equipment and better technology. **Tasers** (13–16) instead of **guns** (10–13), **drones** and **helicopters** (70–73), lapel and dashboard cameras. These are the standard fixes that police reformists offer. Better equipment and better technology to go with better or more education, better and more efforts of understanding **the public** (252–255), more efficient administrative means to ensure accountability and oversight. Better recruitment practices and hiring standards. These are the solutions of police reform. Yet what improvement can we honestly say has come from all of this?

The great accomplishment of police reform is only an improvement if we consider the term a reference to the capacity of police to sanitize and legitimate their violence. Police reform is not simply about making police better, but about making police violence more efficient and more "civilized." **Tear gas** (17–20) provides one such example. The police use of tear gas was deemed a significant reform measure for police violence during the 1960s and 1970s. Commissions at the time saw in tear gas a more hygienic and less lethal form of policing protests and large crowds (201–205). Tear gas was the progressive, liberal technology that would limit the use of force, while still helping police to administer "good order." Unlike the bullet that punctured flesh or the nightstick (55–58) that cracked skulls, tear gas provided police with a weapon that seemed less violent. The use of tear gas, which is depicted as among police reform's great accomplishments, is banned by international law as a form of chemical warfare. It kills and causes long-lasting and significant health and environmental effects. The Taser and the police K-9 (22–24) dog are other such examples. They demonstrate the ways that reform solutions are not real solutions at all, but rather serve to rework the mode and means of violence while keeping violence intact. This is what police reform has given us.

Since the 1960s, police reform has also sought to make the police more diverse and multicultural, or colorblind. If only we could make police more representative of racial, ethnic, and gender demographics, then we could significantly reduce if not eradicate police violence, the reformists' logic goes. A liberal multicultural argument has seized police reform, in which police are encouraged to hire more Black and Brown people and more women to make the police less brutally racist and misogynist. Women, in particular, must be a part of reform efforts because female cops, it is argued, provide a unique skill set and overall different personality than the white male cop. This argument ignores the long history of violence against Black and Brown men and women in places such as Memphis, Cincinnati, Atlanta, Los Angeles, and Washington, DC, which long have had a significant number, if not majority, of Black and Brown cops and even chiefs. As Robin Kelley points out, "It is a rare cop, even among Blacks and Latinos, who sees his or her primary task as working for, or being employed by, poor urban communities of color. Instead, the police work for the state or the city, and their job is to keep an entire criminalized population in check, to contain the chaos of the ghetto (183–184) within its walls, and to make sure the most unruly subjects stay in line. They operate in a permanent state of war."[1]

Police reform does not confront police, but rather attempts to co-opt the communities that hold animosity toward police. It is their rage and resentment that reform seeks to resolve. Reform is not motivated by a desire to see a world without police violence; rather, it is driven by a fear of a world without police. Reform's rhetoric of progress, **order** (83–86) and **security** (86–89), tied as it is to the view of police as the defense of civilization, gives reform both its powerful political authority and its alibi when none of its policies pay off. And so reform seeks to restore the legitimacy of police by destroying the legitimacy of protest against police.

This is not to say that everything under the heading of police reform should simply be dismissed. Not all reforms are created equal. Ruth Wilson Gilmore distinguishes between "reformist reforms" and "non-reformist reforms." The former refers to those reforms that actually bolster and strengthen what one is challenging. "Non-reformist reforms" are "systemic changes that do not extend the life or breadth of deadly forces such as prisons."[2] Is the goal of reform to expand the police powers or constrain them? The abolitionist Mariame Kaba, for example, asks "Are the proposed reforms allocating more money to the police? If yes, then you should oppose them." She goes on: "Are the proposed reforms advocating for MORE police and policing (under euphemistic terms like 'community policing' run out of regular police districts)? If yes, then you should oppose them." If reforms offer technical solutions to police violence, we should oppose them, because it just "means more money to the police. Said technology is more likely to be turned against the public than it is to be used against cops." Finally, she reminds us that "violence is endemic to US policing itself. There are some nice individual people who work in police departments. I've met some of them." But this "is not a problem of individually terrible officers rather it is a problem of a corrupt and oppressive policing system built on controlling & managing the marginalized while protecting property."[3]

Instead of these reformist reforms, Kaba identifies several "non-reformist reforms" that make sense to support and advocate for, such as: reparations to the victims of police violence (and their families), requirements for officers to be held personally liable to cover the costs of violence and death claims, divestment from police agencies and the redirection of those funds to social programs, proposals to disarm the police as well as dissolve local police departments, greater transparency, and the authority of oversight committees to have the power to investigate, discipline, and fire both officers and administrators. These measures do not eliminate police violence. The abolition of the police is the only reform that eliminates police violence, but these non-reformist reforms do strip power from police and refuse reforms that seek only to make police into a more acceptable force.

Reformist reform is premised on the idea that police in its current form—an armed institution of the state that uses violence and coercion to impose bourgeois order—is an indisputable good. It offers the forever-unfulfilled promise of fixing police as a way to defend the order of things and, more importantly, to put a lid on any abolitionist dreams of a world without police. Police reform is the sine qua non of police legitimacy. Without reform there is no police.[5]

Accountability

Cops hate rules. Rules place "irrelevant and unhelpful restrictions" on cops. To cops, rules just "tell us what we shouldn't do . . . don't tell us what we should do" and "give the brass plenty of rope with which to hang us."[1] Rules are the worst if you're a rank-and-file cop. You want to hold cops accountable? Get out of our way.

Rules undermine good police work, cops on **patrol** (170–172) will tell you. It is the rules that force them to lie under oath (see **testilying**, 218–219). It is the rules that force them to plant evidence at the scene (see **throw-down weapon**, 13). It is the rules that force them to play **good cop, bad cop** (195–197) to get a confession (see also **interrogation**, 193–195). According to George L. Kelling, architect of **broken windows** (186–189), rules and regulations, strict supervision, and command and control "are irrelevant to street policing."[2] Accountability begets a tyranny of rules that, according to Kelling, hamstring police and policing. Police work is too messy, and the demands of "order-maintenance," as Kelling liked to call it, are too complex. The many rules and regulations imposed on police fail to anticipate the unseen, everyday work of policing on the street and result in the opposite of accountability. If only there were no rules for cops; rules just get in the way.

The reformist premise behind police accountability begins with the idea that good policing requires independent policies, regulations, and training imposed on cops. But according to cops, this ignores the actual experience of police on the street. Kelling explains that the complaints and the concerns and the demands for accountability by politicians, the public, the media—all of them—are just so ridiculous and counterproductive. They're "oblivious to actual police functioning." They don't "understand the complexity" of policing on the street. Their rules limit police **discretion** (176–178) and make the "real world of policing" more difficult for cops on **the beat** (172–174).[3]

What rich irony. If books came with soundtracks you'd hear a laughter track. Beware police reformists and scholars of **criminology** (261–263) bemoaning rules and regulations when applied to cops. Police is nothing if not a vast and violent bureaucratic institution of armed vigilantes imposing arbitrary rules on everyone but themselves. More rules for **the public** (252–255), none for us. That's accountability to a cop. The late, great David Graeber called this The Iron Law of Liberalism: all demands to reduce bureaucracy in the name of accountability inevitably lead to "more regulations, more bureaucrats, more police."[4] The **thin blue line** (110–112) imagines cops as synonymous with civilization, but police beget bureaucracy, not civilization. What is bureaucracy if not police? What is bureaucracy without police? The state is nothing if not a constantly "ballooning array of legal clerks, registrars, inspectors, notaries, and police officials" making your life miserable and their work less accountable.[5] What better indicator could we find to measure bureaucracy-run-amok than the proliferation of police on **patrol** (170–172)? Fewer than 800,000 cops in the United States in 1992, nearly 1.1 million twenty years later, not to mention the nearly 1.5 million **rent-a-cops** (144–146) in the US.[6]

Cops don't work under a tyranny of rules; we live under a tyranny of police, organized by an institution that refuses to be held accountable but demands accountability from us. The sovereign state delegates its monopoly on legal **violence** (96–100) to police, jailers, and soldiers, who then claim the "right to brush such legalities aside, or to make them up as one goes along." The cops "who enforce the **law** (90–93)," wrote Graeber, "are not really subject to it."[7] That's why justice is blind. She can't watch. She can't take the violence and the bloodletting of police. So she turns away and refuses to hold police accountable. So forget police accountability. It only exists in theory in order to thwart police accountability in reality. Police is only accountable to the power structure that employs it.

Using the Force:
How Police Impose Order

Search

The power to search is among the most wide-ranging of police powers. The Fourth Amendment to the US Constitution places limits on what, who, where, when and how police can search. Chief among these is the requirement that before engaging in a search police must secure a warrant from a court, based on probable cause of criminal activity. But the **reasonable suspicion** (255–257), **plain view** (212–215), automobile, and hot **pursuit** (200–201) exceptions, among others, extend unaccountable **discretion** (176–178) to police regarding searches and thus make the Fourth Amendment all but irrelevant. In practice *and in law* (90–93) the police have carte blanche to search your home or your car, your pockets or your backpack, your **body cavities** (33–34) or your bank account. Indeed the search is a police power always in array. **K-9s** (22–24) at the train station. Body scanners at the airport. Metal detectors at the high school. Drug tests at the workplace. In most cases, searches are conducted based on consent, another exception to the Fourth Amendment limit on unreasonable search and seizure. You can of course refuse to consent to a search, but then you can't drive your car, go to school, collect a wage, or board a plane. Other exceptions to the limits placed on the power of police to search represent after-the-fact justifications of otherwise illegal police searches. Police simply assert powers the law denies them and then launch a "coordinated effort . . . to legitimate their actions by persuading judges, politicians and the public that what they were doing was necessary to curb crime."[1]

Didier Fassin's ethnography of urban policing in France demonstrates the ubiquity of the search as "the usual means [police enter] into contact with their public, whether or not a **crime** (93–96) has been committed."[2] As in the US, there are legal limits to the power of French police to search suspects. "In theory, we have to follow strict rules," an officer told Fassin, "but in practice, the Penal Procedure Code lets us do what we want."[3] One officer told Fassin police could "do what we want." He wasn't exaggerating: Police quite literally can search whatever and whomever and whenever they want because the limits that law places are not limits on searching per se but rather concern the admissibility of any evidence collected during a search. Police can break down your door, ransack your home, rough up your family, and seize your property. The only limit they might encounter is an after-the-fact consideration of the admissibility of the evidence police seized from you.

A search is a tool of intimidation. It is designed to remind a population that they are always at the mercy of police. And this is precisely why constant street searching of poor Black and Latino youth is at the heart of **broken windows** (186–189) policing in the United States. Broken windows policing is the idea that police should use the power of search not to fight crime but to impose **order** (83–86). A judge may throw out any evidence collected, but she cannot go back in time and stop the search from ever happening in the first place. And this is the point of the **stop and frisk** (27–31) search. It is not about crime-fighting or collecting evidence or investigating wrongdoing; it is about information. Search is surveillance and intelligence gathering. It is how the state develops knowledge about a population in order to put that information to work for all sorts of projects that often include those populations' criminalization (see **red squad**, 123–126). And search is a tool of intimidation. It is designed to remind a population that "they are at the mercy of police discretion."[4] The hassle and indignity of the stop and frisk search is designed to impose in its subjects what Fassin calls the "habit of humiliation." When Fassin saw French middle class kids searched—a rare event—he noted how vocal and upset it made them. But when police searched poor, usually Muslim kids in the working-class banlieues that surround Paris, he saw a different reaction. The police search was part of everyday life. The young men knew the drill so they kept their heads down, spoke only when spoken to, and ignored the "abusive or racist comments and aggressive or humiliating treatment."[5] What they were to take away from that unequal encounter was fear, and that is the point.

Armed Friendlies

A sovereign authority constructs an **order** (83–86) based on values, depicted as universal, that conforms to the interests of an economic and social elite. It claims a monopoly on legitimate violence in service to that order and delegates this authority to various branches and apparatuses of the administrative state. A phrase that describes this is "the police powers."

Once delegated, the police power organizes and extends itself across the institutions of the state—across the institutions of police, the military, social welfare, schools, manufacturing, and prisons—across the entire social world. Police must establish beachheads in all places; must concern itself with what happens in every home, heart, and head; must post sentries and recruit spies and snitches in every city or village. The reach of police must be exhaustive, permanent, and potentially infinite. A phrase that describes this is "armed friendlies."

When groups of Native-led activists and organizers declared their intention to tear down statues to Spanish Conquistadors in New Mexico during the summer of 2020, a group of self-described militia "soldiers" declared their intention to stop the plan. As a riot squad of cops from the Albuquerque Police Department (APD) assembled out of sight, activists swung axes at a statue of the genocidal Conquistador Juan de Oñate while a fascist militia policed the protest. A man aligned with the militia groups, Steven Ray Baca, grabbed a woman roughly and threw her to the rocky ground. Some intervened and confronted Baca, pushing him from protestors. Baca, the son of a retired sheriff's deputy and nephew of an Albuquerque cop, began to retreat. He walked backwards down the street holding a pistol and waving it wildly. A man in a black jacket tried to disarm Baca. They scuffled in the street and Baca fell to the ground and as he fell he pointed his weapon at the man. The man swung his skateboard at the gun but missed his target and Baca fired his weapon and hit the man in the abdomen. Police arrived as the man lay bleeding in the street. The first thing they did was fire **tear gas** (17–20) at the protestors.

The shooting came just weeks after thousands of people marched in a Black Lives Matter protest against police violence in Albuquerque. The march began on the campus of the University of New Mexico, whose president gave police permission to post snipers on the roof of a campus building. Meanwhile, Albuquerque police met with a group of armed counterdemonstrators, which included mixed-martial arts fighters who train at the famed Jackson-Wink Academy, including Jon "Bones" Jones. Video of the meeting, posted online, shows a cop recruiting them to assist police against the protestors. Another right-wing militia group, the New Mexico Patriots, also cooperated with police, later telling the press their group had been "working with APD for many years now." They patrolled Albuquerque in squads of armed vigilantes, he explained, under the supervision and cooperation of police. A third group, the recently formed New Mexico Civil Guard, declared its purpose as supporting police through "rapid local lawful response to emergency and dangerous situations" and patrolled the protest in military uniforms with tactical gear and semi-automatic weapons. The day before the Oñate protest, police were heard on the police scanner describing the various militia members as "heavily armed friendlies."

Some saw the various militia groups at the protest as something other than police and therefore condemned police for not "de-escalating" the situation. Police use the word "de-escalation" as a euphemism for violence. This criticism, in other words, condemned Albuquerque police, among the most lethal police departments in the United States, for not using enough violence. "Where were the police?" they asked. Some journalists contributed to and reinforced this false distinction between police and militia by depicting fascist militias as a fringe movement that makes the job of police more difficult.

"Armed friendlies" does not denote a narrow category of right-wing extremism. The phrase offers instead an all-encompassing index of the police powers. It describes the vast and linked networks of actors, institutions, and practices that share, or tolerate, a fascist political ideology rooted in authoritarianism and white nationalism. Armed friendlies seek an active, durable, operational relationship with police. The phrase "active operational relationship" does not imply that armed friendlies appear only in a tactical, support role for **crowd** (201–205) control. While militias often appear prominently during public protests, and while these moments do represent the most public mode of the police-militia operational relationship, the police–militia relationship exceeds this limited view.

The phrase "armed friendlies" (a) indexes the full extent and reach of police, (b) captures a particular police view of the world, and (c) is used by liberal police reformers in a way that illustrates, perhaps better than anything else, the reactionary rot lurking in police reformist thinking.

"Armed friendlies" as an index that captures the full extent and reach of police. The phrase "armed friendlies" catalogues everything that police entail. Police impose order by using violence against the forces of disorder, which police consider a threat because of the potential, according to police, of the forces of disorder to use violence. To police and law, violence doesn't beget violence, violence begets order; or, restated in the language of copspeak, the **force** (102–104) and **deterrence** (228–231) of police establishes "good order." The phrase "armed friendlies," when used to distinguish police from vigilantes, only draws attention away from police—the problem is "armed friendlies," not cops—while simultaneously reinforcing the essential role of police in fabricating order through violence—the solution requires more police and more police violence.

Consider Keith Lee. Lee served in the U.S. Air Force, worked as a **cop** (219–221), and patrolled Afghanistan as a military occupation security guard, or **rent-a-cop** (144–146). He cased the U.S. Capitol building in Washington, DC on January 5, 2020, the day before he stormed it with hundreds of others. Isn't Lee a cop? He worked as a cop and used the language of police when, following the siege of the Capitol, he called the fascist white nationalist groups, the Oath Keepers and III%ers, their "backup." Or maybe Lee's a fascist? He raised money for the Proud Boys and other fascist groups and militias, two groups composed of former police and military, for legal defense and travel costs. Lee is a cop, a soldier, a fascist, an armed friendly. He is all of these things simultaneously, which demonstrates that the category of the "armed friendly" is less a phrase to name a specific kind of reactionary social movement actor and more a way to describe the collected and various roles, networks, and institutions that police require in order to fabricate a racialized capitalist order through violence.

"Armed friendlies" as a phrase that captures a particular police view of the world. Just before the Illinois teenager Kyle Rittenhouse killed a Black Lives Matter supporter in Kenosha, Wisconsin, during a protest following the police shooting of Jacob Blake, a cop in an

urban assault vehicle tossed him a water bottle. "We appreciate you guys," said the cop to the heavily armed Rittenhouse. Moments later police watched the teen shoot two men, kill one, and then walk away. Some critics of the police offered shocked commentary in the wake of the murder. Why did police permit Rittenhouse and other "armed friendlies" to menace Black Lives Matter protestors on the streets of Kenosha with assault rifles? The criticism assumed, as most liberal analyses of law and order do, that police are like other public servants. They serve an order that comes to them from law. Aren't police accountable to law (see **accountability**, 160–162)? This criticism imagines law as a progressive force that, in the abstract, establishes the standards and conditions for an objectively fair and equal social and political **order** (83–86) and then delegates to police the obligation and authority to bring that abstract world of equal justice to life.

Consider the particular phrase—"armed friendlies"—for what it tells us about police. First, the phrase does not include all armed groups. The state of California changed gun laws in the 1960s after Bobby Seale, the co-founder of the Black Panther Party for Self Defense, led a group of Panthers into the California state house armed with unloaded rifles, pistols, and shotguns. Conservative legal scholars claim that the US Constitution establishes a durable right to gun ownership, but police only actively defend the rights of white gun owners. Second, the phrase captures a central claim by police regarding the character and condition of "good order." The order that police fabricate does not *occasionally* require violence, it *is* violence. Police kettle order to life (see **Kettling**, 210–212), choke it to life, and electrocute it to life. Police violence conjures order to life by taking life. Physical death by excited delirium (see **Taser**, 13–16). Social death by incarceration. Political death by disenfranchisement. The phrase "armed friendlies" captures all of this.

"Armed Friendlies" as a phrase that illustrates the reactionary rot of liberal police reformism. Liberalism, as a political ideology, will never confront fascism or fascists because liberals see fascism as they see police brutality, an aberrant act of a confused, individual **bad apple**

(224–227). The way to deal with it, according to liberals, is to condemn the individual while simultaneously celebrating, strengthening, and expanding the institutions where this so-called fringe minority flourish and find shelter. Liberalism requires a world baptized by law's violence, which, like Christian baptism, serves a purification function. Liberalism, particularly the American Exceptionalist version practiced in the United States, presents itself as free from coercion, authoritarianism, and arbitrary violence through its commitment to the rule of law.

> Historically, the process by which the bourgeoisie became in the course of the eighteenth century the politically dominant class was made possible by the establishment of an explicit, coded and formally egalitarian juridical framework, made possible by the organization of a parliamentary, representative regime.[1]

This promise of egalitarianism and freedom from coercion required "the development and generalization of disciplinary mechanisms [that] constituted the other, dark side of these processes."[2]

Liberalism's dark side looks a lot like fascism's public side. Fascism celebrates authoritarianism, violence, and racialized national belonging. Liberalism departs from this only in the way it compartmentalizes and disguises its violence as something illiberal or other-than-violence. Liberals don't separate migrant children from their families, they let law and cops do it. Liberals don't use violence in the street for political purposes, they let cops do it and judges ignore it. Liberalism refuses to confront fascism because fascism constitutes the ever-present dark side of liberal law and order. The phrase that describes all of this is "armed friendlies."

Patrol

It is difficult to see patrolling as a concept. It seems merely to describe the most common police activity. Patrol officers drive patrol cars in order to patrol streets and neighborhoods. As a police practice, it is usually presented as something that merely *takes place*—a standard activity undertaken in a given territory based on a set of preexisting "facts on the ground." There is **crime** (93–96), so police flood the area with patrol officers. Patrolling is what police do. It is self-evident and requires no explanation, and it magically elevates the level of public **order** (83–86) wherever it is practiced.

But none of this is true. In the most famous study of police patrols, the Kansas City Patrol Experiment, researchers increased patrols in one area, eliminated patrols in another, and kept patrols at already-existing levels in a third. They found no difference in reported crime rates as a result of different patrol patterns.[1] If this is true, why do police hold fast to the patrol? Perhaps it is because patrolling feeds the predatory hunger of police. Police are always out on the hunt and in **pursuit** (200–201), preying on neighborhoods and people, hunting dirtbags and checking for things out of place.

Despite what police may say, the patrol is not just a word that describes police activity, but a concept that explains the making of police power. The patrol asks us to consider the police as a set of activities, but we should instead understand the patrol as the way police know and name the world. Consider the origins of the word. It comes to us from the German *Patrolle*, or the French *patrouille*. To patrol, or *patrouiller*, means to tramp through the mud or, literally translated, to paddle in the dirty water. And so the police van is called the "paddy" wagon. The **slave patrol** (143–144) and early police were called "paddy rollers." The patrol, in other words, is not just a police tactic; it works to posit the disorder—the "muddy water" of a crime-infested neighborhood—through which policing justifies itself.

The concept of patrolling advances an idea of space as a set of fixed boundaries within which we find disorder in the absence of police. But what police call disorder does not exist independent of police knowledge of it. Patrol is as much about producing the unruly spaces that need police as it is about imposing order. So what then do we make of the patrol? The patrol should not be understood as a police strategy or tactic that merely responds to a set of seemingly independent, objective facts, such as crime. Rather it is through the concept of the patrol that the idea of disorder is given spatial form. It is through the patrol that certain neighborhoods come to be known to police as disorderly and in need of policing.

To say that the patrol gives spatial form to police power is to say that police *produce* space. What we think of as space is usually depicted as nothing more than a stage on which social life takes place. It is immutable and can be known absolutely. But space is not an empty vessel that comes to us fully formed; space is always political.[2] And yet the most spatial of all police practices, the patrol, is depicted as apolitical. It is merely an effective tactic to establish order. This is how James Q. Wilson and George Kelling describe what the patrol officer does: "Drunks and addicts could sit on the stoops, but could not lie down. People could drink on side streets, but not at the main intersection. Bottles had to be in paper bags. Talking to, bothering, or begging from people waiting at the bus stop was strictly forbidden. If a dispute erupted between a businessman and a customer, the businessman was assumed to be right, especially if the customer was a stranger. If a stranger loitered, [the cop] would ask him if he had any means of support and what his business was; if he gave unsatisfactory answers, he was sent on his way."[3] Patrolling, in other words, is a story about **private property** (81–83). How it is made, how it is defended, and how it comes to be so taken for granted that no discussion of its politics is even necessary.

The concept of the police patrol is a politics of space disguised as an apolitical, compulsory activity that must happen without question. The police patrol gives us the world we live in. This is among the reasons it is so difficult to talk about police. The concept of the patrol evacuates political content from any discussion of police and replaces it with a story of police as indispensable.

The Beat

The beat generally refers to a limited, geographical area in which a **cop** (219–221) is assigned to **patrol** (170–172), either by horse, bike, cruiser, or on foot. To be on duty is to be on the beat. The image of the beat cop or the neighborhood cop is among the most powerful organizing and legitimizing images of policing. The fantasy that there was once a friendly neighborhood cop who knew everyone's name and helped keep the peace while on the beat is the fairytale ideal against which policing in any present moment is always compared. The beat cop is the mythical hero of **order** (83–86) who once worked in the idyllic natural condition of policing to which reformers always demand a return. This Disneyland discourse of policing emerged alongside **broken windows** (186–189) and **community policing** (122–123) as a powerful narrative in the 1980s and 1990s.

The fable of the beat cop places its moral lesson in a geographic logic of racial capitalism. It depicts the truths of capitalism— racism, poverty, and police **violence** (96–100)—as unrelated to capitalism and instead a problem located in the **ghetto** (183–184), and tied to the problem of a criminality usually related to Blackness, Brownness, and Indigeneity. It depicts the solution to the problems of the capitalist city as hidden somewhere in the noble, selfless past of the police. And so it must be the cop, who must emerge from his cruiser, who must swing the **nightstick** (55–58) anew, who must return to the beat, who is our great white hope, who will restore order. Consider how police reformers tell the fairytale:

In the 1970s, American cities felt the consequences of the flight of white families (and others who could afford it) to the suburbs. This flight was in part a reaction to mounting center-city crime . . . Downtowns of many American cities became visibly populated by "street people" of ambiguous origin and vaguely threatening demeanor. "Urban campers" appeared with their cardboard tents in parks and underpasses all over the country. Many street people were apparently mentally disturbed. Where they came from and their actual numbers were subjects of considerable controversy. Some turned to aggressive panhandling while others scrounged through dumpsters for foot. They were attracted by the public facilities and relative safety of downtowns or commercial strips and transportation hubs, and gravitated toward areas where food, shelter and social services were available. This upset area residents and merchants who depended on attracting shoppers, and they demanded that something be done about it. Police inevitably were on the front line in dealing with them.[1]

This is a story of the city told in the passive voice. No one is to blame but the poor who remain. And look! There is the savior, the beat cop. And consider what the story says about what that beat cop is supposed to already know about the city, about **crime** (93–96), and about the job of policing. First, the cop is to understand that the problem of urban crime finds its origins in white flight. In other words, when white people left, crime arrived. Or better yet, the presence of crime is the absence of white people. Next, the homeless and desperately poor are to be understood as of "ambiguous origin," which is a way of saying that the poor always *come from somewhere else*, and this means of course that they never belong *where they are*. They exist independent of the forces and conditions that created the category "homeless." And lastly, all of this threatens commerce, which is what makes it a police problem.

And the solution is the beat. Walking a beat "enables [the cop] to learn about the area and its problems and to become familiar with local hot spots and alternating cycles of troublesome and trouble-free times of day. The reconfiguration also allows them to focus their attention on area residents and issues that concern them specifically."[2] So the beat allows the cop to "learn about the area," but the parable of the beat already has a plot and a cast of characters. There are the "urban campers," many of whom are "mentally disturbed." They are an enemy presence. They have infiltrated a city in which they don't belong. It is the beat cop who will wage a **war** (100–102) "on the front line" to remove them. And there are the shopkeepers, desperate for police protection in a city suddenly without enough white people. And there are the Black and Brown people who live in the former white neighborhoods, which are now called "hot spots," which must be patrolled by the beat cop.

And the point of all this, the point of the beat, is to "take back the streets." The beat seeks to restore order to the city by removing the homeless, by policing the poor, and by targeting Black and Brown people. Without resistance, the beat will make the city white again. Just you wait and see.

Investigation

The special ability police claim in solving **crime** (93–96) through investigation is celebrated as among their most important activities. The investigative power of the police is where the criminal justice system begins. Investigation conjures images of grizzled detectives stalking criminal perps and suspects, chasing down leads and sniffing out clues; or scientific crime scene investigators combing through crime scenes, collecting DNA samples and piecing together evidence. But this is merely a Hollywood fantasy that police are happy to cultivate. Investigation rarely leads to **arrest** (208–210), much less conviction. Most arrests require no investigation whatsoever. Cops don't solve crime, informants do. A suspect, if one is arrested, is most often arrested on the scene of a crime. Frequently a victim or an eyewitness identifies a suspect. This accounts for around 80 percent of all arrests. This leaves 20 percent of "initially unsolved cases" in which, according to a Rand corporation study, investigators play no predominant role.[1] Most "unsolved" cases were eventually "solved," if at all, by passersby or by a witness. In other words, cops "solve" crime *randomly*, not systematically, and usually during a **traffic stop** (73–75), at a **checkpoint** (75–77), or during a **stop and frisk** (27–31).

Forget about crime scene investigation. Special units scour crime scenes for fingerprints and hair samples, conduct ballistics analyses of weapons, and take photographs of everyone and everything. The proliferation of science and technology-driven policing, however, has little effect. This is partly because forensic science is not science. The National Academy of Sciences concluded that the basic procedures behind forensic science are not meaningfully scientific.[2] Fingerprints are not unique. Bite marks do not match an individual's dental characteristics in any scientifically reliable way. Ballistics analyses of weapons cannot systematically match bullets fired from specific weapons. Hair samples do not place an individual at a crime scene. According to the Innocence Project, 60 percent of people exonerated of crimes by DNA evidence were originally convicted of those crimes based on testimony from, and evidence collected by, police forensic scientists.[3] And even when

DNA evidence is collected, it does not follow that police will conduct an investigation. Few police departments devote sufficient resources to manage DNA evidence. In New Mexico, more than 5,000 sexual assault evidence kits, some dating back to the 1980s, languish in police department evidence rooms, untested and unused in criminal investigation.[4] Nearly 7,000 **rape** (41–43) kits sit in evidence rooms in Houston, 12,000 in Memphis, 11,000 in Detroit, and 17,000 in Manhattan.[5]

The fantasy of the CSI unit and the clever detective hot on the trail serves an important function. It extends an authority and gravitas to an otherwise futile and insignificant enterprise. Police rely on this fantasy and trade on its authority whenever they put an innocent person in jail based on a "scientific" investigation.

Discretion

Discretion is the legal authority extended to police to decide what should be done in a particular situation. It refers to the police powers in general: where to **patrol** (170–172), when to use **force** (102–104), who to **arrest** (208–210), who to kill or let live. Considered this way, discretion is just another word for enforcement, one that recognizes the limits of law's reach. After all, what does it matter if **law** (90–93) declares an act unlawful, unless there are police standing by and ready to enforce it? Discretion proposes a view of police as the specialized means to a predefined legal end.

The concept of discretion, however, does more than merely depict police as a means to an end. The concept includes an implicit assumption that the enforcement of law requires special knowledge, skills, and experience. You may know the law, but who knows how to enforce it? Police, we're told. That's who. Thus discretion is two things at once. It is a legal concept that limits the police powers to only those actions that enforce a predetermined law. But it also extends to police the unlimited choice of how to do this. This is why there is little a **cop** (219–221) can do that the law won't find lawful as long as a cop does it while pursuing the ends of good order (83–86). And since only police possess the specialized skill and knowledge necessary to defend order, only police can define discretion. Indeed, courts have consistently refused to define police discretion, since to define discretion would be to limit the power of police.[1] Moreover, part of this reasoning is premised on the idea that there cannot be predetermined, universal codes for handling "police situations," and therefore police are granted nearly unlimited discretion to best handle an incident.

Discretion, then, is the key to understanding the police power as an executive power, and cops as "petty sovereigns" or "everyday executives." Contrary to liberal thought that sees police in liberal democracies as accountable to law, police power is never meant to be restricted by law, and it is the category of discretion that makes this apparent. Rather, police power is the routine application of what John Locke called the prerogative, or the executive power of the sovereign to be free from legal constraints. This is based on the sovereign claim as the sole authority regarding what constitutes an **emergency** (223–224) and **threat** (222–223) to "the public good." Cops have nearly unlimited discretionary power to decide who or what is a threat or emergency and what is the most appropriate or necessary method of response. Even legal concepts such as probable cause and **reasonable suspicion** (255–257), which claim to limit discretion, actually license police intervention. The folk wisdom that police can always find a reason to stop you rings true, especially for those most subjected to the police power.

It is because of discretion that a cop can shoot and kill a twelve-year-old boy on a playground while the boy plays with a toy gun and the law calls that "reasonable under the circumstances." It is because of discretion that a grand jury will refuse to indict a cop who chokes a man to death on the street because the man was selling cigarettes. Discretion does not limit police **violence** (96–100), it justifies police violence as always violence for legal ends. This is true because, as Walter Benjamin explains, discretion comes "with the simultaneous authority to decide these ends itself within wide limits."[2] And as Benjamin makes clear, "The assertion that the ends of police violence are always identical or even connected to those of general law is entirely untrue."[3] In the authority to choose how to enforce **security** (86–89) is an authority to make law itself.

Discretion is often depicted as something cops *use* or *apply*, but it is more accurate to depict discretion as a concept that police *construct* and *defend*. The concept of discretion serves an important political purpose. It limits any consideration of police to individual cops who enforce the law. There is no institution; there are only cops in **uniform** (141–143). Discretion brings the cop into focus while leaving police obscured. This makes any problems with police always only problems of individuals. There may be **bad apples** (224–227), there may be instances of **police brutality** (207 208), but this has nothing to do with police, we're told. This is why discretion has to be understood as a logic of the state, and not merely something individual cops use. Discretion reserves for police an enormous and totalizing authority. Consider the implication. Law establishes what is unlawful in the present and gives to police the authority to choose how to enforce the law in the future. Discretion is law's justification today of police violence tomorrow.

Predictive Policing

Predictive policing refers to the use of computer algorithms based on multivariate geospatial data to model or predict criminal activity. As a theory it fits within what is known as "intelligence-led policing," a mode of policing based on the analysis of quantitative geospatial data, such as **CompStat** (180–182).

Advocates of predictive policing claim that it is scientific, and therefore an objective and unbiased way to fight **crime** (93–96). Its origins are usually found in the 2008 efforts of former Boston, New York and Los Angeles police chief William Bratton who, along with a number of federal agencies, inaugurated a series of symposia on the use of predictive analytics in policing. But efforts to use quantitative geospatial data to map and predict crime go back much further. Predictability emerged in the US as a guiding principle of parole and probation during the 1930s and 1940s, and from there spread into other sectors. And computer software and hardware firms such as Esri and IBM have been developing crime prediction programs since the 1990s. One of the most popular programs currently in use, PredPol, is based on algorithms developed by a research team that includes computer scientists, anthropologists and mathematicians. PredPol, which has raised millions of dollars in venture capital since its launch in 2012, includes advisors from the CIA's venture capital firm, In-Q-Tel, and is in use by dozens of US police departments, including in Los Angeles and Atlanta.[1] Its proponents celebrate it as a "magical" mode of law enforcement they describe as "sci-fi" or "crystal ball" policing.

PredPol's algorithms predict crime based on the idea that criminal activity and seismic activity share similar patterns. PredPol co-founder George Mohler, a professor of mathematics at Santa Clara University, argues that earthquakes are usually followed by aftershocks. These are "clustering patterns" that Mohler's algorithms assume are true also of crime. Mohler claims crime is always followed by what we might call *aftercrimes*, and further, that research in **criminology** (261–263) demonstrates that crime is like a virus that spreads like a contagion. In other words, if crime patterns behave like earthquakes or viruses, then predictive policing deserves the same scientific status as seismology and epidemiology.

The rhetorical purpose of PredPol's claims to science serves a very specific legal effect. At the heart of legal challenges to the police practice of **stop and frisk** (27–31), for example, is skepticism of police claims to prediction. In other words, it is the belief that it is **racial profiling** (24–27), and not knowledge of future crimes, that determines who police choose to stop and frisk. Predictive policing, however, provides seemingly objective data for police to engage in those same practices but in a manner that appears free from racial profiling.

Predictive policing exposes the liberal state's desire for knowledge and intelligence of not merely the past, but the future. We might also reverse this and say predictive policing helps to illuminate a fundamental state anxiety: the fear of *not* knowing or the fear of the unknown. Predictive policing, then, demonstrates the ways police power tries to predict the future out of the fear of the unknown, and so it shouldn't be a surprise that predictive policing locates the **violence** (96–100) of the future in the poor of the present.

CompStat

CompStat, which combines the words "computer" and "statistics," has nothing to do with computers or statistics. It is a neologism that describes a police management philosophy that prescribes the aggressive policing of the poor, usually people of color, as a way to establish **order** (83–86).

CompStat began as a **police reform** (155–160) measure in New York City under William Bratton in 1994. This is how Bratton described the purpose and outcome of CompStat: "We can all celebrate the fact that due to our collective efforts, **crime** (93–96) has been significantly reduced on both sides of the Atlantic. Our insistence that 'Cops Count' is supported by the fact that when properly led, well trained and sufficiently equipped, the police can modify the behavior of the criminal element in our communities. Beyond the saving of lives and the reduction of crime and its victims, we can also appropriately take credit for helping to inject new quality-of-life initiatives into our inner cities, for spurring economic development and for returning large tracts of the urban landscape to the **law** (90–93) abiding."[1]

We could rewrite Bratton's statement as follows: Crime rates accurately describe the behavior of criminals. Police **violence** (96–100) deters this behavior. And this produces order, which is understood as the spatial and social exclusion of the poor from the city through **arrest** (208–210) and incarceration in order to reserve the city for those with economic means.

The whole premise of CompStat begins with the idea that crime rates map criminal behavior and that a drop in crime rates is the miraculous accomplishment of police management. This is claimed as the central success of CompStat, and it's how Bratton became a media darling. He was depicted on the cover of *Time* magazine in a 1996 story that credited him for a dramatic drop in crime in New York: "The drop became a giddy double-digit affair, plunging farther and faster than it has done anywhere else in the country, faster than any cultural or demographic trend could explain. For two years, crime has declined in all 76 precincts."[2] Crime rates, as Bratton and *Time* understand them, are an objective representation of illegal activity. The more illegal activity in a given area, the more arrests in that area, and therefore the higher the crime rate in that area.

Bratton developed CompStat as a way to implement and institutionalize **broken windows** (186–189) policing, which assumes that crime is a function of urban disorder characterized by general lawlessness. In order to create order, police must oppose all forms of "lawlessness," especially the most trivial. CompStat borrowed the broken windows focus on minor crimes, such as jaywalking, littering, public urination, graffiti, and the like, in order to focus police activity around practices designed to enhance what police call "quality of life." This approach assumes that a relationship exists between these minor crimes and more serious ones. Thus CompStat takes credit for any measurable "reduction" in crime rates as a function of the "lawfulness" produced by the deterrent effect of intensified police power directed at the poor.

This is a self-serving premise. Most crime rate statistics are based largely on police arrests, and thus crime rates are a depiction of police behavior, not criminal behavior. Proponents of broken windows policing might reluctantly agree with this statement, but argue that since the police *only* arrest those they suspect of having committed a crime, crime rates still serve as a useful measure of illegal activity. But police arrest or don't arrest, **patrol** (170–172) or don't patrol, target for **stop and frisk** (27–31) or don't target for stop and frisk, always at their own **discretion** (176–178). These are choices by individual police officers, choices that become enforced and monitored by CompStat command and control procedures. Command and control is not just about crime, but about making cops more efficient and prone to make arrests, since they are often judged based on how many people they stop and frisk or pull over and arrest. Individual officer discretion must be understood as always caught within a larger matrix of command and control, and hence the individual actions of cops are always really collective, coordinated actions that result in the very patterns CompStat seeks to impose: some people get arrested and some do not, some groups get targeted and some do not, some neighborhoods come under scrutiny and some do not. This is not about order per se; this is an effort to impose "a new moral order on the poor."[3] Therefore it is not accurate to say that crime rates objectively reveal criminal activity; rather, it is only accurate to say that crime rates describe the social and spatial patterns of the police.

In addition, "crime rates" have a long and notorious history in the promulgation of racist public policy. In the 1960s, Republicans and southern Democrats explained their opposition to the 1964 Civil Rights Act in the rising "crime rates" that they said followed Black civil rights struggles.[4] "Violent crime rates in the nation's biggest cities," according to historian Khalil Gibran Muhammad, "are generally understood as a reflection of the presence and behavior of the black men, women, and children who live there."[5] Crime rates, in other words, reflect racialized patterns of policing, often called stop-and-frisk or quality-of-life policing, which describe the primary approach of CompStat. Police focus their activities in predominately Black and Brown neighborhoods, which results in high arrest rates compared to predominantly white neighborhoods, which reinforces the idea that Black and Brown neighborhoods harbor criminal elements, which conflates Blackness and criminality, which under CompStat leads to even more intensified policing that results in arrest and incarceration, which serves the interests of private capital, which creates the conditions for **gentrification** (184–186). CompStat is policing as capitalist urban redevelopment.

The logic of CompStat was transported to Iraq by the US Army and renamed TERRORSTAT. Broken windows policing is thus a mode of counterinsurgency warfare. Like military counterinsurgency or domestic **community policing** (122–123), CompStat seeks to legitimize police power by penetrating every aspect of life in the city. And since what CompStat claims as its focus—a drop in hypothetical future crime based on some vague relationship to quality of life— nothing, no activity, is ever beyond the police purview. CompStat is policing as domestic, urban counterinsurgency.

Ghetto

Ghetto might come to us from the Italian "borghetto," meaning little town, or it might refer to the Venetian "ghèto," meaning foundry. Whatever its origins, the geography makes sense since we find the first ghetto in Venice in the early sixteenth century. For much of its first few hundred years, a ghetto referred always to a forced enclosure of Jewish people. The ghetto was the home of Jews who were expelled from England in the thirteenth century, and then banished to heavily policed districts in Rome by Pope Pius IV. The Jewish ghetto, in other words, was a place of internment. High walls and Christian guards defined the Venetian ghetto. A ghetto is a spatial enclosure, enforced by the state, designed to control the movement of a specific population.

The Jewish ghetto was an outdoor prison, later perfected by the Nazis. But contemporary use of the word ghetto is generally stripped of this carceral character. A ghetto is just a slum, a place where poor people choose to live. There are no Christian guards closing the gates each night. But this usage conceals the physical coercion and spatial control at the heart of ghetto. In much of the world, the ghetto is a space of social control for poor people. Post-slavery urbanity for Black people in the United States, particularly in Northern cities, was defined by social and spatial exclusion. The idea that the Black ghetto was a neighborhood of choice based on racial and class affinity, and not a function of brute **force** (102–104) and an engine of dispossession, is "segregationist nostalgia [that] ignores the actual conditions endured by the people living there—vermin and arson, for instance—and ignores the fact that the old ghetto was premised on denying black people privileges enjoyed by white Americans."[1]

Police **patrol** (170–172) a district. Police work a **beat** (172–174). Police use force. And the force police use depends on the space they patrol. It is not enough to say that through police the state extends its power over a given territory. The police powers fabricate **order** (83–86) because the police powers *produce* space. The ghetto perfectly illustrates the spatial effects of police power. Just as there could be no Jewish ghetto without Christian guards or Nazi planners and military personnel, there can be no Black ghetto without police. But police ask us to understand this quite differently. Police, we're told, don't make the ghetto; police patrol **crime**-infested (93–96) neighborhoods. But space isn't just inhabited; it is made. It is carried out. Thus to say that policing is a territorial logic is not merely to say that the police powers occur in and across space, but rather it is to say that police carry out police practices—**arrest** (208–210), the use of force, **stop and frisk** (27–31)—in ways that literally make space. Police make and remake the ghetto through **racial profiling** (24–27), which requires spatial profiling. Police identify people who appear out of place and thus become suspicious to police, and this requires more police, more patrols, more surveillance. Police make and remake the ghetto through **broken windows** (186–189) policing, which imagines a space constantly at risk by dangerous people in dangerous places. "The only way to police a ghetto," James Baldwin wrote, "is to be oppressive."[2]

Baldwin wrote that the Black residents of Harlem didn't hate the ghetto because of "disorder" and didn't look to police to rescue them from "crime." The "very presence [of police in Harlem] is an insult, and it would be, even if they spent their entire day feeding gumdrops to children. They represent the force of the white world, and that world's real intentions are, simply, for that world's criminal profit and ease, to keep the black man corralled up here, in his place. The **badge** (106–110), the **gun** (10–13) in the holster, and the swinging club make vivid what will happen should his rebellion become overt."[3] The ghetto, the favela, the shantytown is a prison, and cops are the prison guards.

Gentrification
Police play a fundamental role in making urban space. Police manage the organized displacement of poor people in order to make way for low-income artists, students and hipsters, followed by more affluent white renters, homeowners, and commercial investors. For commercial developers, city planners and politicians, gentrification is the transformation of "blighted" urban space. It is progress because what was once "abandoned" to the poor is now reserved for the affluent. Gentrification increases property values and profits

for landlords and local elites. The urban poor who are systematically evicted from their neighborhoods know that gentrification is not progress. Gentrification is revanchist urbanism: the exacting of revenge against urban undesirables—the homeless, petty criminals, prostitutes, drug users, street youth, and squatters—who stand in the way of a world of privilege and luxury, also known as the investment-backed expectations of real estate speculators. The word gentrification comes from the idea of "the gentry," or the landowning classes. Gentrification is always about the transformation of land use, ownership and the city in the image of the wealthy.

Gentrification, as Neil Smith writes, "portends a class conquest of the city" with appeals for "taking back the streets" in the name of "urban redevelopment" or "reinvestment" in communities that have historically experienced disinvestment in good paying jobs and social infrastructure.[1] Although bohemians looking for cheaper rents are often blamed for gentrification, this view mistakes gentrification as only about the individual preferences for particular places of new residents. Rather, gentrification is a geopolitical and geo-economic process of capital, and not merely people, moving back to the city. Gentrification, then, is capital on the move, and must be understood as a process of uneven development that begins with disinvestment. The historical process of white flight from urban spaces to suburbia, and the disinvestment that followed, including decades of intensive policing of the **ghetto** (183–184), produced the conditions for capital's return: the revanchist city. This revanchist gentrification by capital activates, and is activated by, classed and racialized scripts of degeneracy, often through colonial mythologies of the "Wild West frontier," of "cowboys and Indians," and of courageous but innocent "pioneers" occupying savage spaces. Gentrification becomes a project of civilization, with police often leading the charge by "cleaning up" **public** (252–255) space to secure capital investments and **private property** (81–83) by the forced removal of poor people and activists. The **violence** (96–100) of economies and the economies of violence animate this spatialization of class interests.

Gentrification is always propped up with racialized violence. Police are the armed agents that make so-called revitalization possible in the first place. You can't have gentrification without police, and zero tolerance and **broken windows** (186–189) policing have been at the forefront. Gentrification needs cops because capitalism needs cops. There is perhaps no better example than gentrification to highlight the productive nature of police power. That is, if police power is fundamentally about the fabrication of capitalist **order** (83–86), gentrification provides the grounded site where this is most visible and obvious.[2] The raid, sweep, **arrest** (208–210), eviction, patrol, and police beatings and killings are key weapons of gentrification that make possible the art galleries, yoga studios, gastropubs, and posh bars and restaurants frequented by affluent customers. When rent and property taxes rise, who is called to evict the poor family? Cops. When affluent consumers complain about panhandlers, who is called to evict the disorderly person from the sidewalk? Cops. Who **patrols** (170–172) the revitalized area, keeping a close eye on the burgeoning business fronts? Cops. The policing of gentrification is at once repressive and productive— the violence of police is the violence of building order.

Broken Windows

The phrase "broken windows" in the context of policing refers to a theory of social **order** (83–86) first developed by James Q. Wilson and George L. Kelling in a 1982 *Atlantic Monthly* article in which they depicted "improperly maintained buildings, and broken windows on buildings and cars" as signs of social disruption that, unless addressed, gave implicit license to criminal activity. "Social psychologists and police officers tend to agree that if a window in a building is broken and is left unrepaired, all the rest of the windows will soon be broken."[1] For Wilson and Kelling, one broken window in one building on one street threatens the very fabric of social order and civility.

This theory of broken windows today justifies all manner of aggressive police tactics targeting the poor, often masquerading under the name of **community policing** (122–123). The proponents of broken windows argue that the theory is based on a series of axiomatic statements that go without saying—or should at least go without question—and provide the rationale for the intensive, aggressive policing that has become known as broken windows. These axioms could be defined as follows:

Axiom #1: **Crime** (93–96) and disorder are "inextricably linked," according to Wilson and Kelling, and therefore signs of disorder such as broken windows signal a "breakdown of community controls," which leads to an increase in crime.

Axiom #2: Even if the disorder of broken windows does not lead to an increase in crime, residents *will think it has* and will "modify their behavior accordingly. They will use the streets less often, and when on the streets will stay apart from their fellows, moving with averted eyes, silent lips, and hurried steps."[2]

Axiom #3: Broken windows will result in an increase in crime or a decline in civic life, and either way we will find a deterioration in quality of life, what we will call "urban decay," a condition defined by despair and incivility not dissimilar to previous eras but distinct today because police no longer engage in the maintenance of order and instead focus entirely on crime fighting. In an earlier period, police would impose order in a community "sometimes violently, on behalf of the community. Young toughs were roughed up, people were **arrested** (208–210) 'on suspicion' or for **vagrancy** (189–193), and prostitutes and petty thieves were routed."[3] But the shift from the maintenance of order to law enforcement has left a vacuum.

Axiom #4: Everyone desires order, and order in the city is defined by the values of the community, which are enforced by police. "The citizen who fears the ill-smelling drunk, the rowdy teenager, or the importuning beggar is not merely expressing his distaste for unseemly behavior; he is also giving voice to a bit of folk wisdom that happens to be a correct generalization—namely, that serious street crime flourishes in areas in which disorderly behavior goes unchecked."[4]

Axiom #5: And finally, society "wants an officer to have the legal tools to remove undesirable persons from a neighborhood when informal efforts to preserve order in the streets have failed."[5]

These five axioms are less a theory of broken windows policing than a version of conservative morality imposed by police on the poor—the "importuning beggars" and "prostitutes and petty thieves" who by their very presence threaten the bourgeois order broken windows policing seeks to create. As axiomatic statements, they offer a Hobbesian theory of human nature in which uncivilized, selfish impulses drive behavior. People only behave properly when in the presence of an authoritarian police force, and the threat of violent retaliation that police represent. Broken windows theory is consistent with all conservative social theory in that it is shot through with a wistful nostalgia for an imagined past in which people knew their place and cops did their job. And police of course *must* focus on the poor because, like most conservatives, Wilson and Kelling are "deeply skeptical of the ability of the poor to manage themselves in a civil manner" and so they blame "the moral failings of poor, mostly non-white communities" for everything "wrong" with the city.[6] To the conservative, there is no such thing as poverty, there are only the poor, who individually break windows and collectively produce disorder through their various and many moral failings. They turn tricks, beg for dimes, break windows and frighten the affluent.

Broken windows theory finds the origins of disorder in the 1960s, which to Wilson and Kelling was not the era of civil rights struggle, but a decade of rising crime that flooded American cities with a great wave of disorder. This is why conservative social theory relies on law (90–93) and order. Broken windows theory despises the impolite subject and sends police out into the streets to punish them.

William Bratton, a former police chief in Boston, New York and Los Angeles, was among the most prominent leaders to subscribe to broken windows policing. It was Bratton who brought zero tolerance to the theory. No infraction, no matter how trivial, must go unpunished. Crack down on jaywalking and littering, goes the theory, or watch the murder rate increase.

Broken windows policing reveals the police as not merely coercive and repressive, but productive in that police seek to manufacture a very specific kind of order—one where cities are populated by families and married couples who maintain property, hold down jobs, own homes and raise polite children. It is an order that demands how a place should look, describes what kind of people belong, and targets those who must be excluded. The behaviors that wage labor permits—shopping for groceries, paying your mortgage, buying a ticket to the zoo—are admired. The behaviors that poverty imposes—sex work, panhandling, street vending—are pathologized and policed. The protagonists of broken windows policing are the shopkeepers and taxpayers and property owners whose labor and consumption is productive. They are depicted as cowering in fear from the antagonists of broken windows policing: the woman walking the street, the man selling single cigarettes, and the homeless vet asking for a dollar. Broken windows theory asks us to fear them, teaches us to loathe them.

But this is all just a scam. Broken windows is a street hustle. Bratton and his crowd have us in a game of three-card monte and we keep picking the wrong card, the one depicting a fearful, respectable homeowner, and an earnest property tax payer sweeping broken glass from a stoop. But broken windows policing is not about them; that's just the card they want us to pick. The card they keep palming—the "money card"—is the one that depicts the investment banker, the mortgage broker, and the real estate speculator, who have big plans and investment-backed expectations, but only if broken windows policing can remove the poor. So Wilson and Kelling keep dealing the cards, and Bratton plays the shill, and we're the mark.

Vagrancy

The vagrant is the enemy of police. The police forever hunt the vagrant, see the vagrant everywhere. The police power and the vagrant are bound together, each unthinkable without the other, and it is the intertwined problems of poverty and labor that bind them together. Vagrancy is a **crime** (93–96) of status. It is a crime to be a vagrant and police define who and what one is.[1] The vagrant is a problem for police not necessarily because of his or her actions or for being guilty of a crime, but first and foremost for being poor. The policing of vagabondage, then, provides an exemplar of the police power's administration and criminalization of poverty under capitalism.

In sixteenth- and seventeenth- century England, vagrancy laws emerged as a response to various social disruptions. The most significant of these was the growing *landless* class of uprooted people that emerged from a crumbling feudal order. Thousands upon thousands of "vagrants," and people in other associated categories such as "beggars," "paupers," "prostitutes," and "gypsies," were subjected to intensive legal and state intervention. As the peasant class broke their feudal chains to become "free" to sell their labor for a wage on the new market economy, they found themselves subjected to what Marx famously called the "bloody legislation against vagabondage":

> On the one hand, these men, suddenly dragged from their accustomed mode of life, could not immediately adapt themselves to the discipline of their new condition. They were turned in massive quantities into beggars, robbers and vagabonds . . . hence at the end of the fifteenth and during the whole of the sixteenth centuries, a bloody legislation against vagabondage was enforced throughout Western Europe. The fathers of the present working class were chastised for their enforced transformation into vagabonds and paupers.[2]

This bloody legislation was part and parcel of the **violence** (96–100) of primitive accumulation, and key to this dispossession was the police power, understood as a broad state logic that predated the police as such but remained operative once this institution formed. The central mandate of the police power was to fabricate a general state of prosperity by administering a social order of **private property** (81–83), wage labor, and capital accumulation. Vagabondage was a fundamental **threat** (222–223) to these things. The hunting and capturing of vagrants across Europe, we might say, was the "founding act" of police power, and vagrancy would continue to be a central object of police **pursuit** (200–201) in essentially every historical stage of the police.[3]

Vagrants were said to be "masterless men" because they were idle, lazy, wandering, lawless and dangerous. Vagrants are defined in essence by what they are said to lack. But vagrants are not merely isolated individuals. The vagrant has always been understood as a *class* of the poor, defined by those who refuse to regularly work for a consistent wage even though they are able.

As understood by political and cultural elites at the time, vagrancy was a grave disorder threatening the nascent capitalist order. Vagrants, then, were not merely ordinary criminals that needed some regulation. This growing class of masterless men became the primary enemy in the social war to secure capitalist accumulation, and it was the entire state apparatus of laws such as the Poor Law, workhouses, police, and jails that were charged with mastering the masterless. Vagrancy laws and police statutes were **pacification** (89–90) laws, impositions of work to be enforced by police power, to compel subjects to work, which is to say to produce not merely docile citizens, but docile, rational, and obedient *workers*.

The problem of vagrancy also played a crucial role in the policing and criminalization of freed slaves in the years after chattel slavery was abolished. Freed slaves found themselves freed from slave labor only to sell their labor on the free market. Like the vagrants of Western Europe they found themselves subjected to a version of bloody legislation called the Black Codes. These laws and ordinances were specifically designed, as W. E. B. Du Bois wrote in *Black Reconstruction*, "to make Negroes slaves in everything but name."

> Yet, in the face of this, the Black Codes were deliberately designed to take advantage of every misfortune of the Negro. Negroes were liable to a slave trade under the guise of vagrancy and apprenticeship laws; to make the best labor contracts, Negroes must leave the old plantations and seek better terms; but if caught wandering in search of work, and thus unemployed and without a home, this was vagrancy, and the victim could be whipped and sold into slavery.[3]

As Du Bois makes clear, the mandate of the Black Codes such as **curfew** (38–41) and vagrancy laws was to keep freedmen in an exploitive wage relationship that would maintain their condition of poverty and, for many, slavery in all but name. From the **slave**

patrol (143–144) came the nascent police **force** (102–104) armed with the newly formed vagrancy laws and Black Codes. At times vagrancy laws were not overtly racial, but their application was first and foremost racist as they directly assisted in the political economy of convict leasing and the larger legal order of Jim Crow.

In postwar America during the 1950s and 1960s, vagrancy was a widely used police justification to intervene in the lives of not only the poor, but of those people identified by police as civil rights or anti-war activists, working-class queers, and immigrants. The police use of vagrancy law was not isolated to urban geography, as rural police also often resorted to it. When police sought a nearly foolproof justification to arrest virtually anyone, they found it in vagrancy. Eventually, the Supreme Court struck down vagrancy laws in the early 1970s, at least on the surface. But the broad **discretionary** (176–178) powers of police were sustained.

Vagrancy, vagrants, and vagabondage are not commonly used terms in popular culture or legal doctrine today, but the figure of the vagrant remains a prime object of police power under different names. Police identify people as vagrant-like objects through a very telling vocabulary: the "suspicious person" or "panhandler" or "inebriate," among other terms. Indeed, a central lesson of vagrancy is that vagrancy remains an indispensable police category largely by its vagueness and mutability. Wherever there is police power there will be some criminalized vagrant-like character living outside the wage relation or in search of it. And vagrants are never simply vagrants; they are always merging with other transgressive figures, such as those who cross national borders in search of work. The migrant-as-criminal who is policed as a criminal due only to the status of the migrant-as-migrant must also be seen as belonging to the history of vagrant policing. The modern-day vagrants are also those unemployed workers who have been "laid off" due to capital flight overseas or the austerity of "budget cuts." Or the homeless populations on Skid Row or the destitute loiterers on street corners. Or the prostitutes walking the streets and the hitchhikers wandering the highways. The day laborers and squeegee men of the urban city are also modern-day vagrants. Florida **rent-a-cop** (144–146) George Zimmerman deemed Trayvon Martin a **threat**

(222–223) partly due to his appearing a vagrant as the seventeen-year-old Martin walked through a gated community while wearing a modern day symbol of vagrant thuggery, the hoodie. As long as police haunt urban space, there will be the specter of the vagrant.

Interrogation

Police interrogation is confession-taking. The practice is the single most important factor in police criminal **Investigations** (175–176). "Prosecutors make significant charging decisions, plea bargaining moves, arguments to juries, and sometimes even sentencing recommendations based on confession evidence alone."[1] The most widely used police interrogation training manual explains that taking confessions is so important that the "prosecution may even secure a conviction on the basis of an oral, unwritten, or unrecorded confession with very little corroborating evidence."[2]

And it happens entirely behind closed doors, hidden from view, in windowless interrogation rooms called "the box" where police "exercise and mystify their power."[3] Police confession-taking is openly organized around duplicity and deception. Police create an oppressive atmosphere in the interrogation room in order to carefully stage a drama designed to foreclose any alternative to confession. Police are trained to lie, to deceive, to trick, to play on your greatest fear and your deepest shame. The 1931 Wickersham commission, a federal investigation into police practices, noted that "the inflicting of pain, physical or mental, to extract confessions or statements . . . is widespread throughout the country." **Police reformer** (155–160) August Vollmer, the author of the Wickersham report, wrote a preface to a 1940 interrogation manual that taught police to use emotional manipulation and deception. The police interrogator lies in order to produce the "truth."

A sixteen-year-old confessed to police of the murder of William Gaitan in Los Angeles in 2011, but video evidence placed him miles from the killing.[4] A fourteen-year-old boy, later proven innocent, initially confessed to police of the murder of his twelve-year-old sister in 1998 after police convinced him that he did it but just couldn't remember the act. According to the Innocence Project more than 25 percent of people exonerated of **crimes** (93–96) for which they were convicted initially confessed to the crime during a police interrogation.

Given the uncertainty surrounding confessions and the duplicity of police, what explains the overwhelming legal importance placed on confessions by prosecutors, juries, and judges? How can confessions be simultaneously unreliable and beyond legal reproach? Police training manuals explain that the confidence in confessions lies in the **public** (252–255) trust invested in police. This may be true, but not for the reasons police imagine. The police are a "confession-taking" power, and this is a power with a long political history. The obligatory practice of Christian confession, which first began in the thirteenth century, gave rise to the act of confession as a permanent feature of modern life. Michel Foucault considered confession "one of the West's most highly valued techniques for producing truth." As he argued:

> The confession has spread its effects far and wide. It plays a part in justice, medicine, education, family relationships, and love relations, in the most ordinary affairs of everyday life, and in the most solemn rites; one confesses one's crimes, one's sins, one's thoughts and desires, one's illnesses and troubles; one goes about telling, with the greatest precision, whatever is most difficult to tell. One confesses in public and in private, to one's parents, one's educators, one's doctor, to those one loves; one admits to oneself, in pleasure and in pain, things it would be impossible to tell to anyone else, the things people write books about. One confesses—or is forced to confess. When it is not spontaneous or dictated by some internal imperative, the confession is wrung from a person by violence or threat; it is driven from its hiding place in the soul, or extracted from the body.[5]

It is through confession, we learn, that the authentic version of oneself comes into view. "Tell me the truth of yourself so I can know you," we are told. Whether extracted by priest or police, a confession is imagined as always an unmasking, a revealing of a hidden truth. When finally released by confession and captured by police, truth is established. There is no recanting. There cannot be because it is the only real thing we know about you. From religious confession emerges the pious; from police confession emerges the criminal.

Police confession-taking is not limited to the interrogation room. We are always confessing, because police are always interrogating. All communication between **cop** (219–221) and citizen is an interrogation. The **stop and frisk** (27–31) on the street ("What are you doing here?"), the traffic cop ("Do you know why I pulled you over"?). **Community policing** (122–123), for example, means constant interrogation: walking the neighborhood, visiting schools, playing midnight basketball with kids, asking how things are going.

Police interrogation is a **pursuit** (200–201), a manhunt, and the prey is the *true* you. But what can "true" mean when we learn that deception and **violence** (96–100), or the **threat** (222–223) of violence, lies at the heart of police confession-taking? It means that confession-taking is not about truth-seeking, it is about power.

Foucault called confession "the effect of a power that constrains us."[6] Sometimes that constraint takes the form of a **handcuff** (20–21) to a hot radiator. This is how Jon Burge tortured confessions out of hundreds of Black men in Chicago from 1972 until 1991. Burge, a Chicago Police Department detective, first learned the principles of confession-taking in the US Army while serving in Vietnam and brought this practice with him to Chicago where he ran a squad of detectives who routinely took suspects into basement interrogation rooms and beat them with phone books and poked them with cattle prods (see **Taser**, 13–16). They attached wires coming from small hand-crank generators to the faces and genitals of their victims and electrocuted them. They burned them with cigarettes, beat them with their fists, and waterboarded them before waterboarding had a name. This is the truth of interrogation.

Good Cop, Bad Cop

The phrase "good **cop** (219–221), bad cop" usually refers to a police **interrogation** (193–195) tactic in which two police officers, one acting kindly and one more harshly, interrogate a suspect. The **threat** (222–223) of **violence** (96–100) by the bad cop toward the suspect is intended to generate fear as a way to secure a confession from the suspect. The role of the good cop in this drama is to impress upon the suspect the need to confess as the only way to avoid the violence of the bad cop.

"Good cop, bad cop" is a staple set piece in the police procedurals common on US television. It is compelling because it relies on two widely held views of police. The first is the belief common among police and their allies and even by most police critics and reformers that everything bad about police—police corruption and misconduct—is always a result of the isolated act of a **bad apple** (224–227). It is the bad cop who uses excessive **force** (102–104), who lies under oath (see **testilying**, 218–219), and who plants evidence (see **throw-down weapon**, 13), and therefore **police reform** (155–160) is always an effort either to purge the police of the bad cop or to expel the bad behavior from the bad cop through improved training, supervision, or increased surveillance.

Second, it is the appeal to and promise of the mythical good cop that gives this drama its feel-good character. For police reformers, the good cop is the default category of the police officer. Like children from the womb, all cops leave the police academy as good cops. This is why police reformers always respond to criticisms of police violence by calling for **community policing** (122–123), which just means more police.

But the theatrical power of "good cop, bad cop" comes not from a tension within the police. There is a third character in the interrogation room drama, and it is **law** (90–93) itself. The bad cop is bad only because law, particularly its due process guarantees and the rights it extends to the accused, is depicted as standing *between* police and truth. In other words, what is bad in police is depicted as something rotten in law. This displacement serves as the rationale for all kinds of routine police acts, such as beating confessions out of suspects. Police corruption can only be understood from this vantage point as situational. The bad cop in the interrogation room is merely *playing* a bad cop. This is how police apologists depict themselves as realists and demand reforms that always include an expansion of the criminal justice system. More cops, more prosecutors, tougher criminal penalties, stricter bail standards. And these arguments win the day because the "good cop, bad cop" scenario structures popular conceptions of police as **crime** (93–96) fighters and justice-seekers. But it pays to remember that the good cop is not a stand-in for good policing. Rather the good cop is merely a trope of police reform—perhaps the central trope—that works to seduce us into seeing the world as disorderly and police as the only antidote. "There is no greater fiction than the media version of a good cop."[1]

"Good cop, bad cop" is melodrama and it is meant for all of us. But we are not the audience. We are the suspect sitting in the interrogation room. And the good cop of police reform tells us that we have only two choices: we either let them get tough on crime or we risk unleashing the bad cop. "Don't you see?" we're told. We have only ourselves to blame, not police.

Officer-Involved Domestic Violence

Police violence is always also domestic violence. We should include among the many links between the violence of police and the violence of a partner or a loved one the unequal distribution of both. The subjects of police violence are predominately racialized poor, yes, but also women, girls, and gender nonconforming folks. The power of police is a power modeled on the patriarchal prerogative that claims a monopoly over a familial unit, including and especially women and children. And so cops beat their spouses and their children. But how many? And cops protect the cops who beat their spouses and their children. But how often? "No one knows," according to anti-violence advocate Diane Wetendorf, "the extent to which police officers abuse their wives or intimate partners."[1] We don't know because few ask the question and fewer still seek an answer. Often noted is the lack of research on the topic, namely, the reluctance of researchers to focus on this particular area of state **violence** (96–100). Those who do seek an answer to the question find a state that systematically avoids recording incidents of cops abusing their own family members (just like the state has long refused to systematically record police killings).

Those who do seek an answer estimate that cops commit acts of domestic violence at higher rates than the general population. An influential self-study from the early 1990s found that 40 percent of cops admitted to abusing their intimate partner or children, a rate possibly much higher due to the reluctance to admit wrongdoing. Other studies have found similarly high rates of domestic violence perpetuated by cops. Even the International Association of Chiefs of Police (IACP) identifies "officer-involved domestic violence" as a national problem. So much for the bourgeois dream that police protect women and children.[2]

Cops are not noble protectors of women and children. Cops are not chivalrous knights fighting evil. There is no **thin blue line** (110–112) that cops defend and which makes democracy possible. They don't fight crime or uphold the rule of law. Cops depict themselves as defenders of the status quo, and if this is true the status quo they defend includes their "right" to commit domestic violence. The origins of police offer one explanation for the prevalence of domestic violence among cops. The earliest definitions of the police powers, elaborated in the Greek Polis, modeled the police on the patriarch, the "king of the household" who exercises the sole prerogative to respond to all threats to the house. This authority included the right of the king of the household, understood as an expectation, to use violence against those within the household. Early theorists of the police power understood the imperative at work: the king of the household owes no allegiance to anyone but the King; is accountable to no one but the sovereign; sees violence as productive; and understands the role of the king of the household as impossible without violence, and thus the notion of a patriarchal power at work in the police powers profoundly shaped contemporary legal doctrines of police.[3] As Wendy Brown points out, the prerogative power of police is a fundamentally masculinist power. When it comes to this gendered form of state violence, then, there is never a single "officer involved" but an entire apparatus of violence workers.

All of this falls under the phrase "officer-involved domestic violence," the copspeak phrase of choice when cops want to obscure the politics and patterns of domestic violence committed by police on their families. Like its inspiration, **officer-involved shooting**

(246–248), the term misleads on purpose. It sets out to absolve, rather than acknowledge and accuse, police violence. The phrase takes the pervasive, institutionalized, gendered, legal violence of police as something other than pervasive, institutionalized, gendered, and legal. Officer-involved domestic violence transforms the patriarchal prerogative that underwrites the police power into an unrelated, isolated action of an individual "bad apple" cop. The phrase, like all copspeak, clears the way for the familiar reformist proposals and promises that inevitably follow. The **officer** (227–228) was "involved," sure, but not as an active agent "on the job" backed by the full administrative **force** (102–104) of police and **law** (90–93). And sure, the cops and reformists always say, we might be talking about physical violence, but we're talking about "domestic" violence, which has nothing to do with the police powers or the institution of police in general. The phrase "officer-involved domestic violence" buries the institutional power relations that make police violence against family members so unique and horrifying in the language of reform.

When we refuse the language of copspeak, we recognize that the issue of police violence, whether on the job or in the home, cannot be reduced to police violence against police wives or partners or the children of cops or resolved by empty promises of reform. So much of the liberal commentary on "officer-involved domestic violence" repeats what Black feminist abolitionist Beth Richie calls the "everywoman" thesis that fails to take into account the racial and classed dimensions of gendered forms of oppression and exploitation.[4] Not all women and children are equally vulnerable to gendered modes of violence. As Richie and others note, the police powers not only fail to protect the most vulnerable from domestic violence but actively perpetuate the pattern by divorcing it from police violence more generally. The phrase seeks to direct our attention elsewhere; meanwhile cops fabricate and ruthlessly defend the structural conditions that give rise to gendered oppression and sexual violence.

This willingness of cops and reformists to ignore police violence in all its forms and modes and to actively sacrifice some of the victims of this violence remains a central and active feature of police from its origins to its present moment. Angela Davis defined police as "domestic caretakers of violence," and her definition captures an essential feature of the police powers—its willingness to justify itself in the name of masculinist protection, its willingness to define caretaking as just another mode of coercion.[5]

There is perhaps no more common rejection to demands to abolish police than the claim that doing so would risk the safety of the most vulnerable among us. Who will protect them? The view of the police power as patriarchal protector of women and children is not merely shared by white men, but also shared by some feminists, namely, carceral feminists who look to the state to provide protection from gendered and sexualized forms of interpersonal violence.

Erica Meiners, for instance, compellingly argues that the entire edifice of the carceral state, including the police power, is justified in the name of children and relatedly the white-hetero-nuclear family.[6] In addition, the legal doctrine of *parens patriae*—or the notion that the state is "parent of the nation"—continues providing the juridical justification for the policing and punishing of people cops call "juvenile delinquents," and treated as "wards of the state."

Pursuit

At the heart of police powers lies a predatory animus. Police pursuit is a hunting power. Everyone who has ever been arrested has been hunted. Nine million people worldwide, as of 2016, live lives behind bars, in cages, behind prison walls. Before any of them were incarcerated, they were hunted.

The power to **arrest** (208–210) and detain requires first a hunt. The power of **investigation** (175–176) and **interrogation** (193–195) requires first a hunt. The power to use **force** (102–104), including lethal force, requires first a hunt. This power of pursuit is a "cynegetic power," as Grégoire Chamayou describes it, which "developed largely outside the judicial framework that now justifies it." This is because "police, as a power of pursuit, does not deal with legal subjects but rather with bodies in movement, bodies that escape and that it must catch. Bodies that pass and that it must intercept."[1] The purpose of pursuit is not to enforce the **law** (90–93), but to catch the prey.

Police pursuit, in other words, does not follow or enforce law. It necessarily exceeds it. In pursuit, police have the **discretion** (176–178) to violate law. Police pursuit includes enticement and entrapment: bait cars to catch car thieves, hand-to-hand drug sales to catch drug dealers. The hunt, the pursuit, is depicted as an instrument of law, but it is more accurate to say that law serves the police hunt. Law makes an exception for hot pursuit, which allows police to privilege their hunt over your safety. According the National Highway Traffic Safety Administration, police pursuit resulted in 2,654 fatal crashes between 1994 and 2002, which involved 3,965 vehicles and killed 3,146 people. Of those killed, more than a thousand were bystanders to the hunt.[2] The police hunt includes a prey, and it might require a sacrifice.

There is nothing police do outside the hunt. **Community policing** (122–123) and **police reform** (155–160) are **pacification** (89–90) hunts. The **police helicopter** (70–73) is called the "heavenly prowl car." The military Predator drone hunts for prey. Police hunt their human prey in cars and helicopters with weapons and dogs (see **K-9**) (22–24) and this makes the police hunt more animal than lawful. A deer hunt and a police hunt both end with a trophy shot: the **cop** (219–221) posing with his prey is like the hunter holding his dead deer. We see this in the famous photo of Chicago police officers Timothy McDermott and Jerome Finnigan kneeling beside a Black suspect, posing for a photo. They hold rifles and grin broadly. Between them, on the ground, lies their prey, a Black man held to the floor, his "tongue dangling from his open mouth, antlers fixed to his head."[3] This is the trophy shot that follows pursuit, a picture of domination and, often, death that celebrates the police hunt.

Crowds

There is revolutionary potential in a crowd. It is always the crowd that threatens the **order** (83–86) that police so methodically keep. **Cops** (219–221) are scared of crowds.

We can trace the story of the crowd and the fear it gives police to multiple origins. In the United States the specter of slave collectives and rebellions in the eighteenth and nineteenth centuries stoked fear in the hearts of plantation owners and slave overseers. The **slave patrol** (143–144), the first police in the Carolinas and Virginia, ruthlessly patrolled outside plantations and frequently searched slave quarters for evidence of planned rebellions and collectives. In Europe it was the Paris Commune of 1871 and the lasting obsession it left among reactionary political thinkers and police with crowds and the **threat** (222–223) they posed to bourgeois order. The reactionary French sociologist Gustave Le Bon called the years that followed the Commune the "Era of Crowds." The energy of the Commune and the power of the crowd aimed "to utterly destroy society as it now exists, with a view to making it hark back to that primitive communism which was the normal condition of all human groups before the dawn of civilization. Limitations of the hours of labour, the nationalization of the mines, railways, factories, and the soil, the equal distribution of all products, the elimination of all the upper classes for the benefit of the popular classes, etc., such are these claims."[1] Consider the power and potential Le Bon places in crowds. Only crowds—crowds of escaped slaves or the working class—have the power to upend an entire social order. The "purely destructive nature" of the crowd threatens bourgeois privilege, and it is that privilege that Le Bon calls "civilization" against the crowd.

To police, the potential disorder of a crowd makes it always a threat, always loaded with revolutionary possibility. Le Bon describes a crowd as having a collective mentality. In the crowd people are suddenly put "in possession of a sort of collective mind which makes them feel, think, and act in a manner quite different from that in which each individual of them would feel."[2] Le Bon sees in a crowd a kind of "hypnotic order," and therefore the crowd is always dangerous to bourgeois order. It is in the crowd that a new view of society can emerge, one in which the otherwise stable social forms of capitalism suddenly appear fragile, and egalitarian alternatives might appear possible. It is in the crowd that Le Bon sees the specter haunting Europe. But Le Bon is quick to note that a crowd could be conservative as well. There is no inherent political content to the crowd. Ideas work through a crowd like a contagion and compel people into unpredictable action. According to Le Bon, a person in a crowd is "under the influence of a suggestion, he will undertake the accomplishment of certain acts with irresistible impetuosity."[3] This is the classical view of crowd psychology, one in which crowds are always irrational and dangerous. It is a view that has influenced fascists, commercial advertisers, US presidents and, of course, police—all those who have sought to harness the potential of crowds, or to destroy it.

Le Bon wrote the playbook for police crowd control. Even the peaceful crowd, according to Le Bon, has the capacity for sudden and revolutionary **violence** (96–100). Thus police confront a crowd always with overwhelming **force** (102–104). It is the crowd's possibility of violence, an idea that comes from Le Bon, that police point to in order to legitimize crowd control tactics. Consider the way a police "anti-riot operations guide" begins first with a fear of the unpredictability of the crowd: "Demonstrations and civil unrests can range from simple, non-violent protests addressing specific issues to events, which turn into a full-scale riot . . . Agitators and criminal infiltrators within a crowd can lead to the eruption of violence." To police, the crowd is always about to explode. "With tensions high, it takes just a small (sometimes seemingly insignificant) incident, rumor, or act of injustice to ignite certain groups within a crowd to start a riot, and violent acts."[4] To the police a crowd is a riot about to happen. And so police use force indiscriminately against the crowd, which produces exactly the chaos and disorder that police attribute to the crowd, which in turn rationalizes an expansion and constant escalation of police violence.

But Le Bon also made clear that while crowds are "difficult to govern," there is always a "ringleader or agitator." And so police hunt in the crowd, constantly in **pursuit** (200–201). Consider the testimony of Adrian Jones, a police consultant and "expert" on civil disturbances, when called to testify before the House Un-American Activities Committee in 1967:

HUAC: What countermeasures would you suggest based on your studies during the crowd phase?

Jones: This is a very important time. If countermeasures fail during this phase a riot will ensue. If countermeasures are successful, there will be no riot. One of the basic objectives is either to disperse the crowd or to bring the crowd under control, to maintain contact with the leaders, and possibly to give the dissidents some sort of outlet. For example, let them state their grievances, try to use the leaders in order to control the crowd. Another countermeasure that can be taken during this specific time is to prepare and station riot-control forces to handle any situation, to utilize a clear show of force, to arrest agitators if there are legal grounds, and to identify the riot leaders and to remove them if possible.

HUAC: What about the actual riot or civil disturbance phase?

Jones: Once this particular phase is started, it is very difficult to avoid the use of the force of the state. This force is sometimes applied through batons, riot-control formations, police dogs, and chemical munitions. The procedure of the United States Army is to first use a show of force; then to use riot-control formations; then to consider the use of streams of water; then the use of chemical agents; then fire by selected marksmen; and finally, under very extreme conditions, full fire power.[5]

Along with "full fire power" comes another option. The crowd can be manipulated. Le Bon reminds police that a crowd is imbued with an "excessive suggestibility." Instead of hunting "ringleaders," police can use **red squads** (123–126) to infiltrate the crowd with agents provocateurs. At an anti-war demonstration on the campus of the University of Alabama in 1970, an undercover cop set fire to a campus building and threw firebombs at police. It was entirely the actions of the agent provocateur that police used to justify a crackdown on all protest and **arrest** (208–210) 150 people. In December 2014, "an undercover California Highway Patrol officer who was attempting to infiltrate a demonstration against **police brutality** (207–208) in Oakland pulled a **gun** (10–13) on the protesters after he and his partner were outed and the partner was attacked."

According to eyewitnesses, both officers were inciting protesters to "acts of vandalism."[6]

There is a great irony here. Mainstream social psychology rejects Gustave Le Bon's theories of the crowd, in particular his claim of a collective mind, his notion of a hypnotized order, and his metaphoric use of contagion to explain the crowd's behavior. None of this is true, they say. But when the crowd is made up of police, it seems always true. Against the protest, any imagined individuality of police dissolves into the collective police mind. Each riot-helmeted cop looks like every other **nightstick** (55–58)-wielding cop, each **tear gas** (17–20)-firing cop behaves just like every other flak-jacketed cop. As though hypnotized, the police crowd moves in swarms, attacks in waves, disperses and reassembles according to some invisible force. Police gas protesters in the face who are sitting in a circle. Police beat protesters with truncheons who are following commands. It is not "discipline" or "training" that determines the behavior of police in the crowd, but rather the logic of police—of force—fueled by unlimited power, fueled by the crowd.

Contempt of Cop

Cops claim it's tough to be a **cop** (219–221). It's dangerous work, they say. Not just anybody can be a cop. It takes a special person, they say. "I put my life on the line for you and yours," one Detroit cop said. "I don't have to, but I choose to, so if nothing else, I think I deserve a little bit of respect."

Cops don't deserve respect and deference, they enforce it. "Contempt of cop" refers to both the lack of respect that cops claim to find everywhere they look and also to the violence that cops use on those they claim didn't give them "a little bit of respect." Unlike contempt of court, its juridical inspiration, contempt of cop has nothing to do with **law** (90–93). Like **testilying** (218–219), it's the rationale cops use to ignore law. Cops demand polite obedience and respectful deference and punish those who don't provide it. The phrase captures the blanket justification for the retaliatory arrests and the **rough rides** (31–32) that cops give to a person who "talks back," calls them a pig, or tells them to fuck off.

Contempt of cop illustrates just how damn sensitive, aggrieved, and delicate cops can be. How else to describe the 2015 case of cops in the United Kingdom arresting a club DJ for playing the Peppa Pig theme song and "snorting" like a pig over the microphone? What explains this insecurity? James Baldwin called the authority that cops claim, and that the law extends, a kind of "arrogant autonomy." It grants police *freedom* from **accountability** (160–162) and from the law itself.[1]

What constitutes disrespect? Don't look to law for an answer. The cop on the street, and nobody else, defines the boundaries of the "proper" and its transgression, which makes for a better definition of police **discretion** (176–178) than the version cops offer. On second thought, maybe contempt of cop does have something to do with law. The law's permissive structure grants police virtually unlimited discretionary power to act in whatever way the cop considers "reasonable" in any given situation.[2] This legal permissiveness licenses the everyday tyranny of police discretion operative in contempt of cop. It also predicts the violence that follows because it extends to cops the freedom to intervene, always with the threat of violence, in the lives of those deemed impolite despite what the courts may say after the fact. The prerogative power of police, by its very nature as instrument of the state, always "overflows the banks of law."[3]

Law wants it both ways. It gives cops total discretion on the street to decide who's a **threat** (222–223) and what's an **emergency** (223–224) at the same time that it claims to limit police conduct on the street. US courts have consistently ruled in favor of the right to give "the bird" to a cop so long as it doesn't thwart police work. The Supreme Court has defended rude speech directed at cops. Police should expect and tolerate disrespectful and offensive speech, the courts ruled; but that's just gaslighting. Violence structures law; cops, as Angela Davis explained, are its caretakers. They routinely stop, harass, and arrest people for "digitus impudicus," or the middle finger, and all sorts of other constitutionally protected speech.[4] In November 2005, two Metro DC cops, Liliana Acebal and James Antonio, arrested Lindsay Huthnance outside of a 7-Eleven for saying, as they walked past her, "what a waste of taxpayer dollars." The cops demanded her ID; Huthnance demanded their badge numbers. Acebal and Antonio arrested her for disorderly conduct, which, along with resisting arrest, loitering, and breach of peace, constitutes the quintessential contempt of cop charge.

Cops, those emissaries of oppression, as Angela Davis put it, wear a **police uniform** (141–143) and a **badge** (106–110) and demand obedience and deference because of it. They "know that they are hated," Baldwin wrote, and as a result, "they are always afraid," like fragile little snowflakes armed to the teeth.

Police Brutality
Police brutality is the most commonly used expression to discuss police **violence** (96–100). Although rarely noted, the phrase itself speaks to a certain animalization of police power: the etymological root of brutality is "brute" which in turn evokes an uncivilized, savage beast.

Hence referring to police violence as a form of brutality is at once an identification of the violence of police with an animalistic quality, an uncivilized, beastly violence. The irony here is that the police institution has historically framed itself as the supreme instantiation of civilization. Historically, the term civilization was once synonymous with police—to police is to civilize, to polish or make polite (note the etymological links with police) the uncivilized and impolite brutes threatening white bourgeois **order** (83–86).[1]

More specifically, the charge of police brutality is usually an allegation of excessive violence, or violence that is illegal, or outside of the rule of **law** (90–93), or at least beyond publicly acceptable police practice. Importantly, most cases of so-called police brutality—such as beating a person of color while **handcuffed** (20–21) or shooting an **unarmed** (257–258) homeless person—are most often determined by internal **investigation** (175–176) or by the judicial system to be legal. This fact highlights the pitfalls of the term, since what commonly goes by police brutality works to demarcate between acceptable and unacceptable state violence, and therefore simultaneously works to legitimate all sorts of police violence that might not be deemed excessive or illegal. The problem with police brutality, then, is the way this phrase often works to obscure attention on the normal, routine, and everyday forms of police violence that are internal to the police mandate. Police brutality, as a way to understand police, risks normalizing all sorts of racialized, classed, and gendered legal terror.

Arrest

Arrest is a euphemism for captivity, a term that codifies and dresses up in juridical language a mode of legal **violence** (96–100) via bodily capture. The Oxford English Dictionary defines arrest as "To capture, seize, lay hold upon, or apprehend by legal authority" and "to restrain a man of his liberty, obliging him to be obedient to the **law** (90–93)." To be arrested is to be captured, to be caught and deprived of bodily autonomy (that is, liberty and freedom), however temporarily or prolonged captivity might last. Arrest is not only a mode of state violence, but an initial and primary site of incarceration.

The United States leads the world in rates of incarceration, with nearly 2.5 million people forced into cages called prisons and jails. And they are first forced there by police arrest. You cannot put people into cages without first sending out police to hunt and capture them via the powers of arrest. The entire violence of prison and jail is initiated by the hunting powers of police, a power of **pursuit** (200–201) that often culminates in the captivity of arrest. Hunting always precedes caging.

Arrest is commonly understood as a **cop** (219–221) arresting a person—an individual—but individual arrests are never isolated incidents. The United States of America might as well be called the United States of Arrest, given that at least since 1980 anywhere from 10 to 15 million people are arrested each year. The result is that today there are approximately 70 million people with arrest records, even though most are not arrested for a serious **crime** (93–96) and most are never indicted or charged.

It should not come as a surprise that not all demographic groups are hunted and captured at the same rate. Racial minorities are overrepresented in arrest numbers, and this is a primary factor contributing to the overrepresentation of people of color in prisons and jails, with Black people the most likely to be officially held captive. Police in the St. Louis suburb of Ferguson, Missouri, which came under scrutiny following the police murder of Michael Brown in 2014, almost exclusively arrest Black people. In addition, out of the 21,000 town residents in 2014, 16,000 had active arrest warrants, meaning only 5,000 residents of Ferguson were not fugitives from police power.

Arrest statistics are important not only for the way they mark the racialization of capture, but also, according to the scholar Khalil Gibran Muhammad, for the way they operate as a racist ideology that "proves" Black inferiority or criminality.[2] The *fact* of arrest has come to represent the *fact* of Black criminality. Of course, this is circular: arrest = crime = arrest. What is so often missed is the politics of criminalization, or the ways that arrest statistics are not an accurate marker of racialized criminality but are instead a marker of racialized criminalization projects. Put another way: arrest statistics tell us little about the true or objective nature of crime across demographics. More than anything, arrest statistics tell us very little about criminals, and a hell of a lot more about police. They tell us who police prefer to hunt and capture and what parts of a city are the preferred hunting grounds.

The United States is a nation of captives and has always been a nation of captives, founded on the colonial practice of hunting, capturing, and caging Indigenous and African people. Arrest powers have always been central to these projects, eventually cod ified in the formal police powers granted to cops, with the hunt for vagrants a central part of this project. Arrest is one of the most normalized violences of the capitalist state, and once captured via arrest a criminal record is inevitably chronicled within the archives of the **security** (86–89) state, haunting the captive throughout his or her life. Resisting arrest then requires a steadfast attention to not merely the sensational acts of police violence—**police brutality** (207–208) or even what the Department of Justice calls **justified** (238–240) shootings—but the normal and everyday violence of the capitalist state that is often misrecognized as something other than violence. This is also why a politics of abolition, which often focuses primarily on the cages of prison and jail, must endlessly work toward the abolition of arrest, the abolition of capture—the abolition of police.

Kettling

In his book *The Production of Space*, the French philosopher Henri Lefebvre writes that the modern state "promotes and imposes itself as the stable center," the only essential social formation, the "end and the meaning of history." In other words, the modern state trucks no challenge to its authority. The state refuses even the possibility of the existence of a legitimate challenge to its claim of sovereign authority. As Lefebvre reminds, "there are, however, other forces on the boil . . . seething forces [that] are still capable of rattling the lid of the cauldron of the state and its space."[1]

Cops use this metaphor too—this boiling over of seething forces rattling the lid of the state. The job of police is to keep the lid on that cauldron. It's not for nothing police use the word "kettling" to describe a common police **crowd** (201–205) control tactic. If you've ever marched against police and confronted a line of riot cops wearing helmets and holding truncheons and shields you've been kettled even if you didn't know the term. Cops consider most crowds (except for those convened by the state or capital or **armed friendlies**, 165–170) unruly, unmanageable, and unpredictable. Crowd control, therefore, always begins with intimidation and ends with confrontation. Cops shout into bullhorns while others assemble into formation, forming a riot line marching in lockstep toward the crowd. This is the beginning of the kettle, marked by the synchronizing of the rhythmic striking of their truncheons on their shields. The goal of kettling is to control and contain the crowd, to limit the options of those in the crowd. If the crowd represents "forces on the boil," the police represent the lid of the kettle. These "seething forces" are capable of "rattling the lid," and so police must secure the lid and rob the crowd of the air it needs to breathe. So riot cops compress the crowd, slowly collapsing the space available for maneuver, while, in theory, leaving an escape route—a release valve—that slowly dissipates the crowd.

A kettle follows a bizarre cop logic. It is a tactic police actively use for crowd control but which police refuse to acknowledge as a police tactic of crowd control. It is used against a group of people who, by virtue of their physical proximity to dangerous or potentially dangerous events or circumstances—as determined by police—and who display threatening or potentially threatening behavior—as interpreted by police—are constituted by police as an unruly crowd and therefore must be first encircled and then contained by heavily armed police acting in concert. Mark Neocleous calls the kettle a "preemptive containment," in which police jail people in a kind of "mobile prison the walls of which are made from the actual physical bodies of the police, their truncheons, shields, horses, dogs, and armored vehicles."[2]

Kettling borrows its primary tactic from military strategy—encircling and isolating an enemy. Kettling, like a military siege, establishes a blockade that chokes an enemy off from supplies and support. Kettling often takes one of two forms: either the standard form in which a line of police contain a crowd within a cordon and arrest individuals or a wander-kettle in which a line of police push a crowd away from its target and force-march it until its energy dissipates. Each of these two forms comes with variations. Police use the wander-kettle to force crowds onto bridges or up against embankments, where there is no escape. Police intensify a standard kettling by introducing horses and **K-9**s (22–24). All variations of kettling rely on the full array of police weaponry. Police push the crowd with riot cops, but also with water cannons, long-range acoustic devices that employ painful acoustic waves (see **sound**, 77–79), **tear gas** (17–20), **Tasers** (13–16), and **rubber bullets** (50–55).

The military strategy of encirclement includes also a "general disregard for civilian casualties" and this is true of police kettling as well.[3] On June 1, 2020, thousands of people gathered at Philadelphia police headquarters to protest the police killings of George Floyd and Breonna Taylor, among many others. They marched for hours and by the time they made it to the Benjamin Franklin Parkway, they were 5,000 strong. A line of officers pushed the protestors (wander-kettle) up against a highway embankment bounded by fences on two sides. They moved in, trapping people, and attacked with rubber bullets and tear gas. Kettling isn't crowd control—its **pain compliance** (79–80).

Cops use metaphors to confuse, not to enlighten (see **Predictive Policing**, 178–179). The purpose of a kettle's lid is not to stop the boil, just as the tactic of police kettling rarely includes an escape route for the crowd. In theory, kettling establishes a tactical advantage for police—a police cordon containing the crowd—and police use that advantage to reduce the possibility of violence by limiting a crowd's options to escape or surrender. In practice, police send a wave of riot cops into a crowd without any thought of an escape route, use tear gas at close range once kettled, and then attack the crowd with **nightsticks** (55–58) followed by indiscriminate arrest. Just as the cauldron's lid hastens the boil, so does kettling hasten the chaos. The crowd often panics as cops move in with their dogs and their batons. This is the purpose of kettling: to create the conditions for fear and panic among the crowd because fear and panic are the necessary preconditions police require for "good order."

Plain View

Plain view, or plain sight, refers to an exception to the requirement that police seek a search warrant before conducting a **search** (163–165). The Fourth Amendment protects against unreasonable searches and seizures by the state. Since *People v. Marvin* in 1934, the courts have defined a police search as "a prying into hidden places for that which is concealed." Therefore police must first secure a warrant before engaging in a search. But if evidence of a **crime** (93–96) is in plain view there is no need for an officer to first secure a warrant before conducting a search.

According to the plain view standard, you do not have an expectation of privacy on something that is in plain sight, which would make sense if plain view meant plain view, but it does not. Consider the case of *Texas v. Brown*. Police stopped a car at a traffic **checkpoint** (75–77). A traffic cop shined his **flashlight** (48–50) into a vehicle and saw an opaque balloon in the back seat. This apparently raised the cop's suspicion because balloons are sometimes used to ferry drugs, the officer later claimed. The driver opened the glove compartment to retrieve his driver's license. As he did this, the officer aimed his flashlight into the glove compartment and saw vials of white powder (he claimed). The officer then arrested the driver on suspicion of drug possession and seized the vials and the opaque balloon resting on the backseat. The balloon was later found to contain heroin. But this is a violation of the plain view doctrine. The balloon was plainly visible, but the heroin was not. According to plain view, the officer cannot seize the balloon without a warrant. This is what the defendant's lawyer argued in a suppression hearing. The judge denied the appeal and allowed the evidence for trial. The defendant was convicted of drug possession. The Texas Court of Criminal Appeals, however, disagreed and overturned the conviction based on the fact that the heroin in the balloon was not "immediately apparent" to the officer because it was not in plain view. The Supreme Court later reversed the decision by reinterpreting the plain view doctrine in a manner consistent with the way it was applied by the police officer. According to the Court, the officer claimed he had **reasonable suspicion** (255–257) that the balloon contained heroin and therefore the search and seizure did not violate the unreasonableness standard. In other words, despite the fact that the heroin was not in plain sight, the courts declared the search and seizure legal according to the doctrine of plain view.[1]

What is the relationship of police to **law** (90–93)? The standard view tells us that the police are an instrument of law, that police officers abide by and enforce the law. But the decision in *Texas v. Brown*, and others like it, suggests that the relationship should be understood in reverse. Law is an instrument of police. We are taught the law guides and limits police, but in fact it does quite the opposite. Law grants police cover for many practices *after the fact*. Consider the many doctrines of exception to the Fourth Amendment protection against unreasonable search and seizure by police:

Probable cause: in *Utah v. Strieff* the Supreme Court interpreted probable cause, a standard that purportedly limits police **discretion** (176–178) to stop and search people, as permitting random stops. Police can stop you on the street for no reason, demand your identification for no reason, check you for outstanding warrants for no reason. And if a police officer finds a warrant, they now have a reason to search you. As Associate Justice Sonia Sotomayor explained in her dissent, the warrant search is among the most common ways for police to conduct warrantless searches. "The mere existence of a warrant not only gives an officer legal cause to arrest and search a person, it also forgives an officer who, with no knowledge of the warrant at all, unlawfully stops that person on a whim or hunch." And since "the Department of Justice recently reported that in the town of Ferguson, Missouri, with a population of 21,000, 16,000 people had outstanding warrants against them," the warrant search is a way for police to overcome any limit on police searches and seizures. As Satnam Choongh explains it, "The law does not recognise suspects as having a right not to be stopped, searched, arrested or detained without charge or trial. The law does not proclaim that suspects have an absolute right not to answer police questions, or that they have a right not to be man-handled by the police once arrested. Instead the law speaks primarily in terms of what the police can do to the suspect."[2]

Reasonable suspicion: this standard allows police to **stop and frisk** (27–31) people without a warrant if police have "specific and articulable facts" of a crime. According to the court in *Floyd v. New York City*, New York police based their aggressive stop and frisk policy "on criminal suspect data, of which race is a primary factor." In other words, to police in New York, race establishes reasonable suspicion of crime. NYPD "carries out more stops where there are more black and Hispanic residents, even when other relevant variables are held constant." NYPD cops "are more likely to stop blacks and Hispanics than whites within precincts and census tracts, even after controlling for other relevant variables." NYPD is "more likely to use force against blacks and Hispanics than whites, after controlling for other relevant variables." And finally, "NYPD officers stop blacks and Hispanics with less justification than whites." And half of all stops lead to frisks, while only 1.5 percent of frisks reveal a weapon. And this is a practice that, according to law, conforms to the doctrine of reasonable suspicion that claims to protect people from unreasonable search and seizure.

Plain view, as with probable cause and reasonable suspicion, is not a legal doctrine that limits the police powers; it extends them. And this exposes a fundamental problem of **police reform** (155–160) as a form of pushback against the police powers that relies almost exclusively on law. Reformists constantly seek to hold police accountable and they look to law and the courts to do this. But we know from legal and police history that law does not discipline or limit police. Law trails behind police, lingering in the wreckage, pointing out the broken bodies and the violated rights and explaining why it's all perfectly legal. The only thing in plain view is the fact that police do not follow law; law follows police.

Asset Forfeiture

Asset forfeiture refers to the confiscation of **private property** (81–83) by the state. Police agencies seize assets generated in the course of criminal activity, such as the proceeds of arrests from **War** (100–102) on Drugs policing. In the United States, county sheriff's departments forcibly evict tenants and seize, and subsequently sell, foreclosed property. In addition, police often seize property used in the course of illegal activity, such as a car used to transport contraband of one sort or another. Property is often described as a kind of social relation, but it might also be understood as an ongoing police operation. According to the US Department of Justice, police in 2012 made nearly 9 million arrests for property **crimes** (93–96). And police also seize and acquire property via policing. Confiscated money or seized property is almost always used to expand police— to hire more **cops** (219–221), purchase more equipment, pay for more overtime. The practice of asset forfeiture is described as fairly recent and the logic offered for the practice is simple: criminals should not profit from their criminal activity; instead they should forfeit their right to the money they generate or the property they put to use in the course of their criminal activity.

There is however a longer history and deeper logic at work, and one that reveals the constitutive role of policing in the fabrication of a racialized and propertied **order** (83–86). Throughout the early twentieth century, the broad acceptance of eugenics in the United

States influenced the way rights, including the right to own property, became regulated by the state. Eugenics is usually thought of as a pseudoscience of race, but it should be understood instead as a racialized legal regime of property, or even better, a form of police power that prescribed limited rights to reproduce and own property and restricted these rights, via coercive enforcement, to only those deemed fit. The category of the "unfit" turned on the notion of "tainted" blood. Blood was considered a kind of *property* that marked one's fitness for citizenship or one's proclivity for crime. The "unfit" of eugenics were those defined through a categorical logic—idiot, moron, imbecile, etc.—applied to poor rural whites, Indigenous people, urban Black folk, and the imprisoned. The specter of the criminal haunting white bourgeois society frightened progressives and reactionaries alike. Crime was a sign of corrupted blood. The goal of good order, therefore, required a police **force** (102–104) capable of extending its concern to, and authority over, life itself. Taking property, taking life.

In other words, the eugenic state determined it was illegal to *inherit* the property or genes of those deemed unfit. More than 60,000 men, women and children were sterilized against their will in the United States during the middle of the twentieth century. The Supreme Court in 1927 in *Buck v. Bell* upheld the right of states to engage in compulsory sterilization "for the protection and health of the state." Writing for the majority, Oliver Wendell Holmes argued that "it is better for all the world, if instead of waiting to execute degenerate offspring for crime, or to let them starve for their imbecility, society can prevent those who are manifestly unfit from continuing their kind."

The common practice of asset forfeiture suggests that eugenics remains a guiding logic of police power and a potent source of legal order in the US criminal justice system. Consider that in the United States, nearly one in every 2,000 people is sentenced to life in prison without the chance for parole. Black people constitute nearly 60 percent of all people sentenced to life in jail. That number reaches greater than 70 percent in federal prison.[1] This is a state of affairs that follows perfectly from the logic of eugenics: crime is a genetic disposition associated with poverty and race, and thus the poor are stripped of their property and their ability to reproduce.

The link between race, poverty and asset forfeiture would perhaps be more obvious if it weren't for the influence on the left of libertarian-derived critiques of asset forfeiture, a version which focuses almost exclusively on civil forfeiture. Libertarian groups such as the Cato Institute and the Charles Koch–funded Institute of Justice oppose civil asset forfeiture because of the **threat** (222–223) they say it poses to individual liberty, which for them begins and ends with the right to own private property and the obligation of the state to defend that right. Given this position, one might ask how libertarian critiques of asset forfeiture could possibly ignore a history in which the state has stripped poor people of color of life and liberty. The answer lies in the distinction some libertarians make between criminal and civil asset forfeiture. Unlike criminal asset forfeiture, in which property is seized following a conviction and about which libertarians have no issue, civil asset forfeiture occurs even in the absence of a criminal charge. Thus it should not be a surprise that in 2010 the Institute for Justice would prepare a 123-page study condemning asset forfeiture but never once use the word "race."[2] This is because criminal asset forfeiture **disproportionately** (232–235) affects poor people of color, and libertarians have no significant problem with this; however, the more recent rise among **law** (90–93) enforcement agencies in the use of civil asset forfeiture now impacts corporations, and a white middle class, and this concerns libertarians.

The language of the libertarian critique of asset forfeiture relies on a familiar vocabulary. Evidence for forfeiture is "tainted." The agencies who engage in these practices are "unfit." And the frequency of seizure makes it "compulsory." The libertarian critique of asset forfeiture comes to us in the register of eugenics, and thus the left's embrace of this position, or of libertarian critiques of police more generally (see **militarization**, 139–142), extends progressives' long romance with eugenics in the fabrication of "good order" as a racial order.

Testilying

Testilying is police slang, first coined by New York City police officers, that describes the common practice among police, often encouraged by prosecutors, of lying under oath, otherwise known as perjury. A 1994 investigation of the New York City Police Department by the Mollen Commission concluded that "in-court deception" was widespread among officers, calling it "the most common form of public corruption facing the criminal justice system." It is more than merely corruption, however. Testilying is a form of police **violence** (96–100) because it is a practice intended to incarcerate people innocent of charges against them.

Testilying most often occurs in drug and **gun** (10–13) cases, particularly in areas police call **crime** (93–96)-infested neighborhoods. These are cases in which **arrests** (208–210) are based overwhelmingly on surveillance or confidential informants, and convictions depend almost entirely on police testimony. In studies of the practice, police have described testilying as an ethical grey area within which they believe they work. For example, a police officer will testify under oath that an arrest was based on information obtained from a confidential informant, when in fact there was no informant and therefore no probable cause for an arrest. Police officers do not consider this perjury, thus the word "testilying." Their hands are tied, their argument goes, by a criminal justice system unwilling to give them the **discretion** (176–178) they need to take "bad guys" off the street.

In other words, testilying is not legal, but police consider it **justified** (238–240) when they do it because it gets them around burdensome rules of evidence so that they can "do their job." Law enforcement officers knowingly engage in an illegal practice as a means to enforce the **law** (90–93). What should we make of this contradiction? One possibility is that it does not constitute a contradiction, but rather perjury, and that the violent incarceration of the defendant that follows, serves the central mandate of police: **order** (83–86). To say that order, and not law, is the central category of police is to say also that the rule of law, from the police perspective, is always a secondary or lesser concern than the mandate of fabricating order through the eradication of **threats** (222–223). In other words, the job of police is not to enforce the law or even necessarily follow the law, but rather to make social order itself.[1]

Therefore, testilying might in fact be a violation of law, but this doesn't mean it is in violation of the principles of police. To suggest otherwise is to make the common mistake of assuming that police power first and foremost corresponds to legal **accountability** (160–162). One result of this error is the repeated calls to stop the practice by re-inserting the rule of law alongside administrative **police reform** (155–160). This argument assumes that testilying is a function of institutional incentives to "get the numbers" or "get tough." But if this reformist argument is accepted, the solutions are largely administrative and legal: simply hold police legally accountable and/or remove the institutional incentive, and cops will no longer lie under oath. Interestingly, this logic validates the police justification of testilying by turning police into the victims of an apparently out-of-control system that either demands too much of them or hinders their ability to successfully carry out their job. It too easily and quickly understands testilying as police corruption instead of a practice that is consistent with the internal logic of police: order at all cost!

When law impedes the imperative for order, police ignore the former in the name of the latter, consistent with their political mandate. As Walter Benjamin argued, the police make their own law precisely because the law recognizes its own failures to compel its subjects to act normatively. When we speak of police **discretion** (176–178) to lie under oath in order to take a person's freedom, we are talking about the same decision-making authority that extends to the police the freedom to take a person's life. But we are not talking about law or justice when we speak of such things.

Cop

Even though the word "cop" is perhaps the most common vernacular synonym for police **officer** (227–228), its origins are unclear. One common explanation is that police officers came to be known as "cops" due to their copper **badges** (106–110) or helmets. Another suggests that cop is an acronym for "constable on patrol." More likely, the word cop comes from the Middle French *caper*, meaning "to capture," and from the Latin *capere*, meaning "to seize, to grasp." In other words, the police officer might have become popularly known as a "copper" and then "cop" due to the **arrest** (208–210) mandate of capturing and seizing people and their property.

This origin story of cop locates coercive power as the defining feature of police. Cops hunt humans and place them in captivity. It is likely that "cop" was developed by members of the dangerous classes as a derogatory name for police, later supplanted with a term like "pig". Although today this negative connotation has been lost for the most part, the term "cop" is still often considered by police to be insufficiently deferential to their official authority. Hence "officer" is often thought to be more respectful and stately.

The phrase "to cop" also means "to steal." Thus the word cop contains within it the specter of the criminal, specifically the "thief." It gains meaning in relation to the transgressive subject, whether this is the suspect or fugitive or criminal. Cops and thieves not only imply each other, but actively resemble each other in ways the conventional wisdom of good guys versus bad guys refuses to acknowledge. And let's not forget that some of the first iterations of the police officer were called "thief-takers," or people hired to capture thieves by a process of "taking" to justice the criminal who had illegally taken someone else's **private property** (81–83). Of course, confiscation tactics and **asset forfeiture** (215–217) bring to mind official forms of cop thievery. Cops and crooks, thus, are always intertwined in a dynamic, mutually reinforcing relationship, which is popularly enacted in everything from Hollywood films to the popular children's game cops and robbers, or to the reality show *Cops* and its famous theme song: "Bad boys, bad boys, watcha gonna do, watcha gonna do when they come for you?" As Grégoire Chamayou writes, "This is another great cinematic theme: the mirror relationship between the cop and the criminal, the secret affinity of hunter and hunted, who may go so far as to exchange faces."[1] This is not to say that cops are merely criminals in disguise, even if this is true some of the time. As Michael Taussig argues, "The point is that cops and thieves are erotically intertwined and that the **thin blue line** (110–112) separating them is more like a veil in a striptease . . . What should hold us are the curious properties of the distinction uniting the criminal with the policeman, something Nietzsche, for one, made clear when he argued that the police are worse than the criminal because they do the same things, but in the name of Law."[2] This is why cops and police power constitute a much more difficult political problem than the "bad guys" that cops hate so much.

The drama of cops and robbers relies on an ambiguous status between the two figures while at the same time maintaining that there is a valid distinction. This is the political theater of the thin blue line when cops justify their own crossing of the line between good and evil while simultaneously insisting they are still on the good side of it. So even bad cops are first and foremost cops, not criminals, and the bad things cops do in their official capacity are always set in motion by the **force** (102–104) of **law** (90–93), something not afforded the thief or the crook. Cops have **badges** (106–110), criminals don't, and that distinction, or the way that distinction is produced, makes a world of difference. Or we can turn to a memorable scene in *West Side Story*: "Oh yeah, sure, it's a free country and I ain't got the right. But I got a badge. What do you got?"

Copspeak:
How the Police See the World

Threat

Threat is the category that animates all police power. To engage in policing is to engage in threat management through identifying, responding, containing, and eradicating various threats to a propertied, always racialized **order** (83–86). Always underpinned with the capacity to deploy legal **violence** (96–100), police exercise what is essentially an unlimited power of **discretion** (176–178) when deciding what constitutes a **threat** (222–223), establishing the threat's priority within an endless list of threats, and deciding what course of action to take.

The "threat scenario," to use Bryan Wagner's term, has been the primary standard that US courts apply to police cases, often using hypothetical thought experiments (such as the ticking bomb scenario) to place prevention and necessity at the heart of policing. As Wagner notes, the police are understood as having the discretion to deal with threats to **the public** (252–255) welfare however and whenever they see fit.[1]

Declaring someone or something a threat is one of the most normalized of all powers internal to the police function, and among the most obvious and immediate examples are the routine **stop and frisk** (27–31), or when a **cop** (219–221) rolls up alongside someone and asks them what they are doing in the neighborhood or demands to know where they are going. Of course, the logic of threat is always operative in official justifications of police violence, as the cop only has to claim that he or she felt threatened, or that he or she felt the suspect posed a threat to the public, to justify the violence. In these always unequal exchanges between the "street-level bureaucrat" and the citizen, cops perpetually engage in threat assessment and by extension an assessment of the police response. Given the fact that the courts have consistently refused to define police discretion or set predetermined rules of behavior for police officers, the police prerogative of preventing threats to the propertied order is by extension limitless and boundless.

So let's recognize a stark reality: from the police perspective, only threats matter, which is also to say that only disorder and insecurity matter to police. Not people or rights or **law** (90–93), or even justice, and certainly not the protection of individual lives. The subject deemed a threat might hypothetically say to the cop, "What about my rights?" and the cop can only say, "I don't understand your language. I speak only the language of threats."

Emergency

Police power is always emergency power, a power that police claim is essential to the construction of social **order** (83–86).[1] It is not for nothing that police are often referred to as the "first line of defense" and "first responders" in an endless series of emergencies that go by all sorts of names, from the spectacular to the mundane and comical: disorders and disturbances, **crime** (93–96) and criminals, riots and mobs, gangs and loitering, jaywalking and **vagrancy** (189–193), traffic accidents and violations, noise complaints, public intoxication and drugs, and even the cat in the tree. This is why police are called "emergency responders" and "emergency personnel" who drive "emergency vehicles" and often form "emergency response teams" like **SWAT** (135–139). From the police perspective, anything and everything is an emergency situation.

Etymologically, "emergency" has a long history, but the Oxford English Dictionary makes it clear that the idea evokes a "state of things unexpectedly arising, and urgently demanding immediate action." "Emergency," then, implies urgency, and of course there is the explicitly politico-legal use of the term "state of emergency." But although the "state of emergency" is often declared by a state executive—in essence creating a break between "normal" and "exceptional times" when **law** (90–93) is suspended—the ordinary existence of police is the ordinary instantiation of a permanent state of emergency.

Police power is enshrined into government as an executive power. Police are everyday executives who legally exercise a virtually unlimited power of **discretion** (176–178) to decide on all sorts of emergencies. The implication should be clear: police and the law are not the same, and the rule of law was never meant to fully check the powers of the police, since liberal doctrine has always granted executive power the last word on deciding what and who is a **threat** (222–223) to the public good and the interests of the state. Policing is nothing less than the everyday application of this emergency prerogative.

Bad Apple

Among the most common ways to describe a bad **cop** (219–221) is to call him or her a "bad apple." This is not an innocent phrase. The bad apple metaphor of police **violence** (96–100) condemns the individual bad cop and preserves the perceived righteousness of police as a whole. As a metaphor the expression naturalizes the problem of police violence. It establishes that police violence is no more a political problem than a rotten apple. A bad cop is just an unfortunate fact of nature. It is simultaneously predictable, in that it is bound to happen, and unusual, in that it doesn't describe an entire crop. It condemns police for "unjustified" police violence, but excuses the police as an institution by locating the problem as limited to the individual. After all, an apple tree grows apples, not rotten apples, and thus the bad apple must be understood as an aberration. And just as the orchardist confronts the problem of rotten apples by separating the bad apples from the good apples, so too must police separate the bad cops from the good cops (see **good cop, bad cop**, 195–197). Thus the bad apple theory defines the problem of police violence as a problem of individuals, not police, and therefore gives momentum to **police reform** (155–160) proposals that identify administrative solutions designed and carried out by police brass that focus on police **professionalization** (113–115), such as higher wages, more training, better equipment, and **community policing** (122–123), among others.

The bad apple theory is politically persuasive, however, because it is understood as more than just a metaphor. It is offered as an accurate depiction of the way police violence works, a depiction found as often in liberal political discourse as in the rhetoric of police chiefs and conservative **law** (90–93) and **order** (83–86) politicians. Few scholars take the theory seriously, but it is popular among some journalists as a common sense way to explain the violence of police. Consider the bad apples study by FiveThirtyEight, a website that uses quantitative methods to answer, mostly, sports and political questions. "Until recently," the article explains, "[the bad apple] theory was difficult for civilians to investigate, but department data on complaints against officers obtained through a legal challenge shows that police misconduct in Chicago is overwhelmingly the product of a small fraction of officers and that it may be possible to identify those officers and reduce misconduct."[1] The study went on to confirm the bad apples theory by noting that only a small fraction of Chicago cops were "ill-intentioned or inclined to misconduct or violence, while the majority of officers are good cops."

Just like all efforts that purportedly confirm the bad apple theory, the FiveThirtyEight approach assumes that all, or at least a statistically representative sample of all, police misconduct comes into view through complaints lodged against police with official **police oversight** (146–149) agencies. In other words, the approach accepts the key premise of the theory: unjustified police violence is always and only a problem of individual decisions by bad cops. If this is true, then the only way to disprove the bad apple theory is to prove that all police officers are bad apples.

So, how do we get around the bad apple theory of police violence? One way would be to recognize that the bad apple theory poses the question of police violence as one always limited to **police brutality** (207–208). In other words, there is good police violence and bad police violence. The bad apple cop is the cop who engages in unjustified police brutality. The good apple cop uses good **discretion** (176–178) to engage in **justified** (238–240) police violence.

Another way to understand the bad apple theory would require taking the data on police complaints seriously, but not in the way the FiveThirtyEight study does. Recent Chicago police complaint data show that police misconduct complaints are more likely to be upheld if lodged by white people than by Black or Hispanic people.

According to the *Chicago Reporter*, "Allegations by whites are nine times more likely to be upheld than those by blacks and almost three times more likely than those by Hispanics." And perhaps more importantly, "allegations of improper **arrest** (208–210) and lockup procedures are much more likely to be made by African-Americans and are sustained less than two percent of the time."[2] Thus police complaint data confirms the differentially racialized nature of police complaint adjudication. And this reveals that police violence must be understood as institutional, not individual. It is an administratively organized adjudication of police complaints that acknowledges the police violence by individual officers as a problem only when identified by white complainants, and that cannot see a problem when complaints are lodged by people of color. Thus the violence of individual officers occurs in a context of institutional indifference.

And this is made clear in the research on police complaint procedures that demonstrate that certain groups resist filing complaints not only because they suspect those complaints will not be taken seriously (the institutionalization of indifference), but also because they fear retaliation by police (the institutionalization of violence). This is individual violence matched with organized indifference, also expressed as individual indifference matched with organized violence.

A study of sex workers in South Africa concluded that "the highest levels of violence against sex workers come from the police." Among the women interviewed, one in three "described being forced to have sex with police officers" (see **rape**, 41–43). The pattern included indifference and retaliation when women complained. As one woman explained, "When I complained to the captain about how I was hurt when they arrested me he said '*Ag dis maar net hoere en hy kan nie n saak van n prostituut aaneem nie.*' [Oh they are only whores and he can't take a case made by a prostitute.]" Another said, "They just laughed at us."[3]

A national report on racist violence against Aboriginal people in Australia concluded that "Aboriginal-police relations have reached a critical point due to the widespread involvement of police in acts of racist violence, intimidation and harassment."[4] As a result of organized violence by police, few members of Aboriginal communities are willing to complain. "The fear of retaliation against the complainant, or a witness, or their families, combine to discourage all but the rare person from pursuing complaints."[5]

On October 11, 1994, Kim Groves, a thirty-two-year-old mother of three children, saw New Orleans police officer Len Davis pistol-whip seventeen-year-old Nathan Norwood just blocks from her house. The next day Groves identified Davis in an official misconduct complaint. And the day after that, Davis hired a local drug dealer named Paul Hardy to shoot and kill Groves. There's small choice in rotten apples.

Officer

The common title applied to individual police, "Officer," is quintessential copspeak. From the Latin *officiarius* and *officium*, the word describes a person said to possess an authority based on a circular logic: an individual cop's authority is official because the cop holds an official position of high *office*. More directly, the *oficier* of old French is today's *officer*, which of course isn't reducible to the police officer. Pay attention and you'll find "officers" everywhere you look. The loan officer at the local bank, the chief executive officer (CEO) of local firms or Fortune 500 companies, and even the human resources officer at a nonprofit organization. Despite the ubiquitous use of the term, the phrase is most closely associated with cops and soldiers, the most recognizable agents of official **force** (102–104) who, as Frantz Fanon put it, "speak the language of pure force." Fanon wrote about police and soldiers in a colonial context, where the honorific title of "officer" authorizes and enshrines state **violence** (96–100) under the sign of the *officium*.

Far from a simple honorific or descriptive title, the word "officer" operates as a euphemism designed to underwrite the violence work of cops and soldiers. Officers of all sorts require a uniform. The judge dresses up the violence of legal interpretation by donning religious-cum-secular robes. The cop dresses up official police violence by wearing an official **uniform** (141–143) and an official **badge** (106–110). With the uniform and the badge comes the **gun** (10–13) and the

nightstick (55–58), and the expectation to use them. The cop holds an official office, a *legitimate* authority, and as a result the rough "street justice" and the bloodletting the cop doles out with the **flashlight** (48–50) or the **K-9** (22–24) can only ever be legitimate and official in the eyes of the state. Officers know best, so the logic goes, because officers are official representatives of the *official* state.

Listen carefully when the courts or liberal reformists confront public outrage over a cop's violence. They seek no escape from the straitjacket of their circular logic, and instead fall back on their **bad apple** (224–227) theory of police violence. An officer can never be a bad cop, in other words, because an officer is always also a "gentleman."—The British relied on this phrase—"an officer and a gentleman"—in eighteenth-century court martial hearings related to scandalous behavior and the violation of official protocol or decorum by military officers. The liberal defense of police at work here blunts any structural critique of the state apparatus as a violent regime. In place of this, we get the bad apple theory of state violence.

When we use the words "police officer," we transform the bully-in-uniform to an esteemed, respectable, polite, official representative of social order and polite society. We normalize and enshrine the organized cruelty of policing with the pomp and ceremony of relentless police violence. We speak like a **cop** (219–221). We submit, always under the threat of official violence, to a relation of deference, of obedience, of respect, and even admiration. This is why the cop demands we call them *officer*, especially those of us who "don't wear the uniform." If the more colloquial "cop" suggests a vernacular withholding of deference and respect for the "person in uniform," then officer works to enshrine the cop with reverence, regard, and legitimate authority. The use of the word "officer" appears rather innocent, but don't be fooled. It's copspeak designed to insidiously normalize the quotidian violence of police.

Deterrence
Deterrence is a foundational principle of criminal **law** (90–93) and **criminology** (261–263) as a school of thought. The theory of deterrence, in short, claims people *choose* to obey or transgress the law

based on calculating the possible pains and pleasures of their actions. The modern state, therefore, strives to prevent legal transgressions by increasing the pains of punishment or decreasing the pleasures of transgression. Criminologists usually distinguish between general and specific deterrence, the former directed at a general population and the latter directed at specific individuals. Deterrence, then, is a utilitarian choice theory about **crime** (93–96) prevention through **threats** (222–223) of a swift, certain, and severe punishment.

Deterrence is really a state euphemism for official strategies and tactics of fear and terror. As the novelist J.M. Coetzee points out, deterrence is etymologically linked to terror. The verb "deter" comes from the Latin *terrere*, meaning "to frighten," and then *deterrere*, which means "to frighten from, discourage from." Deterrence is part and parcel of political power, from nuclear containment doctrines of the Cold War to the wars against crime, drugs, and terror itself. In terms of criminal law, the terror of deterrence is often associated with a "tough on crime" policy, with the usual examples being "three strikes" laws, mass incarceration, capital punishment, mandatory sentencing, and efforts to increase the number of police officers. But using these as the only or primary referents for domestic deterrence fails to account for the ways that deterrence-as-terror is an animating logic of the most routine, workaday operations of law and **order** (83–86) politics, including police power.

Although criminal deterrence is most often associated with state punishment, and therefore formal sanctions like prison, jail, and even fines, if we locate prevention of threats as one of the oldest and essential structuring logics of police power—and here we should recall the "preventative police" of the eighteenth century—then the terror logic of deterrence can more easily be understood as not merely a punishment or carceral logic, but a police logic. The distinction is important, and one implication here is that punishment, to the extent it is obsessed with future or potential transgressions, can itself be understood as a logic of police power/terror. To punish in order to deter future transgression is a police power in the way it aims to prevent potential, future threats to the social order. Prison, then, might also be understood as not merely an institution of punishment, but about policing the larger population, and rational choice thinkers see the population as always containing an unlimited pool of potential criminals.

Of course, articulated by officials as crime prevention, deterrence as a normalized form of **public** (252–255) terror guides most all police activity. As a National Institute of Justice report states, "The police deter crime when they do things that strengthen a criminal's perception of the certainty of being caught." Note here how there seems to be a conflation or confusion between the criminal and the general population. Hence the routine vehicular **patrol** (170–172), hot spots policing, foot and bicycle patrol, and the **police helicopter** (70–73), for instance, are all projects of deterrence, or frightening the population into compliance. But deterrence is operative in more "velvet glove" scenarios, like public relations campaigns and even **community policing** (122–123), such as police officers reading books to public school children or organizing midnight basketball, or anti-drunk driving commercials, or the seat belt campaigns of "click it or ticket." Thinking about deterrence in specific relation to police power, it is clear that most things police do are guided by the logic and goal of frightening people into consent and compliance, however harmless the means might appear.

Deterrence theory originated with the reformist Enlightenment liberal social contract theorists of the seventeenth and eighteenth century, like Hobbes, Bentham, and Beccaria. Challenging spiritual and theological understandings of transgression and the arbitrary, brutal forms of punishment divvied out by monarchical regimes, these theorists argued that people are rational, self-interested, autonomous individuals who exercise free will in choosing their actions in any given circumstance. The job of the state, then, was to fulfill its role in the social contract of deterring individuals by punishing them in ways that contribute to the "greater good." These theorists were interested in establishing the legitimacy of the modern liberal state, and its corresponding order of **private property** (81–83) and wage labor, by offering humane forms of law—the punishment should fit the crime, so to speak. But as Poulantzas has argued, "This 'State based on law,' conceived as the contrary of unlimited power, gave birth to the illusory opposition Law/Terror," which didn't banish violence from the social order, but merely recoded this terror within bourgeois "rule of law."

Today, the debate over deterrence is largely reduced to a simplistic, positivist, and apparently straightforward question: "Does deterrence work?" In general, research establishes that swift, certain, and severe punishment is not nearly as effective at deterring crime as its advocates often claim. But this line of questioning should be refused for the ways it mystifies, legitimates, and normalizes public terror. It is a prompt for magical thinking, not empirical science, since we can't say for sure why people didn't commit a crime. Yet whenever police and prosecutors appeal to deterrence, they are participating in this mysticism, always pointing to those who aren't committing crimes as proof that deterrence works.

The logic of police deterrence transforms thinking about the criminal law—and prevention and punishment—into an issue only concerned with the modification of the means of deterrence. For example, if the answer to the question "Does the deterrence of patrol work?" is "No, patrol doesn't deter crime," it doesn't necessarily follow that police will stop patrolling. It only means that the police will then proceed to adjust or modify their methods of patrol by establishing a new type of police presence. This is exactly how practices like hot spots policing, directed patrol, and **broken windows** (186–189) policing emerged—as **reforms** (155–160) to ostensibly make deterrence more effective. If the answer to our question is "Yes, patrol does deter crime," then we go down a path of easily legitimating strategies of public terror in the name of **security** (86–89).

Therefore, the problem of deterrence is a political problem regarding the ways the liberal state fabricates a racialized, propertied order by aiming to frighten its subject population—"the people"—into compliance through symbolic and material threats to human bodies. When state officials speak in the name of "crime prevention" through deterrence, they are simply talking euphemistically about frightening people into submission.

Disproportionate

The word "disproportionate" is commonly used by critics of police or by journalists who cover police as a way to describe the racial disparities in the use of **violence** (96–100) by police. In the aftermath of the police killing of Alton Sterling and Philando Castile, for example, journalist Wesley Lowery noted that "blacks were killed at rates disproportionate to their percentage of the U.S. population. Of all of the unarmed people shot and killed by police in 2015, 40 percent of them were black men, even though black men make up just 6 percent of the nation's population."[1] "Disproportionate" is also used to criticize police officer **discretion** (176–178) in the use of violence. In September of 2012, an Albuquerque police officer **Tasered** (13–16) a seventy-five-year-old man after a confrontation at a bus station. Officers ordered the man to leave. He initially refused but finally agreed, and when the elderly man raised his cane in order to rise up from the bench where he was sitting, an officer Tasered him. A sergeant later praised the Tasering as "exceptional" policing. The Department of Justice disagreed, concluding in a report on police use of **force** (102–104) in Albuquerque that a "lack of **accountability** (160–162) in the use of excessive force promotes an acceptance of disproportionate and aggressive behavior towards residents" and, in particular, "that APD officers used Tasers in a manner that was disproportionate to the **threat** (222–223) encountered."[2]

The use of the adjective "disproportionate" appears to interrupt police claims to unlimited discretion in the use of violence, and it focuses needed attention on the racialized patterns of police violence. The use of the word "disproportionate" echoes the use of words like "excessive" or "unjustified" in its refusal to accept prima facie police claims about violence. Disproportionate demands independent and objective criteria when judging the use of violence by police.

But be cautious when using the term disproportionate. Like excessive and unjustified, the word disproportionate questions or condemns individual decisions by police to use violence *at the same time* that it accepts without question the right, even the need, of police to use violence in general. For example, police violence is usually depicted as **justified** (238–240) or unjustified, excessive or appropriate. The problem is not violence per se, but excessive violence. This is the problem of words such as excessive and unjustified, but disproportionate is even more troubling for the way it *affirms* police violence as not just an accepted given, but also, frighteningly, a *social good*. When we describe the "disproportionality" of police violence, we depict the issue as one in which the problem is not police violence, but the distribution of police violence. And this leaves us in a strange position. If disproportionality is the problem, the solution is not an end to police violence but a more *equitable distribution* of that violence.

Disproportionality as a concept is persuasive because, when applied in some contexts, it reveals the effects of institutional biases. For example, the US Department of Education reported in 2014 that "students of color are suspended more often than white students, and black and Latino students are significantly more likely to have teachers with less experience who aren't paid as much as their colleagues in other schools."[3] Black and Latino students are disproportionately more likely than white students to have an inexperienced, underpaid teacher. Students of color are disproportionately more likely to be suspended than white students. If educational attainment is our concern, people of color are disproportionately less likely to graduate from college than white people. Poor people are disproportionately less likely to graduate from high school than wealthy people. In this example, educational attainment is the independent or controlled variable. We might expect to find implicit or explicit biases in the school system that limit the educational attainment of poor people and people of color. More white and wealthy students in advanced placement courses, for example, or a hostile campus climate to people of color, or poorly trained teachers in majority minority schools. And if we found these things—and we surely would if we looked honestly—the solution would be to adjust the independent variable. In other words, the solution would be to find effective means to distribute educational attainment more equitably.

Now, consider what happens when the independent variable is police violence. Consider the subtle shift that happens when the word disproportionate describes the racial disparities of police violence rather than the racial disparities of educational attainment. Police, we know, use violence disproportionately against people of color. This is true. But when we say that police use violence disproportionately against people or color, we imply that this disproportionality of violence is the problem. In doing so we establish "police violence" as the independent variable, like educational attainment. Just as the issue is not the college degree per se but the disproportionate access to the degree by people of color, so too the issue is not police violence per se but the unequal *distribution* of police violence. The solution to the problem of disproportionate school achievement by race or income is not to abolish educational attainment but to better redistribute the benefits of school, to improve access to school; in short the solution is to redistribute the social good of educational attainment.

This is not what critics of police violence intend when they use the word "disproportionate" in claims of racial disparity, but it is the logic of the argument: we identify some social good (educational attainment) whose unequal distribution or unequal access by race establishes a specific disparity that causes social ills. To say that police violence is disproportionately experienced by race is to say that the *maldistribution* of police violence causes social problems. We're left asking strange questions: What proportion of police violence would be acceptable? Should we be content to have police kill Black people in proportion to their representation in the general population? It's no wonder this logic of disparity gets us nowhere politically. Conservatives respond to every report that finds racial disparity in police violence with their own report that claims Black people commit disproportionately more **crime** (93–96) than whites and therefore, they argue, the distribution of police violence might be calibrated just as it should be. The logic of disparity contributes to, rather than interrupts, the familiar conservative **law** (90–93) and **order** (83–86) narrative of Black communities as difficult to police. When we identify the problem as disproportionality, we risk legitimizing a logic that gives us **racial profiling** (24–27) and **stop and frisk** (27–31). Disproportionality limits any analysis of police violence precisely as police prefer, because to say that police violence is disproportional is to demand that we better distribute it to the population that deserves it, not abolish it.

Ferguson Effect

Also called the "viral video effect," the "Ferguson effect" is a theory advanced by police leaders that attempts to link the anti-police protests that began in the United States in 2014 to an increase in violent **crime** (93–96), particularly murder, that they say followed. St. Louis, Missouri police chief Samuel Dotson coined the phrase following the protests of the killing of Mike Brown by Ferguson police officer Darren Wilson in August of 2014. "The criminal element is feeling empowered by the environment," claimed Dotson, and he called it "the Ferguson effect."[1] Right-wing pundits quickly took up the claim. When protests increase, they claim, **arrest** (208–210) rates go down, and crime rates go up. Police can't "do their job" because, as conservative author Heather McDonald argued in the *Wall Street Journal*, the protests in Ferguson represented a new "demonization of **law** (90–93) enforcement." The Ferguson effect was real, she claimed, and it's "happening across the country as officers scale back on proactive policing under the onslaught of anti-cop rhetoric."[2]

The Ferguson effect is an argument in defense of police homicide. Police kill someone and protests erupt. And these protests against police killing, according to the argument, restrain police from "doing their job." It is a lament more than an argument: "If only police could continue to kill as they have." It is an argument that holds fast to the idea that police kill people as part of their job and that this killing is crucial to **order** (83–86) and **security** (86–89). Police must kill people, in other words, and must be free of any scrutiny (which is to say, no protests) when they kill people, because killing people is the way order is made and kept. Thus the only problem with police killing is not the act of killing, but rather that the large and popular protests that sometimes follow them have a "chilling effect" on police officers, who are now afraid to "do their job"—which means afraid of killing people—and this encourages an emboldened criminal element. The police killings may not be legal or consistent with the rule of law but they produce order, and order is the job of police. This is the logic of the Ferguson effect.

The former director of the Federal Bureau of Investigation, James Comey, took up Dotson's claim and became among the most vocal proponents of the theory, asserting in a 2015 speech that the Ferguson effect produced a "chill wind blowing through American law enforcement over the last year." He called for a return to "actual, honest-to-goodness, up-close 'What are you guys doing on this corner at one o'clock in the morning?' policing."[3] We should remember that this was precisely the kind of policing Darren Wilson was doing when he killed Mike Brown, or that Timothy Loehmann was doing when he killed twelve-year-old Tamir Rice. In other words, police need to kill, must kill, and if this makes you angry, if this makes you distrust police, that's your problem. Keep it to yourself.

Furtive Movements

Furtive movements can get you killed, harassed or **arrested** (208–210). Just ask the family of Amadou Diallo, the Guinean immigrant who was shot and killed in 1999 when officers said he made a furtive movement for his **gun** (10–13). Of course, the gun turned out to be a wallet, since police were demanding he identify himself. But this fact isn't of concern for **cops** (219–221), since officer safety and the elimination of a perceived **threat** (222–223) take precedence over everything else. Furtive movements—a fleeting movement of a hand, a turning of the waist, a glance of the eyes—marks the line between freedom and captivity, life and death.

What exactly are furtive movements? "Furtive" implies actions that are stealthy, secret, shifty, cunning and underhanded. It describes a state of guilty nervousness. And since in the eyes of police everything and anything can be deemed a furtive gesture, you're always a threat. A furtive movement is whatever a cop says it is. The courts have consistently ruled that officers can violently intervene based solely on their perception of danger and threat. Furtive movements, therefore, do not reveal criminal intent but rather are gestures that a "reasonable" officer would find consistent with going for a weapon, even if that weapon were a wallet or a cellphone. The officer only has to claim after the fact that he or she thought you were going for a weapon in order to license bodily intervention, whether it is a routine **stop and frisk** (27–31), a **Taser** (13–16) to the neck, a bludgeoning by a **nightstick** (55–58), or a deadly shooting. Furtive movement is the legal category that justifies and legitimates the police killing of so many people with impunity.

Given the highly racialized and classed nature of police power, it is not a coincidence that police most often see people of color and other marginalized populations as prone to furtive movement. Indeed, officers frequently cite the "waistband grab" as justification for **violence** (96–100) against people of color, such as the unarmed Ricardo Diaz Zeferino who was shot and killed by police in Gardena, California in 2013. In July 2015, the *Huffington Post* compiled a list of at least twenty cases since 2010 where police **justified** (238–240) the killing of **unarmed** (257–258) people of color with the "reaching for the waistband" explanation.[1] Interestingly, to those populations most subjected to racist police violence, the very presence of police officers can actually produce fear, a fear officers then perceive as furtive and "threatening."

It is so easy to think of the "furtive movement" justification as evidence of first and foremost the conscious or unconscious bias of individual police officers. Similarly, it is easy to chalk up the furtive movements justification as a boilerplate excuse deployed by biased officers to justify, and to lie about, their violent, racist actions after the fact—just another case of a **bad apple** (224–227) cop. But the justification of furtive movements is not only about individual bias or individual decision-making. It is a legal doctrine, sanctioned by **law** (90–93) and legal rules and precedent, and built into the police institution and workaday routines of policing. Furtive movement is law's blank check that police cash to justify their lethal force. The doctrine of furtive movements is animated by law and put into practice by police **discretion** (176–178).

Cops have the sole prerogative to decide what is or is not a furtive movement. You might think what you are doing—say, reaching into your pocket to obtain your wallet—is the right or sensible thing to do. But the only thing that matters in the police encounter is the cop's perception of your actions.

The doctrine of furtive movements is also a mode of political address to a larger public. After a cop kills someone **the public** (252–255) is asked to consider the incident from the cop's perspective. The police interpret and narrate the incident to the public, telling us the officer mistakenly thought that reaching for a wallet was really reaching for a gun, and so it is the officer with whom we must empathize: "See, wouldn't you have thought the same thing? Don't you now understand that this killing, however tragic, is actually understandable and justified? Yes, there is a body lying in a pool of blood, but it is the cop with whom we must sympathize." "Furtive movements" is just another way in which we are told to see the world like a cop.

Justified

The use of **violence** (96–100) by police is often judged, whether by police, district or state attorneys or anti–police violence activists, as either justified or unjustified. The justified/unjustified binary establishes a continuum of police violence as either good and therefore justified, or bad and therefore excessive.

The language of police violence as either justified or unjustified is how police want you to talk about police violence, because the question of justification is a question only police can answer. This is because the decision to use violence is evaluated, by police and **law** (90–93), according to the **use-of-force continuum** (258–261), which establishes a seemingly objective and independent standard against which all police violence is judged. The continuum begins with a **cop**'s (219–221) order: "Put your hands up," or "Get out of the car," or "Show me your ID." If a subject is compliant but police use force anyway, the violence is excessive, and therefore unjustified. But when police officers confront a "noncompliant" subject, they are authorized to use escalating force, up to and including lethal force, until compliance. On its surface, the use-of-force continuum appears to hold police accountable. It appears to protect **the public** (252–255) from the **bad apple** (224–227) cop. But the continuum does quite the opposite. It invests in a police officer the *sole* **discretion** (176–178) to choose when, where, and how to use violence based on a police officer's interpretation of **noncompliance** (245–246). And remember that any limit placed on the police use-of-force standard is a limit only imposed after the fact. Law may deem it unjustified, but only after the blood has been spilled

According to the continuum, for example, police are justified if a person is armed and a **threat** (222–223), which is why law extends to police the discretion to define not only who is a threat, but also to define what armed means and what **unarmed** (257–258) means. You might be armed, and therefore a threat, if you raise your hands while holding a cellphone, like Daniel Tillison, or even if you have nothing in your hands at all, like Terrence Crutcher. When we judge police violence as either justified or unjustified, we weigh only what police officers think and if they fear for their lives. In other words, the question of justification asks us to see the world solely through the eyes of police, never through the eyes of their victims. Was Tamir Rice scared? Did he fear for his life? Yes, of course he was scared. But this is immaterial to law. What matters to law is how the **cop** (219–221) felt.

On the rare occasion police violence is declared unjustified, it is always depicted as a question of individual volition. Unjustified police violence is always the result of an independent decision by a bad apple cop who chose to engage in **police brutality** (207–208). This is why when **police reform** (155–160) measures are proposed in the wake of police brutality cases, they almost always focus on the mythical bad apple, not police in general. Fire the bad apples, raise hiring standards to avoid hiring new bad apples, and improve training in order to teach current police officers how not to be a bad apple.

Police violence, whether justified or unjustified, is always rare and exceptional, rather than routine and everyday. No district attorney investigates a **handcuffing** (20–21). And rarely a **chokehold** (58–60) or a **rough ride** (31–32) or a hog-tying, unless you die as a result. It's not violence, it's policing, which is to say that policing is always violence.

The justified/unjustified binary is animated by the logic of innocence and guilt. Did he have a knife? Then he must be guilty. The killing must be justified. When we see the world this way, like a cop,

only the innocent deserve our sympathy, and it is perfectly acceptable, even preferable, that police kill those deemed guilty. But just
like armed versus unarmed, guilty and innocent are cop categories.
As Ruth Wilson Gilmore explains, "By campaigning for the relatively
innocent, advocates reinforce the assumption that others are relatively or absolutely guilty and do not deserve political or policy
intervention . . . Such advocacy adds to the legitimation of mass
incarceration and ignores how police and district attorneys produce
serious or violent felony charges, indictments, and convictions. It
helps to obscure the fact that categories such as 'serious' or 'violent'
felonies are not natural or self-evident, and more important, that
their use is part of a racial apparatus for determining 'dangerous-
ness.'"[1] The problem is not *only* that police kill the innocent, but
also that police determine who is guilty, who is innocent, and who
must die.

And **police oversight** (146–149) will not save us. It does not
confront the problem of police violence; it only confronts "unjustified" police violence. The unjustified/justified binary works to bind
the two together. Unjustified violence is kin to justified violence.
The proposals of police reform—improved training, better equipment, and more cops on **the beat** (172–174)—promise to make the
unjustified killing of today the justified killing of tomorrow.

No Humans Involved (NHI)

Police use the classifying acronym NHI to refer to suspected gang
members and Black-on-Black **crime** (93–96). "No humans involved,"
they say. According to Sylvia Wynter, the acronym banishes the poor
and Black people from the category of the human: "Humanness and
North Americanness are always already defined, not only in optimally White terms, but also in optimally middle class."[1] In the early
1980s, LAPD officers used **chokeholds** (58–60) to kill sixteen people
during routine arrests, twelve of whom were Black. When a reporter
asked Los Angeles police Chief Daryl Gates to explain why LAPD
officers were choking so many Black people to death, he explained
that "the veins and arteries do not open up as fast in blacks as they
do in normal people."[2] In other words, according to Gates it was

impossible for LAPD officers to commit a crime against a Black person, because there were "no humans involved."

W. E. B. Du Bois wrote of "the color line" as the "central problem of the twentieth century." And the use of NHI by police and other **violence** (96–100) workers demonstrates that this line is not a metaphor, but rather a line literally policed by the state. This racist language marks people of color as less than human, and it was (and remains) prevalent among police in Miami, St. Louis, Phoenix and, particularly, Los Angeles, where the use of the term has been carefully documented. In the late 1980s, LAPD officers began referring to murders of gang members by rival gangs as NHI. Following the beating of Rodney King in 1991, the Christopher Commission investigated racist violence at the LAPD. The subsequent report devoted page after page to examples of racially motivated police violence rationalized by a pattern of racist speech. LAPD officers routinely used epithets to describe Black and Latino people as animals. The practice was so widespread in fact that officers typed their racist epithets directly into a mobile communications system they knew to be monitored by supervisors. In one communication profiled in the report, officers discussed killing Black people: "Everybody you kill in the line of duty becomes a slave in the afterlife." For police to say of Black deaths that there are "no humans involved" is to deny Black personhood. What does it say about police power that it routinely engages in the discursive production of Black people as less than human and prescribes violence as the means to an end that culminates in a return to Black slavery?

But NHI in the police lexicon refers also to the murder of women they consider prostitutes, whose slayings they describe as "misdemeanor murders," a reference to the total lack of concern regarding their deaths throughout the criminal justice system. Donna Gentile was one of forty-five women **raped** (41–43) and murdered in San Diego between 1985 and 1992. Gentile, who was both a sex worker and a police informant, was found strangled and choked to death after she testified against police. Her killer or killers had violently forced gravel into her mouth. Few of the murdered women were sex workers, but San Diego police referred to all of the women as prostitutes.[3]

The police project thus is fundamentally a politics of personhood. NHI reveals the ways that police power is intimately bound up with the category of the human. But it is not simply that the police exterminate an already existing person through dehumanizing language that seeks to justify (if not celebrate) acts of repression against those who police consider nonhuman. Rather, police power can more usefully be understood as a power that actively produces the very category of the human by conjuring up its opposite: animals, savages, brutes, rodents, slaves and even inanimate objects like "trash" and "scum" and "filth," for instance. Or snitches who need to eat gravel.

Establishment definitions of police power generally imagine police authority as limited to deciding who to identify as a **threat** (222–223), and when to use **force** (102–104). But the violence marked with the acronym NHI reveals that police power defines the limits of the human, and includes the authority to decide who is or isn't one. Identifying threats is also to identify who might or might not be a person. Policing is the work of death.

Deadname

When Albuquerque cops arrest trans women of color, particularly Native women, the police bring the women to the Metropolitan Detention Center in Bernalillo County (Albuquerque, New Mexico) where jailers place them in holding cells with men. The jailers write their deadnames on booking sheets and use pronouns interchangeably—sometimes she's a male, sometimes he's a female.

This is not a result of confusion or embarrassment by police or jailers or a product of their ignorance. Policing has always been about classification and its imposition—naming the vagrant (see **vagrancy**, 189–193), identifying the transient, cataloguing the criminal. If police decide you are not a person, you are a deviant. You are part of a population that constitutes a **threat** (222–223). You require management by police. Other categories of people include those who are disposable. And if you're a trans woman of color, you are presumed by police to be a sex worker. Cops and jailers do this routinely, but for transgender people, even well-meaning bystanders participate in this policing. Your family threw you out. Your school expelled you. The local businesses call the cops on you. The straight woman in the bathroom claims you are a pedophile. The neighborhood association fears for its property values because of you (see **gentrification**, 184–186). You live a life made impossible by all.

Native and working class trans women of color and trans people forced to live on the street navigate a world of hostile exclusion. A spatial exclusion—"you don't belong here." An existential exclusion—"What are you?" An emotional exclusion—"Calm down. What's wrong with you?" And a legal exclusion—"We invented criminal trespass for you." These are all forms of exclusion that license violence against trans people. To Morgan Bassichis, Alexander Lee, and Dean Spade, the conditions of trans living are found in its impossibility.

> According to our legal system, the media, science, and many of our families and religions, we shouldn't exist! Our ways of living and expressing ourselves break such fundamental rules that systems crash at our feet, close their doors to us, and attempt to wipe us out.[1]

Try surviving that.

Eric Stanley, in *Captive Genders: Trans Embodiment and the Prison Industrial Complex*, writes that "some, perhaps many, trans/queer people, as a result of experiencing relentless violence, are in favor of incarceration and believe in its claims of safety."[2] Consider that claim. How bad is the street that the grinding dehumanization of incarceration constitutes a better, safer place?

A woman sits in her black SUV at a streetlight on the west side of Albuquerque in February 2020. She sees a woman in a white shirt throw a rock that shatters her rear window. She calls police who arrive and find a trans woman named Penelope waiting. "Handcuff me and arrest me," Penelope tells the cop when he finally arrives. "I just want to go to jail," she says.

The cop brings Penelope to the detention center, where jailers call her only by her deadname and place her in a holding cell with men. The way many trans women survive men's jail is by trading sex for protection, which is the way many trans women survive the street. If subsequently convicted, incarcerated, and transferred from jail to prison, the sexual **violence** (96–100) intensifies. "COs [correctional officers] use the transgendered prisoners to keep the violence rate down."[3] A trans woman named Kim Love took a charge to protect someone else and was sent to prison. "If you look like a female, she explained, they'll force you into a sexual relationship. They threw her in a cell and "They told me that's gonna be your husband, and that's where you're going to be."[4]

Penelope threw a rock in order to escape the street for jail. But days after she was incarcerated police were called back to the jail. There'd been a commotion. A jailer had entered Penelope's cell to "discuss his [sic] discharge plan," as the cop wrote in his criminal complaint, when Penelope spit in the jailer's eyes and yelled, "You are a fucking bitch." The jailer turned to leave as Penelope kept yelling. "You bitch! Fuck you!" Police charge Penelope with battery. From street, to jail, to prison.

It's as if cops and jailers have directed all of law's violence toward trans women of color. As if they've been saving it up, conserving it all, collecting and caring for it, keeping it at the ready, until they finally find a trans woman on whom they can unleash it. As if order requires this violence; as if the nation needs defending from trans women of color.

Cops and jailers use epithets such as "Miss Thing" or "he/she" to dehumanize trans women. On their criminal complaints they record a woman's deadname and then sometimes they cross it out or they write AKA ("also known as") after the deadname. Police limit self-determination to those they consider redeemable, not those they treat as disposable.

The extreme violence directed at trans people confounds most efforts at description. When police or vigilantes kill poor trans men or trans women and especially trans people of color they are often "shot, stabbed, or bludgeoned, even after death." It's not enough to kill them. "The purpose of these attacks was not simply to terminate life, but to punish and torture for gender-non-conformity."[5]

A group of children play with friends in Gallup, New Mexico, in June 2009 and find a trash bag that contains Frank Yazzie's torso. Whoever murdered Yazzie, a Navajo trans man, dismembered him after murdering him. Searchers find another bag three days later that contains the rest of his body. No cop will ever "solve" Yazzie's murder (see **starlight tour**, 46–48). Organizers ask a trans woman on the street near the Albuquerque Indian Center in 2014 if the cops harass her. She looks at them without patience. "What the fuck do you think?"

Noncompliance

Police is a power premised on an imaginary world of disorder, populated by unpacified subjects, who can be restored only through its application. When police speak of noncompliance, they speak of these fictional subjects in a state of disorder. It is a word that permits only one alternative to disorder, only one solution to non-compliance: police. Only police produce the pacified, compliant subject. Without police there will be disorder; without police you will be noncompliant.

"Noncompliance" reveals the impossibility of an equal exchange between a **cop** (219–221) and a subject.[1] It describes the moment after the police use of **violence** (96–100)—after the **handcuffs** (20–21) are tightened, the **Taser** (13–16) fired, the **chokehold** (58–60) applied. Anything other than complete obedience and respectful deference is noncompliance, usually referred to as "resisting **arrest** (208–210)." Noncompliance is not just the absence of compliance, but the way cops legitimize police violence. **Pain compliance** (79–80) is another word for terror.

Policing seeks to turn unpacified subjects into polite subjects and uses pain compliance to do so. A ninety-pound **K-9** (22–24) is set loose on you. If you move at all—turn to run, cover your face, strike the dog—you will be charged with resisting arrest. You are mauled by a trained attack dog, left bleeding, flesh torn from your body, because you were noncompliant.

Or imagine that you are Sandra Bland. Texas state trooper Brian Encina pulls you over in July of 2015 for failing to signal a lane change. You're sitting in your car, smoking a cigarette, waiting for him to return with your ticket. Encina walks back to your car and orders you to put out your cigarette. What? "Why do I have to put out a cigarette when I'm in my own car?" you ask. Encina is now agitated and he orders you to get out of the car, but you refuse. You are now non-compliant and things escalate quickly. Encina starts shouting and grabbing at your car door. "I am giving you a lawful order." He pulls open your door and grabs at you, yanking you out of the car. You pull back, struggling to stay in the car. And Encina keeps shouting, and he's pointing his Taser directly at you. "I will light you up! Get out! Now!"

Encina arrests you and transfers you to the Waller County, Texas jail where they find you three days later hanged to death in your cell. In the wake of your death, the *New York Times*, while pointing out that Encina had no reason to fear for his safety and thus no reason to order you out of the car, notes that he had "almost complete **discretion** (176–178)" to do so and that you were "legally obligated to get out when asked."[2] In other words, forget what the **law** (90–93) may say; it's what the cop says that matters. As far as law is concerned, you were noncompliant and thus your death was your fault.

According to the Texas Department of Safety, Encina did not comply with official policies and procedures and was fired for his actions. Encina is out of a job for being noncompliant; Bland is dead for being noncompliant. And this is the key point. "Non-compliance" is not descriptive; it is prescriptive. It does not merely describe a deviation from a normative behavior; it describes a condition under which police can kill you.

Officer-Involved Shooting

Language, George Orwell reminds us, is always political. It can be used to "make lies sound truthful and murder respectable." The euphemism, he wrote, is the weapon of choice: "Defenseless villages are bombarded from the air, the inhabitants driven out into the countryside, the cattle machine-gunned, the huts set on fire with incendiary bullets: this is called *pacification* (89–90)."[1]

Consider the phrase "officer-involved shooting," which does not refer to shootings that merely involve police, but refers exclusively to situations in which an officer fires a weapon at a person. It is an intentionally misleading phrase used to obscure the patterns and politics of police **violence** (96–100). And its use is not restricted to police. "A bad usage," according to Orwell, "can spread by tradition and imitation even among people who should and do know better." And so journalists, particularly local TV journalists, happily repeat the copspeak daily, which serves to further obscure police violence.

The syntax of the phrase does not just obscure responsibility, it works to divert our attention from police entirely.[2] The phrase equates the perpetrators of violence—police—with its victims. And so instead of any scrutiny of police actions, professors of **criminology** (261–263) wonder after the cops' feelings and worry over their suffering: "What goes through police officers' minds when they are involved in shootings? How does facing deadly **force** (102–104) affect what they see, hear, and feel?"[3] Orwell would marvel at the work such a question does, transforming homicide into "facing deadly force."

We're asked to empathize with cops, to see and feel like a **cop** (219–221). And the obfuscatory syntax of "officer-involved shooting" is usually paired with the active voice that describes the person who the cop shot. He menaced officers; he threatened officers; she made **furtive movements** (236–238); he went for a **gun** (10–13); she wouldn't show her hands. Paired together, we find a grammar of exoneration. "How can agency leadership expect law enforcement personnel involved in one of the most critical incidents in their lives, who are operating under stress and fear, to remember what just happened in a rapidly evolving event?" asks *Police Chief Magazine*. "This is not a realistic expectation. What also must be realized is that civilian eyewitness testimony may be based on beliefs and values and may not be a fair replication of the actual facts."[4] In other words, what police think is realistic and fair: that cops have total **discretion** (176–178) to use violence because of their training and expertise. What victims of police violence think is unrealistic and unfair: that cops should or even could explain why they used violence in any single instance because of the trauma they suffer.

A critical inquiry into the usage of "officer-involved shooting" reveals it as a familiar ploy of copspeak. The grammar of copspeak offers a *phrase* ("officer-involved shooting") that obscures an *act* (police killing a human being). This ploy individualizes at the same time that it anonymizes police violence. There are other such words and phrases in the copspeak glossary. **Community policing** (122–123), **deterrence** (228–231), **force** (102–104), **broken windows** (186–189), **crime** (93–96) and more. These are all words that not only obscure real relations of violence but reserve for police permanent virtue, and an always-pure authority. Most criticisms of the phrase "officer-involved shooting" complain that the phrase releases the cop from blame or culpability. But in this way the syntax accidentally reflects a real truth: there is a dreadful inevitability to police violence. "Officer-involved shooting" is copspeak in fatal voice.

Challenge Coins

The **violence** (96–100) of police conditions the work of police. Cops don't only use violence, they celebrate it, they memorialize it. As museum conservators curate collections, cops curate their sadism, turning their brutal quotidian violence into horrifying objects of art. Don't believe it? Ask a **cop** (219–221) to see their coin collection. On second thought, don't talk to cops (see **interrogation**, 193–195); instead, find it online yourself.

Online you'll find images of cop coins and lots of them, example after example of the routine, there-for-all-to-see cruelty of police power. Badges and coins and commemorative medallions, considered by some to have military origins, are enormously popular with police. There are hundreds upon hundreds of coins of every shape and size. Some are sanctioned and official and issued by departments, while others are unofficial, underground, and hidden from view. The sanctioned coins are designed and produced by department brass or city officials. The underground coins are made by individual cops or their supporters. In both cases, they usually venerate a specialized unit, or a specific department or precinct, or a historical event. Many commemorate direct physical violence. Many of the coins appear quite innocent, even harmlessly nostalgic, like those that depict majestic precinct buildings next to a department's name adorned with an American flag and predictable copspeak like "protect and serve."

If, metaphorically speaking, you flip over the seemingly "politically correct" coins, you find in plain view policing's quotidian sadism. Take for instance the coins of the New York Police Department (NYPD), the department responsible for some of the most well-known and racist challenge coins. The most infamous come from the notorious Street Crime Unit, whose members in 1999 hunted down and killed the **unarmed** (257–258) Guinean immigrant, Amadou Diallo, with a barrage of forty-one gunshots. The coin they minted to celebrate their murder is shaped like a police **badge** (106–110). It includes the unit's motto, "We Own the Night," and a quote by Ernest Hemingway: "There is no hunting like the hunting of man, and those who have hunted armed men long enough and like it, never care for anything else thereafter."[1] The Hemingway quote is popular with cops. It shows up alongside the Jamaican flag on a challenge coin for the NYPD's 67th precinct, along with a reference to "Fort Jah," a racist reference to the large West Indian and Rastafarian population of East Flatbush. Two cops, guns drawn, hunt a Black man in dreadlocks on the coin. Look closely and you'll see the hunted man's shadow on the coin taking the shape of a deer. "Let the Games Begin" it reads, a reference to "The Most Dangerous Game," a short story about the hunting of humans.[2]

NYPD challenge coins often depict police as hunter-settlers colonizing a frontier against "savage Indians." In typical settler fashion, police always see themselves as under attack, and this often figures into the designs and typography of their coins. "Fort Apache," the cop colloquialism for NYPD's 41st precinct in the South Bronx, makes an appearance on a number of challenge coins. On one, arrows pierce the side of the precinct building as though under attack. Another takes the shape of an arrowhead. Ralph Friedman, known as the NYPD's "most decorated detective," mostly because he killed four people and shot at more than a dozen others, gets his own challenge coin: an American flag flies in the background surrounded by two pistols, a pair of **handcuffs** (20–21), and four skulls, each with a bullet hole in the forehead. A banner stretches across the top of the coin and reads "4x justified," commemorating Friedman's confirmed kills.

The challenge coin is not just an NYPD thing; rather, it is part and parcel of police across the United States. A Minneapolis challenge coin, released by police soon after the 2020 uprisings in response to the police murders of George Floyd, depicts a Robocop-looking riot cop gripping his **nightstick** (55–58) on which is written the phrase "Operation Restore Order."

The year of Covid saw a bumper crop in cop coins. Soon after the protests surrounding the police murder of Breonna Taylor in 2020, a Louisville-based company produced a challenge coin depicting nightstick wielding riot cops standing in front of a burning city; the phrases "hold the line" and "the strongest steel is forged in the hottest fire" are embossed across the coin. On the coin's flip side, the phrases "uphold the constitution" and "protect the city" share space next to the department's official logo. A Los Angeles Police Department (LAPD) challenge coin displays a skull in a police helmet above the phrase "hats and bats," an obvious reference to the nightstick as a baseball bat by another name. This same phrase, "hats and bats," appears also on Baltimore challenge coins that commemorate the city's riots of 1968 and 2015. The LAPD's **CRASH** (128–130) unit had its own challenge coins, one of which has a menacing red-eyed skullhead wearing a cowboy hat alongside playing cards, graphically celebrating CRASH members as frontier outlaws who gamble with the lives of the racialized poor. The homicide division for the Long Beach police has a challenge coin that depicts a large vulture perched on a gravestone marked with the radio code for murder, 187, alongside the phrase "Our day begins when your day ends."

What should we make of this? On its surface, the challenge coins appear insignificant and juvenile. But don't dismiss the challenge coins too quickly. They pull back the curtain on the hidden economy of cruelty among police, an economy of cruelty the writer China Miéville calls a "social" or "surplus sadism," a "scandalous, invested sadism, enjoying its own cruelty."[3] Start looking and you'll see this sadism among police everywhere. Take the police T-shirt, for example, a related if more public artifact of police sadism.[4] Cops and their **thin blue line** (110–112) supporters, including **armed friendlies** (165–170) who love the vigilante symbolism of The Punisher comic book, celebrate the legal violence they mete out against populations that they criminalize. Their T-shirts catalogue their cruelty. "We get up early to beat the crowds," reads one. "Scumbag Eradication Team," reads another. Like drunk fraternity brothers, they brag online about their shirts. One bragged about owning a T-shirt inscribed with the words "**Police Brutality** (207–208) . . . the fun part of policework." T-shirts regarding police **K-9** (22–24) are particularly illuminating in this regard, with examples like "here to bite your ass not to kiss it" or "I can't fix stupid but my partner can bite it," as well as "K-9: teaching idiots not to run one bite at a time." And in an homage to Trump: "Make America Bite Again."

Both challenge coins and T-shirts (to take just two examples) offer ample evidence of the social sadism running through the twisted emotional life of policing's violent prerogative. This is not a matter of a few **bad apple** (224–227) cops. This is about an institution constructed around a social order premised on relations of **private property** (81–83), white supremacy, and class hatred, which together constitute the glue that holds the police powers together. This is about social sadism, a view of police that shifts our attention away from individual psychology and toward an analysis of police focused on political economy and political power—on capitalism itself. "Our everyday and surplus sadisms," Miéville writes, "are inextricable from capitalism's history of racist violence." The idea of a surplus sadism draws our attention to the ways that police violence always includes an "excess" that isn't always functional or serves a practical purpose. As Miéville states: "the sadism of capitalism is a deep grammar, and it is always functional. And/but it is never only functional." Cops don't just kill, they destroy. The coins and T-shirts let them return to the scene over and over again, like serial killers celebrating their kill and mocking the dead. They make racist jokes about unsheltered people. They make jokes about running over the flowers that people leave to honor Michael Brown. They make jokes about their K-9 pissing on Brown's street memorial. In this excess we find the nature of police.

Challenge coins and T-shirts are not just trivial symbols and decorative trinkets. They don't merely celebrate violence. Like the police **badge** (106–110), they reaffirm and sanction police sadism as essential to good order. Nearly all coins or T-shirts make this clear, one way or another, such as the T-shirt that Las Vegas police made following their 2003 murder of Orlando Barlow. Barlow was babysitting his girlfriend's children when police arrived with their guns and demanded he surrender. Barlow complied with police commands, left the house on his knees with hands in the air and his back to police, which is when **Officer** (227–228) Brian Hartman shot him in the back and killed him. The cops celebrated by making and selling T-shirts that included the words "Baby's Daddy Removal Team." Not to be outdone, scores of NYPD cops wore T-shirts celebrating the murder of Eric Garner in 2014. After NYPD cop Daniel Pantaleo choked Garner to death, his fellow cops made shirts that included the words "I can breathe," mocking Garner's dying words, "I can't breathe." They also made one that read "I can breathe . . . because I obey the law."

The coins and the T-shirts get at the heart of police power and illustrate one of Miéville's key points, namely, that evil often manifests itself as the

> party-goer; boisterous; braying; a frat alumnus; a bully who loves being a bully; a successful professional, lip-smacking at the misery of those s/he hurts; one who is increasingly happy to cop to that enjoyment, to proclaim it, to perform it.[5]

This is the lesson of the challenge coin and other artifacts of police sadism. The need to perform, for themselves and others, the joys and pleasures of inflicting violence. Their challenge coins, the currency of a capitalist system that police violence fabricates and defends, shimmer as though polished with the blood of their victims.

The Public
The idea of the public is crucial to **law** (90–93) and **order** (83–86) mythology. Police authority is a public authority in that the very existence of the police is thought to come from the consent or desires of

the people. Robert Peel, the original gangster credited with forming the first modern police **force** (102–104), save for the earlier **slave patrol** (143–144), famously quipped that "the police are the public and the public are the police." Of course, the public always wants public safety and public decency, so this demand by the people explains why police officers, as public officials and public authorities, are always working at all costs toward the public good and public order. Police officers are also public employees who work for the public in public space and in public view while simply trying to do their best with low salaries, high stress, real dangers, and lots of negative public opinion. **Cops** (219–221) are always getting frustrated with the public because the public simply demands too much from police, their public servants. Not only must they reduce or eradicate **crime** (93–96) but they must also respect civil liberties and submit to public **accountability** (160–162) and public **oversight** (146–149). The police work for the public, but when push comes to shove, to hell with the public. They just can't really understand the unique challenges of being a cop, so it is best the public just trust cops and respect police.

This fetish of "the public" is nothing but political deception, what Nina Power calls a "bad joke." "The police are not the public, and never were," she explains. "They were always just police."[1] This bears repeating over and over again because the fetishization of the police as somehow forming out of the consensual desires of some mystical entity called the public is so insidious and normalized that it holds sway over most all discussions of police **violence** (96–100) and **police reform** (155–160). As Christopher Wilson demonstrates, the public is not some objective entity that simply corresponds to police power, but is a political construction often created by police, elite sponsors like business owners, and journalists. That is, the police and their cadre of stakeholders are often responsible for constructing the very public they claim to represent and serve, and of course the very publics, or anti-publics, that apparently threaten the public good. In this formulation, "the police officer actually *becomes* the public's representative, agent of its own desire for order."[2] That is, in their noble duties of securing public order, the police are simply following the wishes of the public, as if the police are saying,

"We killed this person because you asked us to," or "We are busting people for selling untaxed cigarettes and jaywalking because you have given us those orders." How dare the public complain and criticize police for injustice or injuries to members of the public.

The public belongs to that other fairytale about the democratic state: the social contract. This is also why the notion of the public is fraught with confusion: it simultaneously refers to private individuals agreeing among themselves to consent to be governed by, and unquestionably obedient to, a sovereign authority. This process, liberal state theorists argue, renders the modern state a public authority that is of the people and for the public good. In this view, the public simultaneously refers both to state authorities and their subjects, the policers and the policed. This abstraction that the state is borne out of some mystical public authority provides an illusory account of how law, because it is of the people, holds police accountable to the people while making humane and civil the violence of the liberal state. One insidious problem with the mythology of the public, then, is how it makes any alternative to the police, or really the administrative, coercive state itself, seem impossible, and downright foolish. We need the police, or the police must operate in such and such way, because certain publics require police.

At the same time, the public can never really be the police because the fairytale requires a partition between both entities—a public made up of private individuals pursuing their own interests and of public officials who reject pursuing their own private interests in the name of the public good through their own **professionalization** (113–115) and **badge** (106–110) of honor. Police advocates frequently argue that actual members of the public shouldn't interfere with the practice of policing, while trusting that the police, as the real public, always know best the public good. Moreover, the public is an object of police concern because it is often found wanting in its alliance with and support of the police, setting off police efforts to rectify this by all sorts of strategies and tactics to win hearts and minds, like **Officer Friendly** (132–135) and **community policing** (122–123).

The idea of the public enshrines in police an abstract foundation of consent and mutual agreement at the same time that the threat of public disorder is found in the public. Here it is easy to speak of the highly racialized, classed, and gendered dynamics of the public. For instance, the public that consents to police is supposed to include all people, but the public that threatens order is only some people. It could be panhandlers in one place, or sex workers in another, or Native homeless trans women in another. Poor people, the jobless, the homeless, and a multitude of racial others are first and foremost constructed as public enemies, and therefore not a part of other bourgeois, frequently white publics consisting of obedient workers, consumers, clients, customers, and good citizens.

The power of the public is its malleability to be many things at once: orderly and disorderly, obedient and unruly, threatening and nonthreatening. When certain publics take to public space to resist or contest the public authority and its role in inequality and injustice, then it is only a matter of asserting public order, or the **security** (86–89) of the public good, over public space and public assembly. It is through constructing the public that police defend their unlimited **discretion** (176–178), deflect calls for **oversight** (146–149), define **threats** (222–223) and **emergencies** (223–224), distinguish between a rioter (who gets a **Taser** (13–16) to the stomach) and a citizen (who gets a sticker), and claim to be merely imposing the normative values of the public that guide policing and its never-ending cycles of reform. If the police are of the public, it is a very limited, insular, and narrow public of accumulation and **private property** (81–83). The police want to cut down the insurgent public and plant in its place other publics like the consuming public, the working public, and the obedient public.

Reasonable Suspicion
This is how law books explain "probable cause": A police officer may stop and **search** (163–165) a person only if objective facts and circumstances, known to the officer, would lead a reasonably cautious person to conclude that a **crime** (93–96) had been committed. Most importantly, the right to engage in that search is only permitted with a search warrant issued by the independent judgment of a judge or magistrate. This view advances the idea that the law protects you from police.

But probable cause does not protect you from police, especially if you are a person of color or you are poor, and God help you if you are both. Police will lie on search warrants (see **CRASH**, 128–130); they will lie in court (see **testilying**, 218–219). They will plant evidence and concoct "anonymous tips." And they will get their search warrant. But liberals, not just conservatives, will never tire of the myth. They will assure you time and again that the law will protect you, that law will constrain police power. But **law** (90–93), like the irrigation water that a farmer carefully draws into her field, knows its master and nourishes only police power.

And making law consistent with police practice was what the Supreme Court had in mind in 1968 when it established a different standard than probable cause for police stops and searches in *Terry v. Ohio*. In that case the Court ruled that a police officer could **stop and frisk** (27–31) a suspect on the street without a search warrant, and without violating the Fourth Amendment prohibition on unreasonable searches and seizures, as long as the stop was based on "specific and articulable facts." But despite subsequent court rulings regarding what constitutes "specific and articulable facts," the court has never provided a definition of this different standard, reasonable suspicion, thus leaving it up to police to define. Thus the power to stop, to search, to seize, to **arrest** (208–210), is entirely at the **discretion** (176–178) of police. Are you in a "crime-infested" neighborhood? Are you running? Are you walking? Are your movements evasive? **Furtive** (236–238)? Are your hands in your pockets? Are you congregating on a street corner? Are you by yourself? Are you walking down an alley? Are you whispering in someone's ear?

But before we conclude that reasonable suspicion constitutes an expansion of police powers, let's remember that cops have always stopped and frisked people on little or no evidence, particularly Black people. Terry didn't create the police stop, it legitimated it.[1] The practice is built into policing. Reasonable suspicion is just a way to explain the exercise of police power.

The courts endlessly defer to police practice and experience, and thus the concept of reasonable suspicion is embedded deeply in policing and law as an institutional imperative to conflate race and criminality. Recall that "reasonable suspicion" emerged as a new legal standard during the civil rights struggles of the 1960s. Law and **order** (83–86) politicians responded with tough-on-crime proposals based on the claim that probable cause **handcuffed** (20–21) police and limited their ability to do their job during this period of rising Black crime.

Without reasonable cause there would be no **predictive policing** (178–179). The rise of the computer modeling of crime by police is a direct result of the only limit that the standard of reasonable suspicion places on police. A hunch or intuition does not itself establish reasonable suspicion, unless it can be rendered as a statistical probability by a computer algorithm. The condition of poverty also does not establish reasonable suspicion, unless it is rendered as a statistical probability by a computer algorithm. And the result of reasonable suspicion and the practices it permits, such as **broken windows** (186–189) policing and **CompStat** (180–182) and **racial profiling** (24–27), is not lost on the people constantly stopped and frisked. As Michelle Alexander writes, "For black youth, the experience of being 'made black' often begins with the first police stop, **interrogation** (193–195), search, or **arrest** (208–210). The experience carries social meaning—*this is what it means to be black.*"[2]

Unarmed

According to the police **violence** (96–100) counting project, *Mapping Police Violence*, 102 unarmed Black people were killed by police in 2015. This means that of all the Black people killed that year, almost one in three were unarmed, which is five times the rate that police kill unarmed white people. The most high-profile police killings of Black men and women over the last thirty years—for instance, those of Amadou Diallo, Sean Bell, Oscar Grant, Mike Brown, Rekia Boyd, Eric Garner, Freddie Gray, Tamir Rice, John Crawford III, Walter Scott—are all tied together through the fact that this state violence was directed against unarmed people of color.

But we should be careful when using unarmed as the primary or sole criterion to judge and protest police killings. It is a term that hides a deceptive logic designed to justify the police killings of those persons deemed armed, which characterize the overwhelming majority of police killings.

Put in more direct terms: the category of unarmed, as a means of politicizing police killings, risks depoliticizing the killing of armed people, a category that shouldn't be taken for granted. For example, what exactly do police mean when they declare a person armed? In 2015, according to the *Guardian*, police killed 1,140 people in the United States, and 853 of these victims were considered by police to be armed. Although the majority were listed as possessing a firearm or knife when police killed them, over 200 of these armed people were said to possess "other weapons." One of the most common weapons was a car. Other weapons included flagpoles, steel pipes, bicycle chains, or replicas of firearms, including toys such as water pistols.

From the police perspective, everyone is always potentially armed, and as the racialized demographics of the victims starkly show, police see people of color as the most likely of all. Remember, police officers killed Sean Bell because his friend had just mentioned going to get a **gun** (10–13). Darren Wilson described the body of Michael Brown as essentially a weapon in "demon" form, and of course police claimed they thought twelve-year-old Tamir Rice's toy gun was an actual gun.

To engage in a debate about police violence structured by an armed versus unarmed binary is to be seduced into thinking like police. The result is that all other forms of police violence are normalized and obscured as "nonevents," stripped of any political content. It is to conclude that there is a who and a how that police *ought* to kill.

Use-of-Force Continuum

The use-of-force continuum is common in police parlance as a way to describe and prescribe an escalating progression of police **violence** (96–100). The continuum begins with the mere presence of one or more officers. An officer makes a verbal command. "Show me your hands," for example. If the person does not comply with the order, the officer escalates force, using first nonlethal and finally, depending on the **threat** (222–223) and the circumstances, deadly force.

The continuum is taught to police officers in training, and it is invoked by police in response to public outrage following the unjustified use of force. It is often an effective tactic in these situations because on its face it purports to merely explain when and why an officer would be justified in escalating force in any given situation. It appears to describe an "if this, then that" cause and effect relationship. In this way, police can depict the use-of-force continuum as an objective way to evaluate the choice by a police officer to use force. We're told that it is a kind of checklist that not only governs police behavior but also allows for the independent evaluation of police behavior. It judges whether force was warranted and therefore **justified** (238–240). This is the appeal of the use-of-force continuum: it appears on its surface, particularly to police reformers, to actually challenge **police brutality** (207–208) through the creation of **professional** (113–115), regulatory standards that independently evaluate and criticize police violence. Those who hold fast to this view, however, forget that police violence is not an abstraction. Police escalate their force not because of some objective set of standards or checklist that they merely apply, but rather because an officer or a group of officers decides to tackle a person to the ground and **Taser** (13–16) him in the back, chooses to restrain a noncompliant motorist in a **chokehold** (58–60), or lets loose a **K-9** (22–24) police dog on a person in a mental health crisis who is acting erratically. In all of these cases, the use-of-force continuum would prompt one to ask, "What justification did the officer have to use force?" And the only way to answer that question would be to consider the encounter from the perspective of the police officer, not the victim. The use-of-force continuum thus invests the officer not only with the authority to choose when and how to escalate **force** (102–104), but also with the authority to evaluate whether it was justified. From this we can see that the use-of-force continuum masquerades as a kind of safe standard theory of police force that promises to hold police accountable but, in practice, serves to inoculate police officers from any and all sanction.

Despite all of this, the use-of-force continuum does reveal a profound contradiction in how police defend the **discretion** (176–178) to use force. On the one hand, the continuum proposes a set of standards that limit police violence, but the police have long claimed that police power cannot and should not be defined or limited in advance. Any given circumstance could pose a threat or create disorder, and thus, the argument goes, police should be given wide latitude to use their discretion however they deem fit. What do we make of this apparent contradiction? In practice, the continuum serves only to protect police from any and all judgment, but it is also a theory elaborated by police that, at its most basic level, admits that police should be limited in their day-to-day discretion to use force. This is the genius of the use-of-force continuum: it admits that police use of force should be limited and regulated by independent standards, and this satisfies advocates of **police reform** (155–160), but it also reserves for police the right to establish those standards. And that satisfies police.

And this is not all that it does. Note the similarity between the use-of-force continuum for police officers and what the military calls "escalation of force." Like police departments, the military defines a set of abstract conditions under which soldiers are permitted to use deadly force. A progression of force is predicated on the presence of "resistance" to officer (or soldier) authority at each step along the force continuum. These similarities are not an accident but instead point to a more general and historical correspondence between the police and the military. Police reformers and even many anti–police violence activists imagine that the police and military are and must remain distinct institutions, forever divided by a bright line that separates the different purposes they serve (that is, the police should "keep the peace" domestically while the military should "defend American interests" abroad). But this view ignores both what the police and military *actually* do and how similar those things really are. "Police officers and military veterans are kindred spirits," writes Mark Clark for *Police Magazine* in a January 2014 article that explains that military skills are in high demand by police departments. The skills learned on the battlefield, it turns out, translate directly to **the beat** (172–174). And police and military share more than personnel, they also increasingly share similar tactics (see **SWAT**, 135–139), training, and equipment (see **militarization**, 139–142). The similarity in how the police and military escalate force tells us that these similarities are not just in style but also in substance. In other words, police look and behave like the military because police and the military do the same things and share the same goals. The police and military use violence to occupy territory. Military outposts in hostile territory and police substations in "**crime** (93–96)-infested" neighborhoods. The military engages in **pacification** (89–90) in order to win "hearts and minds." The police engage in **community policing** (122–123) in order to secure community support for police authority. And, most importantly, the police and military decide when, where and how to use violence and reserve for themselves the right to call it justified.

Criminology

If anyone understood the bloody truth of criminology, which describes itself as the academic home for the scientific study of **crime** (93–96) and criminals, it was George Jackson, who in 1961 received an indeterminate prison sentence of one year to life for stealing seventy dollars from a gas station. Before prison guards shot and killed Jackson in an escape attempt, they caged him for ten years, nearly nine of which were in solitary confinement. Criminology helped construct Jackson as a criminal, and his torture via solitary confinement is a form of captivity long **justified** (238–240) by criminological knowledge. In his letters from prison, Jackson suggested that we "burn all of the criminology and penology libraries and direct our attention where it will do some good." He was convinced that the discipline of administrative criminology failed to properly admit that "racism is stamped unalterably into the present nature of Amerikan sociopolitical and economic life" and that "criminals and crime arise from material, economic, sociopolitical causes."[1] For Jackson, administrative criminology is not an objective and neutral academic discipline, but a political project of the capitalist state that is part and parcel of the class **violence** (96–100) carried out daily by all of its actors, stem to stern. From his vantage point, the scholarly project known as criminology did little more than underwrite the legal terror that fabricates a racial capitalist **order** (83–86).

Our era, the era of daily police killings and the mass caging of Black and Brown men and women, is the era of the rise of criminology and criminal justice as academic fields, one that explicitly animates liberal notions of reform that always result in more people in cages, more people on parole, and more people on probation. Criminology serves a legitimating function to the patterns of police violence because it takes crime for granted. The "prison didn't come to exist where it does just by happenstance," argues Jackson. "Those who inhabit it and feed off its existence are historical products."[2] They are products of criminology's history.

In the United States during the late 1960s and early 1970s, criminology grew with help from the Law Enforcement Administration Act (LEAA) that funded both local police agencies and academic units. Today criminology and criminal justice departments litter university campuses like so many candy bar wrappers and beer cans. It certainly isn't a coincidence that criminologists regularly work with and conduct research for police and prisons and other law enforcement organizations on program evaluations, to say nothing of the Department of Justice and other large police departments like the NYPD that maintain their own research departments. This is what criminology was always meant to do. College students who major in criminology in the United States can get a Bachelor's degree, and even a Master's and PhD, without ever taking one *required* course on police violence or the racist history of prisons. If anything, these courses are usually listed as electives, relegating the material violence of police and prisons outside the fundamental historical premises of the discipline. Of course, as an academic major, criminology also is primarily responsible for generating new recruits who will staff police departments, jails and prisons, and parole and probation offices. They are "cop shops" and they provide degrees for future police and prison guards.

Criminology exists to legitimate the amorphous, cruel state juggernaut known as the "criminal justice system." Take a class in criminology or read a textbook from the field and consider Michel Foucault's argument about the discipline. He was asked once in an interview, "You are very hard on criminology, its 'garrulous discourse,' its 'endless repetitions' . . . 'Have you ever read any criminological texts?'" he responded: "They are staggering. And I say this out of astonishment, not aggressiveness, because I fail to comprehend how the discourse of criminology has been able to go on at this level. One has the impression that it is of such utility, is needed so urgently and rendered so vital for the working of the system, that *it does not even seek a theoretical justification for itself, or even simply a coherent framework*. It is entirely utilitarian."[3]

The work of abolishing police and prisons might require that we first abolish criminology. There is no escaping the fact that the history of academic, administrative criminology is a history of police violence and putting people in cages. The history of academic criminology is the legitimation of the violence of capitalism and the capitalist state, all in the name of "better" policing, "more humane" prisons, "more democratic" rules and laws. The history of criminology is a history of state violence in the name of **reform** (155–160) and progress. The history of criminology is a history of the security state, whose grant dollars flood criminology departments staffed by academics who gleefully write crime reports and policy evaluations, all the while justifying this affair as an unfortunate but necessary arranged marriage in the name of progress and knowledge. The history of criminology is a story of the distrust of the poor and love for the liberal administrative state.

George Jackson, caged and killed by the state, understood this better than most. So next time the streets erupt in flames, heed his words and stoke the fire with criminology textbooks and criminal justice treatises. Man the barricades against the riot **cops** (219–221), but also the criminology professors who justify the police response and offer only piecemeal reforms on ways the cops restore its legitimacy. And only then, as George Jackson said, can we finally "direct our attention where it will do some good."

Epilogue:
On a World Beyond Police

Copspeak is all around us. Nearly everything we think we know about police comes to us through a vocabulary patrolled by police. It is safe to say that, to one degree or another, we all have a cop in our head. A cop who sees the world through the lens of security. Who is obsessed with order. Who sees threats, crime, and disorder everywhere they look. The purpose of *Police: A Field Guide* has been to challenge the world of copspeak. Our contention is that a rigorous critique of police and police violence must take the language of police seriously; must take into account the ways the vocabulary of police reform often sets the very terms of debate, blunts any criticism, and makes any alternative to business as usual all but impossible. This book challenges the police definition of reality by refusing its official language and rejecting the seemingly common-sense vocabulary of police.

We are not the first to offer an alternative to the lexicon of copspeak. "Fuck the police" emerged as the unofficial motto of the 1992 riots in Los Angeles following the acquittal of the white police officers who beat Rodney King. It was written on signs and shouted at police and graffitied everywhere on walls throughout South Central LA. Activists and protesters chanted these words in Seattle in 1999, in Ferguson and Baltimore in 2014 and 2015, and in Baton Rouge and Minnesota in 2016. Following the murder of Michael Brown in Ferguson, street signs and businesses were frequently tagged with FTP.

"Fuck the police" is a direct challenge to the police demand that the ideal police subject be polite and polished. It offers rage against political histories of racist state violence and the police occupation of the ghetto. Marvin X Jackmon's poem "Burn Baby, Burn" was one powerful early example, written after the 1965 Watts riots:

Black people.
Tired.
sick an' tired.
tired of being
sick an' tired.
Burn, baby burn . . .

"Fuck the police" expresses the anger and fatigue of the oppressed, and refuses the passive, depoliticizing language of police reform. "Fuck the police" is all about refusal. It refuses to be polite, refuses to defer to police, and refuses to believe it will all somehow get better through reform.

We end with "fuck the police" because, as the terms in this book make clear, police power has always given itself the task of fabricating order by civilizing the "uncivilized." "Fuck the police" strikes at the heart of this white bourgeois order by affirming a subaltern politics of the impolite, disobedient, and disrespectful. To the extent that police have come to be synonymous with civilization and order, "fuck the police" isn't merely a negation of the police, but a demand for justice that calls into question the legitimacy of the very social order that police are tasked with producing and reproducing. It is the anthem of large-scale riots and mass mobilizations, and the transcript to the most ordinary interactions with a cop on the street. But it is more than just a shout, song, or tag. It is an expression that condenses into three words the cruel political economies of racial capitalism, and the radical despair, rage and insurgency of the oppressed.

To shout "fuck the police" is to invoke a political vision of a world without cops, a demand for a better future, even if we aren't exactly sure how that future should look. But at least we know what it must not include: certainly not police as we know it, and not prisons full of people arrested by police, and not a world of order and security for only a privileged few. The language of copseak gives us police reform, which just gives us more police. "Fuck the police," on the other hand, demands the abolition of police and a more just order than what's offered by racial capitalism. This is a demand that requires being attentive to the enormous power of the modern state, and the ways it works to maintain and legitimize an unequal social order. Abolition rejects the fetish of security that animates all life and death under capitalism.

The goal of "fuck the police" is to reduce and eventually replace the police and prison industrial complex, that vast overlapping set of institutions that shape politics and society through the constant expansion of jails, prisons, parole and police, and in its place to offer alternative ways of dealing with inequality, violence, and racism. Yet abolition cannot offer a definitive end, because police and prisons lie at the heart of the capitalist state, which is always evolving, adapting and reconstituting itself in response to resistance and insurgency. Abolition must therefore continuously make and remake itself in response. And along the way, confront the individuals, institutions, systems and interests engaged with the capitalist state, because a different kind of order must not only include an end to the killing of people of color and the poor, and an end to their daily harassment and routine violence at the hands of the police. It must be an order in which the public good is not found in private property; in which public funds go toward education and healthcare for all, instead of more police and bigger cages. Abolition is achievable in the form of an organized political struggle that rejects police reform and instead challenges business as usual in the current political economy.

This view is dismissed by liberals and conservatives alike as too utopian, unrealistic, or naïve, just as "fuck the police" is dismissed as an expression of juvenile angst. Critics of abolition point to the absence of alternatives to police. Who will you call when you fear for your life? Only the police stand between order and disorder; only police patrol the thin blue line. Liberals and conservatives alike invoke these anxieties to argue for the persistence of police power. Cops for them are just like capitalism: there is no alternative.

This lack of imagination is what gives police reform its authority. Of course, police abolitionists and police reformists can agree on some points: limiting the police use of force, ending racial profiling, or halting stop and frisk. But where they diverge is on whether the

institution of police is inherently democratic and socially benefi-
cial, and whether it can be fixed. Reformists fail to recognize what
empirical research so clearly demonstrates: police, as well as prisons, do very little to actually reduce crime and make ordinary people
any safer. The police are not an institution essential for democracy;
they are an institution for maintaining an order of racial capitalism
and have never strayed from this mandate since the days of the slave
patrols and colonial militias. Where police reform seeks only to
transform the way policing happens, police abolition seeks to transform what police are.

Police abolition is not an abstract concept. Most people go
through their everyday life without much contact with police,
although this isn't true for the poor, oppressed, and marginalized,
for whom police are "enemies of the population," as James Baldwin
put it. For them abolition is a distant dream. Reformists, who refuse
to even consider that a world without police and private property
might actually be a safer and more democratic world than the one
we know today, never get tired of telling poor communities,
routinely terrorized by police, to simply be patient, follow police
orders, and work harder to escape the ghetto. The "pious calls to
'respect the law,'" wrote James Baldwin, "always to be heard from
prominent citizens each time the ghetto explodes, are so obscene."[1]
Whether in Detroit in 1967 or Ferguson in 2014, insurgent movements of poor Black and Brown people know that police reform
always leads to more criminalization, harassment, arrest and police
killing in their communities, "no matter how many liberal speeches
are made, no matter how many lofty editorials are written, no matter
how many civil rights commissions are set up."[2] They know that
the everyday terror of police violence is no aberration. So, "fuck the
police." The only way to improve the police is to abolish it.

Notes

Preface to the Second Edition

1 Jacobin, "Debating the 'Defund the Police' Language," Youtube, December 11, 2020.
2 Simone, AbouMaliq and Edgar Pieterse, *New Urban Worlds: Inhabiting Dissonant Times*, Polity, 2017.
3 Krausch, Meghan, "The Movement to Defund the Police Won't Go Away When Biden Takes Office," *Truthout*, January 16, 2021.

Introduction

1 See Williams, Kristian, *Our Enemies in Blue: Police and Power in America*, AK Press, 2015; Murakawa, Naomi, *The First Civil Right: How Liberals Built Prison America*, Oxford University Press, 2014; Neocleous, Mark, *The Fabrication of Social Order: A Critical Theory of Police Power*, Pluto Press, 2000.
2 Marx, Karl, *Capital: A Critique of Political Economy*, Vol. 1 [1867], Ben Fowkes, trans., Penguin, 1976, 899.
3 Monture-Angus, Patricia, "Standing against Canadian Law: Naming Omissions of Race, Culture, Gender," in Comack, Elizabeth, ed., *Locating Law: Race/Class/Gender Connections*, Fernwood, 1999, 93.
4 Huggins, Martha K., Mika Haritos-Fatouros and Philip G. Zimbardo, *Violence Workers: Police Torturers and Murderers Reconstruct Brazilian Atrocities*, University of California Press, 2002.
5 Neocleous, Mark, "The Police of Civilization: The War on Terror as Civilizing Offensive," *International Political Sociology* 5:2 (2011), 144–59.

1. WEAPONOLOGY

Gun

1 Correia, David, "'Killer Cop' Competition Comes to Albuquerque," *La Jicarita*, August 26, 2014.
2 Dunbar-Ortiz, Roxanne, *An Indigenous Peoples' History of the United States*, Beacon Press, 2014.

3 Umoja, Akinyele Omowale, *We Will Shoot Back: Armed Resistance in the Mississippi Freedom Movement*, NYU Press, 2013.

Throw-Down Weapon

1 Boyer, Peter J., "Bad Cops," *New Yorker*, May 21, 2001.

2 Clifford, Stephanie, "NYPD Under Investigation for Routinely Planting Guns on Suspects and Fabricating Circumstances of Arrests," *New York Times*, January 17, 2015.

Tear Gas

1 Sollom, Richard, Holly Atkinson, Marissa Brodney, Hans Hogrefe and Andrea Gittleman, *Weaponizing Tear Gas: Bahrain's Unprecedented Use of Toxic Chemical Agents Against Civilians*, Physicians for Human Rights, 2012, 1.

2 Rejali, Darius, *Torture and Democracy*, Princeton University Press, 2009, 290.

3 Knappen, Theo, "War Gases for Dispersing Mobs," *Gas Age-Record* 48:19 (1921), 702.

4 Feigenbaum, Anna, "100 Years of Tear Gas," *Atlantic*, August 16, 2014.

5 Pinsky, Mark, "If Pepper Spray Isn't Lethal, Why All the Deaths?" *Los Angeles Times*, June 18, 1995.

6 Feigenbaum, "100 Years of Tear Gas."

Handcuffs

1 Goodman, Amy, "As Chicago Pays Victims of Past Torture, Police Face New Allegations of Abuse at Homan Square," *Democracy Now!*, May 15, 2015.

K-9

1 Wall, Tyler, "Legal Terror and the Police Dog," *Radical Philosophy* 188 (2014), 2–7.

Racial Profiling

1 Martinot, Steve and Jared Sexton, "The Avant-Garde of White Supremacy," *Social Identities* 9:2 (2003), 170.

Stop and Frisk

1 Wilson, James Q. and George L. Kelling, "Broken Windows," in Dunham, Roger G. and Geoffrey P. Alpert, eds., *Critical Issues in Policing: Contemporary Readings*, Waveland Press, 2015, 458.

2 Ibid., 456.

3 Ibid.

4 Ibid., 457.

5 "Investigation of the Baltimore City Police Department," Report of the Civil Rights Division of the United States Department of Justice, August 10, 2016, 24.

6 Ibid.

7 Fassin, Didier, *Enforcing Order: An Ethnography of Urban Policing*, Polity, 2013, 92.

Rough Ride

1 Donovan, Doug and Mark Puente, "Freddie Gray Not the First to Come out of Baltimore Police Van with Serious Injuries," *Baltimore Sun*, April 23, 2015.

Body Cavity Search

1 Simons, Pamela Ellis, "Strip-Search: The Abuse of Women in Police Stations," *Barrister* 6 (1979), 8.

No-Knock Warrant

1 *Richards v. Wisconsin*, 520 US 385 (1997).

2 Norwood, Candice, "The War on Drugs Gave Rise to 'No-Knock' Warrants. Breonna Taylor's Death Could End Them," *PBS News Hour*, June 12, 2020.

3 See Ristroph, Alice, "The Constitution of Police Violence," *UCLA Law Review* 64 (2017), 1182.

Curfew

1 Parenti, Christian, *Lockdown America: Police and Prisons in an Age of Crisis*, Verso, 1999, 135.

2 Williams, Kristian, *Our Enemies in Blue: Police and Power in America*, South End Press, 2007.

3 Loewen, James W., *Sundown Towns: A Hidden Dimension of American Racism*, The New Press, 2013.

4 Wacquant, Loïc, *Punishing the Poor: The Neoliberal Government of Social Insecurity*, Duke University Press, 2009, 68.

5 Mitchell, Don, *The Right to the City: Social Justice and the Fight for Public Space*, The Guilford Press, 165, 172.

Rape

1 Ritchie, Andrea, "Say Her Name: What It Means to Center Black Women's Experience of Police Violence," *Truthout*, September 18, 2015.

Lynching

1 Wells, Ida B., "Lynch Law in All Its Phases," *Our Day*, 1893.

2 Gilmore, Ruth Wilson, "Race, Prisons and War: Scenes from the History of US Violence," *Socialist Register* 45, 2009, 74.

3 Murakawa, Naomi, *The First Civil Right: How Liberals Built Prison America*, Oxford University Press, 2014, 31.

4 Gilmore, "Race, Prisons and War," 75.

5 Wagner, Bryan, *Disturbing the Peace: Black Culture and the Police Power after Slavery*, Harvard University Press, 2010, 18.

Starlight Tour

1 Chamayou, Grégoire, *Manhunts: A Philosophical History*, Princeton University Press, 2012.

Flashlight

1 Schivelbusch, Wolfgang, "The Policing of Street Lighting," *Yale French Studies* 73, 1987, 61–74; Browne, Simone, *Dark Matters: On the Surveillance of Blackness*, Duke University Press, 2015.

Rubber Bullets

1 Puar, Jasbir, *The Right to Maim*, Duke University Press, 2017.

2 Wilson, Mark, "The Lethal History of Rubber Bullets—and Why They Should Never be Used on Peaceful Protesters," *Fast Company*, June 5, 2020, fastcompany.com.

3 Ibid.

4 Ibid.
5 Haar R. J., V. Iacopino, N. Ranadive, et al., "Death, Injury and Disability from Kinetic Impact Projectiles in Crowd-Control Settings: A Systematic Review," *BMJ Open* 7 (2017), 1–9.
6 Arnold, Amanda, "'Rubber Bullets' Are Not Rubber," *The Cut*, June 5, 2020.
7 Gramenz, Jack, "Photojournalist and Author Linda Tirado Blinded in Minneapolis Protests," *The Chronicle*, May 31, 2020.
8 Freskos, Brian, "Police Should Never Use Rubber Bullets Against Civilians, Experts Say," *The Trace*, June 3, 2020, thetrace.org.

Nightstick

1 Johnson, Marilynn, *Street Justice: A History of Police Violence in New York City*, Beacon Press, 2004, 41.
2 Winton, Richard, "How the Rodney King Beating 'Banished' the Baton from the LAPD," *Los Angeles Times*, March 2, 2016.
3 Studley, Joe and Kelly Goff, "Complaint Filed After Rough Jaywalking Arrest Video Goes Viral," *NBC Los Angeles*, September 15, 2015
4 Hermann, Peter, "Baltimore Police Retire the Twirling Nightstick, Ending a Century of Use," *Baltimore Sun*, March 27, 1995.
5 Ibid.

Chokehold

1 Rejali, Darius, *Torture and Democracy*, Princeton University Press, 2007.
2 Skolnick, Jerome H. and James J. Fyfe, *Above the Law: Police and the Excessive Use of Force*, The Free Press, 1993.

Lapel Camera

1 Foucault, Michel, *Discipline and Punish: The Birth of the Prison*, Vintage Books, 1995, 228.

Data Center

1 McQuade, Brendan, *Pacifying the Homeland: Intelligence Fusion and Mass Supervision*, University of California Press, 2019.
2 Correia, David and Keegan James Sarmiento Kloer, "Albuquerque

Police Engaged in Secret Intelligence Gathering Operation, Leaked Documents Show," *AbolishAPD*, September 7, 2020, abolishapd.org.

Police Helicopter

1 Meilinger, Phillip S., *10 Propositions Regarding Air Power*, Air Force Historical Studies Office, Washington, DC, 1995.

Traffic Stop

1 Epps, Charles, *Pulled Over: How Police Stops Define Race and Citizenship*, University of Chicago Press, 2.
2 Report on the Findings of the Department of Justice Civil Investigation of the Albuquerque Police Department, US Department of Justice, April 10, 2014.

Checkpoint

1 Coleman, Matthew and Austin Kocher, "Detention, Deportation, Devolution and Immigrant Incapacitation in the Us, Post 9/11," *Geographical Journal* 177:3 (2011), 229.
2 Stuesse, Angela and Matthew Coleman, "Automobility, Immobility, Altermobility: Surviving and Resisting the Intensification of Immigrant Policing," *City & Society* 26:1 (2014), 59.
3 See *Illinois v. Lidster*, 540 US 419 (2004) and *United States v. Martinez-Fuerte*, 428 US 543 (1976).
4 Dyson, Michael Eric and Paul Elliott, *Come Hell or High Water: Hurricane Katrina and the Color of Disaster*, Basic Civitas Books, 2007, 153.
5 Williams, Kristian, *Our Enemies in Blue: Police and Power in America*, AK Press, 2015, 171.

Sound

1 McGreal, Chris, "Israel's Use of 'Sound Bombs' Causing Miscarriages in Gaza," *The Irish Times*, November 3, 2005.
2 Goodman, Steve, *Sonic Warfare: Sound, Affect, and the Ecology of Fear*, MIT Press, 2012.

Pain Compliance

1 Esmeir, Samera, *Juridical Humanity: A Colonial History*, Stanford University Press, 2012, 140.
2 Ibid., 145.
3 Scarry, Elaine, *The Body in Pain: The Making and Unmaking of the World*, Oxford University Press, 1985, 4.
4 Neocleous, Mark, *The Fabrication of Social Order: A Critical Theory of Police Power*, Pluto, 2000.

2. THE OATH

Private Property

1 Smith, Adam, *Lectures on Jurisprudence*, Oxford University Press, 1978, 5.
2 Ibid., 398.
3 Ibid., 5.

Order

1 Neocleous, Mark, *The Fabrication of Social Order: A Critical Theory of Police Power*, Pluto Press, 2000, x.
2 Wilson, James Q. and George L. Kelling, "Broken Windows," in Dunham, Roger G. and Geoffrey P. Alpert, eds., *Critical Issues in Policing: Contemporary Readings*, Waveland Press, 2015, 456.
3 Rodríguez, Dylan, "The Political Logic of the Non-Profit Industrial Complex," in Incite! Women of Color Against Violence, ed., *The Revolution Will Not Be Funded: Beyond the Non-Profit Industrial Complex*, South End Press, 2007, 25.
4 Baldwin, James, "A Report from Occupied Territory," *Nation*, July 11, 1966.
5 Ibid.
6 Razack, Sherene, *Dying from Improvement: Inquests and Inquiries into Indigenous Deaths in Custody*, University of Toronto Press, 2015, 14.
7 Benjamin, Walter, *The Arcades Project*, Harvard University Press, 1999, 473.

Security

1 Neocleous, Mark, *Critique of Security*, McGill-Queen's University Press, 2008, 24.

2 Benjamin, Walter, "Critique of Violence," in *Reflections: Essays, Aphorisms, Autobiographical Writings*, 1978, 287.

Pacification

1 Neocleous, Mark, "The Dream of Pacification: Accumulation, Class War, and the Hunt," *Socialist Studies/Études socialistes* 9:2 (2013), 18.

2 Razack, Sherene, *Dying from Improvement: Inquests and Inquiries into Indigenous Deaths in Custody*, University of Toronto Press, 2015, 32.

3 Dafnos, Tia, "Pacification and Indigenous Struggles in Canada," *Socialist Studies/Études Socialistes* 9:2 (2013), 59.

4 Ginger, James D., et al., "Use of Force Policy, Supervision and Management at the Albuquerque Police Department," *Special Report of the Independent Monitor*, September 16, 2016, 14.

Law

1 Miéville, China, *Between Equal Rights: A Marxist Theory of International Law*, Brill, 2005, 101.

2 Pashukanis, Evgeny, *Law and Marxism: A General Theory*, Pluto, 1987, 58.

3 Ibid., 59.

4 Benjamin, Walter, "Critique of Violence," in Demetz, Peter, ed., Edmund Jephcott, trans., *Reflections: Essays, Aphorisms, Autobiographical Writings*, Schocken Books, 2007, 286.

5 Poulantzas, Nicos, *State, Power, Socialism*, Verso, 1980, 77.

Crime

1 Crystal, Joseph, "How Police Reinforce Misconduct," *New York Times*, August 15, 2016, A19.

2 Hall, Stuart, et al., *Policing the Crisis: Mugging, the State, and Law and Order*, Palgrave Macmillan, 2013, 316.

3 Murakawa, Naomi, *The First Civil Right: How Liberals Built Prison America*, Oxford University Press, 2014, 13–14, 3, 6.

4 MacKinnon, Catharine A., "Reflections on Sex Equality Under Law," *Yale Law Journal* (1991), 1303.

Violence

1 Butler, Judith, *Precarious Life*, Verso Books, 2006.

2 Bittner, Egon, *The Functions of the Police in Modern Society*, National Institute of Mental Health, 1970, 46.

3 Cover, Robert M., "Violence and the Word," *Yale Law Journal* (1986), 1601–29.

4 Calder Williams, Evan, "Objects of Desire," *The New Inquiry*, August 13, 2012.

5 Marx, Karl, *Capital: A Critique of Political Economy, Vol. 1* [1867], Ben Fowkes, trans., Harmondsworth, 1976, 926.

War

1 Rodríguez, Dylan, "The Terms of Engagement: Warfare, White Locality, and Abolition," *Critical Sociology* 36:1 (2010), 165.

2 Johnson, Lyndon, Special Message to the Congress on Crime and Law Enforcement, March 9, 1966.

3 Murakawa, Naomi, *The First Civil Right: How Liberals Built Prison America*, Oxford University Press, 2014, 5.

4 Quoted in Baum, Dan, *Smoke and Mirrors: The War on Drugs and the Politics of Failure*, Little, Brown, 1996, 13.

5 Kelley, Robin, "Slangin Rocks, Palestinian Style," in Nelson, Jill, ed., *Police Brutality: An Anthology*, W. W. Norton & Company, 2001, 24–5.

6 Bush, George W., Remarks on the 2002 National Drug Control Strategy, Washington, DC, February 12, 2002.

7 Neocleous, Mark, *War Power, Police Power*, Edinburgh University Press, 2014.

Jurisdiction

1 Foucault, Michel, *The Birth of Biopolitics: Lectures at the Collège de France, 1978–1979*, Michel Senellart, ed., Palgrave Macmillan, 2010, 7.

2 Cover, Robert M., "Violence and the Word," *Yale Law Journal* 95:8 (1986), 1601.

The Badge

1 Taussig, Michael, *Walter Benjamin's Grave*, University of Chicago Press, 2006, 177.

2 Williams, Paul F., "Notable Speech: Honor of the Badge," *FBI Law Enforcement Bulletin*, August, 2012.

3 Taussig, *Walter Benjamin's Grave*, 178.

4 Hobbes, Thomas, *Leviathan* [1651], Penguin Books, 1984, 358.

Thin Blue Line

1 Comaroff, Jean and John Comaroff, "Criminal Obsessions, after Foucault: Postcoloniality, Policing, and the Metaphysics of Disorder," *Critical Inquiry* 30:4 (2004).

2 Jackson, George, *Soledad Brother: The Prison Letters of George Jackson*, Chicago Review Press, 1970.

Professionalization

1 Potter, Claire Bond, *War on Crime: Bandits, G-Men, and the Politics of Mass Culture*, Rutgers University Press, 1998, 35.

2 Kuzmarov, Jeremy, *Modernizing Repression: Police Training and Nation Building in the American Century*, University of Massachusetts, 2012.

3. MODELS OF POLICING

Police Gangs

1 *Thomas v. County of Los Angeles*, 978 F.2d 504 (1992), Findings of Fact and Conclusions of Law, 11.

2 Kolt, James G., *The Los Angeles County Sheriff's Department*, Los Angeles: A Report by Special Counsel James G. Kolts and Associates, 1992, 323.

3 O'Connor, Anne-Marie and Tina Daunt, "The Secret Society Among Lawmen," *Los Angeles Times*, March 24, 1999.

4 *Thomas v. County of Los Angeles*, Findings of Fact and Conclusions of Law, 1.

5 National Gang Intelligence Center, *2013 National Gang Report*, Washington, DC, 2013, 31.

Asset Protection Officer

1 Bureau of Labor Statistics, US Department of Labor, *Occupational Outlook Handbook*, Security Guards and Gambling Surveillance Officers, bls.gov/ooh/protective-service/security-guards.htm.

Community Policing

1 Fielding, Nigel G., *Community Policing*, Oxford University Press, 1995; Cordner, Gary, "Community Policing: Elements and Effects," *Police Forum*, 5:3 (1995), 1; and Trajanowicz, Robert C., "Understanding Community Policing: A Framework for Action," *U.S. Bureau of Justice Monograph Series*, 1994, 1.
2 President's Task Force on 21st Century Policing, *Final Report of the President's Task Force on 21st Century Policing*, Office of Community Oriented Policing Services, 2015.
3 Williams, Kristian, "The Other Side of the COIN: Counterinsurgency and Community Policing," *Interface* 3:1 (2011).
4 Platt, Tony, et al., *The Iron Fist and the Velvet Glove*, Center for Research on Criminal Justice, 1975.

Red Squads

1 Donner, Frank J., *Protectors of Privilege: Red Squads and Police Repression in Urban America*, University of California Press, 1990, 14.
2 Goldman, Adam and Matt Apuzzo, "NYPD: Muslim Spying Led to No Leads, Terror Cases," *Associated Press*, August 21, 2012.
3 Conroy, John, *Unspeakable Acts, Ordinary People: The Dynamics of Torture*, University of California Press, 2000.
4 Ackerman, Spencer, "Guantánamo Torturer Led Brutal Chicago Regime of Shackling and Confession," *Guardian*, February 18, 2015.
5 Slahi, Mohamedou Ould, *Guantánamo Diary*, Hachette UK, 2015.

Qualified Immunity

1 *Nixon v. Fitzgerald*, 457 US 731 (1982).
2 *Butz v. Economou*, 438 US 478 (1978).

CRASH

1 Board of Inquiry into the Rampart Area Corruption Incident, Los Angeles Police Department, March 1, 2000.
2 Cannon, Lou, "One Bad Cop," *New York Times Magazine*, October 1, 2000.
3 Davis, Mike, *City of Quartz: Excavating the Future in Los Angeles*, Verso, 1990, 286–7.

COINTELPRO

1 April 26, 1976 Report of the United States Senate Select Committee to Study Governmental Operations with Respect to Intelligence Activities.
2 September 15, 1969 memorandum from San Diego Field Office to J. Edgar Hoover, Senate Report, "Using Covert Action to Disrupt and Discredit Domestic Groups."
3 August 28, 1964 Memo from J. Edgar Hoover to all SACs, Senate Report, "The Development of FBI Intelligence Investigations."
4 August 4, 1967 memorandum from Hoover to all SACs, "The Development of FBI Intelligence Investigations."
5 August 28, 1968 memorandum from Hoover to Chicago SAC, Senate Report.

Officer Friendly

1 The National Child Safety Council, "Friendly Police Program."
2 "The Officer Friendly Program: Bridging the Divide Between Police and the Public," YouTube video, posted by Neil Rockey, April 8, 2016.
3 Sweeney, Annie and Angie Leventis Lourgos, "Officer Friendly Back on City Beat," *Chicago Tribune*, January 21, 2010.
4 Neocleous, Mark, "'A Brighter and Nice New Life': Security as Pacification," *Social & Legal Studies* 20 (2011), 191–208; Williams, Kristian, "The Other Side of the COIN: Counterinsurgency and Community Policing," *Interface* 3:1 (2011), 81–117.
5 Ibid.; Platt, Tony, et al., *The Iron Fist and the Velvet Glove,* Center for Research on Criminal Justice, 1975.

SWAT

1 Kraska, Peter B. and Victor E. Kappeler, "Militarizing American Police: The Rise and Normalization of Paramilitary Units," *Social Problems* 44:1 (1997), 2.

2 Ibid., 1.
3 Parenti, Christian, *Lockdown America: Police and Prisons in the Age of Crisis*, Verso, 2000, 112.

Militarization

1 Platt, Tony, et al., *The Iron Fist and the Velvet Glove*, Center for Research on Criminal Justice, 1975.

Police Uniform

1 Cox, Ana Marie, "Ice Cube Might Have Dinner with the President," *New York Times Magazine*, August 6, 2015.
2 Barthes, Roland, *The Language of Fashion*, Bloomsbury, 2013.
3 Calefato, Patrizia, "Signs of Order, Signs of Disorder: the Other Uniforms," in Bonami, Francesco, Maria Luisa Frisa and Stefano Tonchi, eds., *Uniform: Order and Disorder*, Charta, 2000.

Slave Patrol

1 Hadden, Sally E., *Slave Patrols: Law and Violence in Virginia and the Carolinas*, Harvard University Press, 2003.
2 Quoted in Williams, Kristian, *Our Enemies in Blue: Police and Power in America*, AK Press, 2015, 65.
3 Singh, Nikhil Pal, "The Whiteness of Police," *American Quarterly* 66:4 (2014), 1093.
4 Chamayou, Grégoire, *Manhunts: A Philosophical History*, Princeton University Press, 2012.
5 Durr, Marlese, "What is the Difference Between Slave Patrols and Modern Day Policing? Institutional Violence in a Community of Color," *Critical Sociology* 41:6 (2015), 875.

Rent-a-Cop

1 Joh, Elizabeth, "When Police Moonlight in their Uniforms," *Los Angeles Times*, October 13, 2014.
2 Williams, Kristian, *Our Enemies in Blue: Police and Power in America*, AK Press, 2015, 179.
3 Spitzer, Steven and Andrew T. Scull, "Privatization and Capitalist Development: The Case of the Private Police," *Social Problems* 25:1 (1977), 18.

4 Evans, R., "World Has More Private Guards than Police," *Reuters*, July 7, 2011.

5 Spitzer and Scull, "Privatization and Capitalist Development," 27.

Police Union

1 Walker, Samuel, "The neglect of police unions: exploring one of the most important areas of American policing," *Police Practice and Research* 9:2 (2008), 95–112.

Dinkheller

1 Supreme Court of Georgia, *Hall v. Brannan.* 284 Ga. 716 670 S.E.2d 87, Decided: November 3, 2008.

Police Reform

1 Wilson, Christopher P., *Cop Knowledge: Police Power and Cultural Narrative in Twentieth-Century America*, University of Chicago Press, 2000.

2 Kelley, Robin, "Slangin Rocks, Palestinian Style," in Nelson, Jill, ed., *Police Brutality: An Anthology*, W. W. Norton & Company, 2001, 49.

3 Gilmore, Ruth Wilson and Craig Gilmore, "Restating the Obvious," in Sorkin, Michael, ed., *Indefensible Space: The Architecture of the National Insecurity State*, Routledge, 2008, 145.

4 Kaba, Mariame, "Police 'Reforms' You Should Always Oppose," *Truthout*, December 7, 2014.

5 Vitale, Alex S., *The End of Policing,* Verso Books, 2017; Schrader, Stuart, "The Liberal Solution to Police Violence: Restoring Trust Will Ensure More Obedience," *The Indypendent*, June 30, 2015.

Accountability

1 Wilson, James Q., *Varieties of Police Behavior*, Harvard University Press, 1968, 279.

2 Kelling, George L., *"Broken Windows" and Police Discretion*, US Department of Justice, Office of Justice Programs, National Institute of Justice, 1999, 16.

3 Kelling, *"Broken Windows" and Police Discretion*, 2.

4 Graeber, David, *The Utopia of Rules: On Technology, Stupidity, and the Secret Joys of Bureaucracy*, Melville House, 2015, 11.

5 Ibid., 11.

6 Bureau of Justice Statistics, *Program Report: National Sources of Law Enforcement Employment Data*, US Dept. of Justice, Office of Justice Programs, October 4, 2016.

7 Graeber, *Utopia of Rules*, 214.

4. HOW POLICE IMPOSE ORDER

Search

1 Neocleous, Mark, *The Fabrication of Social Order: A Critical Theory of Police Power*, Pluto, 2000, 97.

2 Fassin, Didier, *Enforcing Order: An Ethnography of Urban Policing*, Polity, 2013, 87.

3 Ibid., 91.

4 Ibid., 7.

5 Ibid., 87.

Armed Friendlies

1 Foucault, Michel, *Discipline and Punish: The Birth of the Prison*, Alan Sheridan, trans., Random House, 1977, 222.

2 Ibid., 222.

Patrol

1 Kelling, George L., et al., "The Kansas City Preventive Patrol Experiment," Police Foundation, 1974.

2 Lefebvre, Henri, *The Production of Space*, Oxford, 1991.

3 Wilson, James Q. and George L. Kelling, "Broken Windows," *Critical Issues in Policing: Contemporary Readings* (1982), 395–407.

The Beat

1 Skogan, Wesley G., et al., *On the Beat: Police and Community Problem Solving*, Westview Press, 1999, 10–11.

2 Ibid., 58.

Investigation

1 Greenwood, Peter, "The Rand Criminal Investigation Study: Its Findings and Impacts to Date," Rand Corporation, July, 1979.

2 Edwards, H. and C. Gotsonis, "Strengthening Forensic Science in the United States: A Path Forward," Statement before the United State Senate Committee on the Judiciary, 2009.

3 Jones, Jonathan, "Forensic Tools: What's Reliable and What's Not-So-Scientific," *Frontline*, April 17, 2012.

4 Gallagher, Mike, "NM's Stunning 'Rape Kit' Backlog," *Albuquerque Journal*, November 15, 2015.

5 Graham, David, "Rapists Go Free While Rape Kits Go Untested," *Atlantic*, February 24, 2015.

Discretion

1 Dubber, Markus, *The Police Power: Patriarchy and the Foundations of American Government*, Columbia University Press, 2005.

2 Benjamin, Walter, "Critique of Violence," in *Reflections: Essays, Aphorisms, Autobiographical Writings*, 1978, 286.

3 Ibid., 287.

Predictive Policing

1 Bond-Graham, Darwin and Ali Winston, "All Tomorrow's Crimes: The Future of Policing Looks a Lot Like Good Branding," *San Francisco Weekly*, October 20, 2013.

CompStat

1 Bratton, William J. and Sean W. Malinowski, "Police Performance Management in Practice: Taking COMPSTAT to the Next Level," *Policing* 2:3 (2008), 259.

2 Lacayo, Richard, "Crime: Law and Order," *Time*, January 15, 1996.

3 Vitale, Alex and Brian Jordan Jefferson, "The Emergence of Command and Control Policing in Neoliberal New York," in Camp, Jordan and Christina Heatherton, eds., *Policing the Planet: Why the Policing Crisis Led to Black Lives Matter*, Verso, 2016, 158.

4 Murakawa, Naomi, "The Origins of the Carceral Crisis: Racial Order as 'Law and Order' in Postwar American Politics," in Lowndes, Joseph,

Julie Novkov and Dorian Warren, eds., *Race and American Political Development*, Routledge, 2008.

5 Muhammad, Khalil Gibran, *The Condemnation of Blackness*, Harvard University Press, 2010, 1.

Ghetto

1 Coates, Ta-Nehisi, "The Case for Reparations," *Atlantic*, June, 2014.
2 Baldwin, James, "Fifth Avenue, Uptown," *Esquire*, July, 1960.
3 Ibid.

Gentrification

1 Smith, Neil, *The New Urban Frontier: Gentrification and the Revanchist City*, Routledge, 1996, 25.
2 Neocleous, Mark, *The Fabrication of Social Order: A Critical Theory of Police Power*, Pluto Press, 2000.

Broken Windows

1 Wilson, James Q. and George L. Kelling, "Broken Windows," in Durham, Roger G. and Geoffrey P. Alpert, eds., *Critical Issues in Policing: Contemporary Readings*, Waveland Press, 2015, 457.
2 Ibid., 458.
3 Ibid., 460.
4 Ibid., 461.
5 Ibid., 464.
6 Vitale, Alex and Brian Jordan Jefferson, "The Emergence of Command and Control Policing in Neoliberal New York," in Camp, Jordan and Christina Heatherton, eds., *Policing the Planet: Why the Policing Crisis Led to Black Lives Matter*, Verso Books, 2016, 158–9.

Vagrancy

1 Beir, A. L., *Masterless Men: The Vagrancy Problem in England 1560–1640*, Methuen, 1985, xxii.
2 Marx, Karl, *Capital: A Critique of Political Economy, Vol. 1*, [1867], Ben Fowkes, trans., Penguin, 1976, 896.
3 Chamayou, Grégoire, *Manhunts: A Philosophical History*, Princeton University Press, 2012.

4 Du Bois, W. E. B., *Black Reconstruction in America 1860–1880*, Harcourt, Brace and Company, 1935, 67.

Interrogation

1 Leo, Richard A., *Police Interrogation and American Justice*, Harvard University Press, 2008, 3.

2 Inbau, F. E., J. E. Reid and J. P. Buckley, *Criminal Interrogation and Confessions*, Williams & Wilkins, 1986, 176.

3 Leo, Richard A., "Miranda's Revenge: Police Interrogation as a Confidence Game," *Law and Society Review* 30:2, (1996), 261.

4 Elinson, Zusha, "False Confessions Dog Teens," *Wall Street Journal*, September 8, 2013.

5 Foucault, Michel, *History of Sexuality, Volume 1: An Introduction*, Pantheon, 1978, 59.

6 Ibid., 60.

Good Cop, Bad Cop

1 Lovell, Jarret S., *Good Cop, Bad Cop: Mass Media and the Cycle of Police Reform*, Criminal Justice Press, 2003, 42.

Officer-Involved Domestic Violence

1 Wetendorf, Diane, *Abusive Police Officers: Working the System*, 2015, abuseofpower.info/Wetendorf_Working2015.pdf

2 Johnson, Leanor Boulin, "Statement of Leanor Boulin Johnson," in *On the Front Lines: Police Stress and Family Well-Being*, Hearing Before the Select Committee on Children, Youth, and Families, House of Representatives, 102 Congress, First Session, May 20, 1991, U.S. Government Printing Office 1991, 32–48; Neidig, Peter H., Harold E. Russell and Albert F. Seng, "Interspousal Aggression in Law Enforcement Families: A Preliminary Investigation," *Police Studies: The International Review of Police Development* 15:1 (Spring 1992), 30–38.

3 See for instance, Dubber, Markus, *The Police Power: Patriarchy and the Foundations of American Government*, Columbia University Press, 2005.

4 Richie, Beth E. *Arrested Justice*. New York University Press, 2012.

5 Davis, Angela Y. *If They Come in the Morning . . . : Voices of Resistance*. Verso Books, 2016. APA

6 Meiners, Erica R., *For the Children? Protecting Innocence in a Carceral State*, University of Minnesota Press, 2016.

Pursuit

1 Chamayou, Grégoire, *Manhunts: A Philosophical History*, Princeton University Press, 2012, 90.
2 Rivara, Frederick P. and Chris D. Mack, "Motor Vehicle Crash Deaths Related to Police Pursuits in the United States," *Injury Prevention* 10:2 (2004), 93–5.
3 Linnemann, Travis, "Proof of Death: Police Power and the Visual Economies of Seizure, Accumulation and Trophy," *Theoretical Criminology* 21:1 (2016), 14.

Crowds

1 Le Bon, Gustave, *The Crowd: A Study of the Popular Mind*, Fischer, 1897, 9.
2 Ibid., 15.
3 Ibid., 18.
4 Hunsicker, A., *Behind the Shield: Anti-Riot Operations Guide*, Universal Publishers, 2011, 40.
5 Testimony of Adrian Jones, "Subversive Influences in Riots, Looting, and Burning," House Un-American Activities Committee, October/November 1967.
6 Ho, Vivian, "Undercover CHP Officer Pulls Gun at Oakland Protest after Outing," *San Francisco Chronicle*, December 11, 2014.

Contempt of Cop

1 Baldwin, James, "A Report from Occupied Territory," *Nation*, July 11, 1966.
2 Ristroph, Alice, "The Constitution of Police Violence," *UCLA Law Review*, 64:5 (2017), 1182; see also Neocleous, Mark, *A Critical Theory of Police Power: The Fabrication of Social Order*, Verso, 2021.
3 Poulantzas, Nicos, *State, Power, Socialism*, Verso, 1980.
4 Robbins, Ira P. "Digitus impudicus: The middle finger and the law." *UC Davis L. Rev.* 41 (2007): 1403.1464.

Arrest

1 Neocleous, Mark, *War Power, Police Power*, Edinburgh University Press, 2014.

2 Muhammad, Khalil Gibran, *The Condemnation of Blackness: Race, Crime, and the Making of Modern Urban America*, Harvard University Press, 2010.

Kettling

1 Lefebvre, Henri, *The Production of Space*, Blackwell, 1991, 23.

2 Neocleous, Mark, "Kettle Logic," *Critical Criminology* 29:2 (2021), 191.

3 Sørli, Scott, "The Political Aesthetics of Police Kettling," *Tripwire: A Journal of Poetics* 8 (2014), 139.

Plain View

1 *Texas v. Brown,* 460 US 730 (1983).

2 Choong, Satnam, *Policing as Social Discipline,* Clarendon Press, 1997, 217.

Asset Forfeiture

1 See Nellis, Ashley and Jean Chung, "Life Goes On: The Historic Rise in Life Sentences in America," The Sentencing Project, 2013; and Murakawa, Naomi, *The First Civil Right: How Liberals Built Prison America*, Oxford University Press, 2014.

2 Williams, M., et al., *Policing for Profit: The Abuse of Civil Asset Forfeiture*, Institute for Justice, 2010.

Testilying

1 Neocleous, Mark, *The Fabrication of Social Order: A Critical Theory of Police Power*, Pluto Press, 2000.

Cop

1 Chamayou, Grégoire, *Manhunts: A Philosophical History*, Princeton University Press, 2012, 91.

2 Taussig, Michael, *Walter Benjamin's Grave*, University of Chicago Press, 2010, 178.

5. COPSPEAK

Threat

1 Wagner, Bryan, *Disturbing the Peace: Black Culture and the Police Power after Slavery*, Harvard University Press, 2010, 7.

Emergency

1 Wall, Tyler, "Ordinary Emergency: Drones, Police, and Geographies of Legal Terror," *Antipode* 48:4 (2016).

Bad Apple

1 Arthur, Rob, "How to Predict Bad Cops in Chicago," FiveThirtyEight.com, December 15, 2015.

2 Emmanuel, Adeshina and Jonah Newman, "Police Misconduct Complaints by Whites More Likely to Be Upheld," *Chicago Reporter*, November 10, 2015.

3 Fick, Nicolé, "Enforcing Fear: Police Abuse of Sex Workers When Making Arrests," *SA Crime Quarterly* 16 (2006).

4 Human Rights and Equal Opportunity Commission Report of the National Inquiry into Racist Violence (1991), 213.

5 Wooten, Hal, "Aborigines and Police," *UNSWLJ* 16 (1993), 291.

Disproportionate

1 Lowery, Wesley, "Aren't More White People Than Black People Killed by Police? Yes, but No," *The Washington Post*, July 11, 2016.

2 US Department of Justice Civil Rights Division, "Report on the findings of the Department of Justice Civil Investigation of the Albuquerque Police Department," April 10, 2014, 36, 16.

3 "Expansive Survey of America's Public Schools Reveals Troubling Racial Disparities," Report of the Department of Education, March 21, 2014.

Ferguson Effect

1 Byers, Christine, "Crime up after Ferguson and More Police Needed, Top St. Louis Area Chiefs Say," *St. Louis Post-Dispatch*, November 15, 2014.

2 MacDonald, Heather, "The New Nationwide Crime Wave," *Wall Street Journal*, May 29, 2015.

3 Comey, James B., "Law Enforcement and the Communities We Serve: Bending the Lines Toward Safety and Justice," Speech delivered at the University of Chicago Law School, October 23, 2015.

Furtive Movements

1 Delaney, Arthur, "Ricardo Diaz Zeferino's Death Shows The Danger Of Owning A Waistband," *Huffington Post*, August 22, 2015.

Justified

1 Gilmore, Ruth Wilson, "The Worrying State of the Anti-Prison Movement," *Social Justice Journal*, February 23, 2015.

No Humans Involved (NHI)

1 Wynter, Sylvia, "No Humans Involved: An Open Letter to My Colleagues," *Voices of the African Diaspora* 8:2 (1992), 14.
2 Associated Press, "Urban League in Los Angeles Asks Police Chief Suspension," *New York Times*, May 12, 1982.
3 Mydans, Seth, "Police Criticized in San Diego Killings," *New York Times*, September 22, 1990.

Deadname

1 Bassichis, Morgan, Alexander Lee, and Dean Spade, "Building an Abolitionist Trans and Queer Movement with Everything We've Got," in Stanley, Eric A. and Nat Smith, eds., *Captive Genders: Trans Embodiment and the Prison Industrial Complex*, AK Press, 2011, 48.
2 Stanley, Eric A., "Fugitive Flesh: Gender Self-Determination, Queer Abolition, and Trans Resistance," in *Captive Genders*, 19.
3 nemec, blake, "No One Enters Like Them: Health, Gender Variance, and the PIC," in *Captive Genders*, 345.
4 Ibid., 304.
5 Saffin, Lori A., "Identities Under Siege," in *Gender Captives*, 204.

Noncompliance

1 Calder Williams, Evan, "Objects of Derision," *The New Inquiry*, August 13, 2012.
2 Lai, Rebecca K. K., et al., "Assessing the Legality of the Sandra Bland's Arrest," *New York Times*, July 22, 2015.

Officer-Involved Shooting

1 Orwell, George, *Politics and the English Language* [1946], Benediction Classics, 2010, 22.
2 Lennard, Natasha, "Some NYPD Officer-Involved Shooting Narratives Just Don't Fly," *Vice News*, May 19, 2014.
3 Klinger, David, "Police Responses to Officer-Involved Shootings," Report submitted to the National Institute of Justice, *NIJ Journal* (2006), 253.
4 Tracy, Drew J., "Handling Officer-Involved Shootings," *Police Chief*, June, 2016.

Challenge Coins

1 Wall, Tyler, "Superpredators: Police on the Hunt," *Verso Blog*, March 30, 2018.
2 Campbell, Jon, "NYPD Defends 'Challenge Coins' That Call East Flatbush Precinct 'Fort Jah'," *The Gothamist*, August 30, 2020.
3 Miéville, China, "On Social Sadism," *Salvage*, December 17, 2015, salvage.zone.
4 Balko, Radley, "What Cop T-Shirts Tell Us About Police Culture," *The Huffington Post*, December 6, 2017.
5 Miéville, "On Social Sadism."

The Public

1 Power, Nina, "The Public, the Police and the Rediscovery of Hate!" *Strike!*, December 5, 2013.
2 Wilson, Christopher P., *Cop Knowledge: Police Power and Cultural Narrative in Twentieth-Century America*, University of Chicago Press, 2000, 70.

Reasonable Suspicion

1 Harris, David A., "Factors for Reasonable Suspicion: When Black and Poor Means Stopped and Frisked," *Indiana Law Journal* 69 (1993), 659, fn6.
2 Alexander, Michelle, *The New Jim Crow: Mass Incarceration in the Age of Colorblindness*, The New Press, 2012, 199.

Criminology

1 Jackson, George, *Soledad Brother: The Prison Letters of George Jackson*, Lawrence Hill Books, 1994, 18.

2 Ibid.

3 Foucault, Michel, *Power/Knowledge: Selected Interviews and Other Writings, 1972–1977*, Pantheon, 1980, 47.

Epilogue

1 Baldwin, James, "A Report from Occupied Territory," *Nation*, July 11, 1966.

2 Baldwin, James, "Fifth Avenue, Uptown," *Esquire*, July 1960.